American Sāmoa

100 Years Under The United States Flag

American Sāmoa
100 Years Under The United States Flag
Written by J. Robert Shaffer

Designed and Published by

 ISLAND HERITAGE
P U B L I S H I N G
Honolulu, Hawaii

Phone: (808) 487-7299
Fax: (808) 488-2279
e-mail: hawaii4u@islandheritage.com

ISBN: 0-89610-339-0
First edition, First printing — 2000

American Sāmoa

100 Years Under The United States Flag

Centennial Edition
By J. Robert Shaffer

Governor's Message

In Pacific Ocean terms American Sāmoa is quite small. In the world's terms, our five beautiful islands may seem very small indeed. Yet, despite its diminutive size, American Sāmoa could be considered one of the richest places on earth.

Our culture and our heritage give us our wealth. Our country is found in the hearts and minds of our people – wherever they may be. Our islands, the sea surrounding us, the shores which glisten in the sunlight, the endless parade of clouds which bring beauty to the sky and rain to the soil, all serve to make this home of ours a very special place.

Among these riches there is one more aspect which makes our territory unique: our relationship with the United States of America.

Those chiefs who signed the Deed of Cession in 1900, ceding our islands to the United States, gave their descendants the greatest gift anyone could ask for – the gift of being American. As a student of history, I continue to be amazed at the wisdom and foresight of our traditional leaders who, at the turn of the century, clearly understood the international forces at play in Sāmoa between Germany, Great Britain and the United States. Since the American flag was first raised on Sogelau Ridge on the morning of April 17, 1900, American Sāmoans have stood tall, proud and loyal as members of the American family.

The year 2000 marks the 100th anniversary of American Sāmoa as a territory of the United States. Our Centennial year will surely be a very special time for American Sāmoans everywhere.

Today many American Sāmoans live in the United States to take advantage of both the educational and employment opportunities that exist there. Thousands of American Sāmoans presently serve in the United States Armed Forces, a proud legacy that began during World War II and continues through today.

Many American Sāmoans have been away for a long time. Others were born far from home. For those who were born in Sāmoa, this book will provide a glimpse of our long and gloried history. For those who have never been in Sāmoa, the book will provide visual images of our land, our people and our culture. For those who left the islands many years ago, I hope this book will evoke memories of your childhood.

It gives me great pleasure to present the Centennial edition *American Sāmoa – 100 Years Under the United States Flag*. I hope this book finds its way into the homes not only of American Sāmoans everywhere, but all those who have come to American Sāmoa and found it to be the special place it truly is.

TAUESE P.F. SUNIA
Governor of American Sāmoa

Acknowledgments

Publishing a special Centennial book on the 100-year history of American Sāmoa is a tremendous undertaking. A project of this magnitude could not succeed without the support and assistance of a dedicated group of special people.

First and foremost, I must extend a very special "fa'afetai tele lava" to Governor Tauese P. F. Sunia, not only for his foresight and vision on recognizing the importance of publishing this book, but also his enthusiastic support and personal effort to insure this book would be completed.

Over the past three years a select group of people have generously given of themselves, their knowledge, special skills, and insights into Sāmoa's culture, history, art and traditions. I especially wish to express my gratitude to Dr. Frederic K. Sutter, whose color photographs bind the pages of this book together. Dr. Sutter spent nearly three decades photographing Sāmoa's people, culture and way of life. He graciously opened his extensive photographic library to me and made his photographs available for publication in this book. Dr. Sutter's kind donation of his photographs made the broad scope of this book possible.

The desire to display Sāmoa's cultural arts on these pages was an integral part of the book's planning from the very beginning. In this regard, Reggie Meredith Malala responded to my every request for assistance. The artistic textures and themes which grace the pages of this book were made possible because of Reggie's efforts – efforts too numerous to even recount.

The intent of this special Centennial publication was to provide the reader with a capsulized overview of American Sāmoa's 100-year history as a U.S. territory. While it was not my intent to make this book a scholarly historical publication, I did want to provide enough historical data to illustrate the events which shaped American Sāmoa's march through the century. It would have been impossible to find certain historical facts and insure their historical accuracy without the assistance of Stan Sorensen. Many of the historical facts printed on these pages are the result of Stan's research for his "Sāmoan Historical Chronology 1606-1998." Stan also assisted in the identification of individuals and places in the historical photos – not an easy task.

I wish to extend a very special "mālō!" to Island Heritage for their extraordinary effort in producing this book. To E. Lynne Madden, Executive Vice President, for sharing my vision on the theme, scope and importance of this book. To Art Director and Designer Micki Fletcher who, with remarkable artistic insight, brought the myriad of elements all together so wonderfully, turning my vision into reality. And to Brian Lavelle, Senior Account Executive of the Custom Products Division, who coordinated this entire project, truly a remarkable feat.

Finally, to Lieutenant Governor Togiola Tulafono, who shared his insights with me on the more subtle aspects of Sāmoan culture. Such insight provides an especially valuable contribution to this book.

My deepest gratitude goes to these special people. Without their help this project could not have succeeded.

Fa'afetai mo le galuega māe'a! Mālō lava le tautua!

ROB SHAFFER
Tutuila, American Sāmoa

16

30

48

75

86

187

Contents

201

7

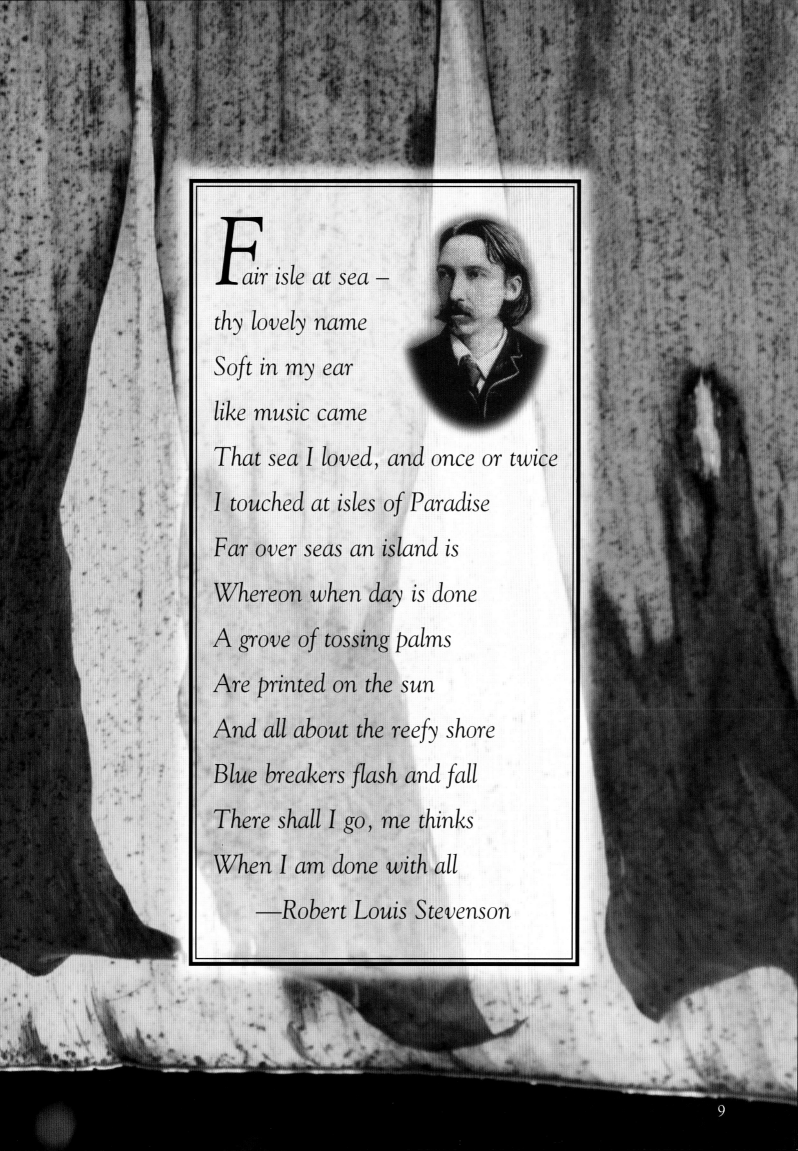

*F*air isle at sea –

thy lovely name

Soft in my ear

like music came

That sea I loved, and once or twice

I touched at isles of Paradise

Far over seas an island is

Whereon when day is done

A grove of tossing palms

Are printed on the sun

And all about the reefy shore

Blue breakers flash and fall

There shall I go, me thinks

When I am done with all

—Robert Louis Stevenson

Ua tofo i tino matagi lelei

'A favorable wind is felt on the body.'

The joy of expectation. — Proverb

Introduction

pproximately forty thousand years ago the discovery and settlement of the Pacific islands began. The pioneer settlers in what is now New Guinea found a climate cooler than today's and hence somewhat different types and locations of vegetation and animals. By about 10,000 years ago, however, those natural elements had changed when the final Ice Age ended and sea levels rose to their present heights, allowing the plants and animals to evolve into what they were when Western explorers arrived in the 16th century.

Those earliest migrants were dark brown to black in skin color with curly to frizzy black hair. They derived from peoples who lived in small groups that were scattered from Timor and Moluccas westward into mainland Southeast Asia and northward into the Philippines. Their stone tools were made by flaking and they subsisted by hunting and gathering wild animals and plants. Reflecting on the wide scattering of their various groups, their languages must have been numerous and exceedingly diverse. Their watercraft must have been of enough size and stability to transport families across the sixty to eighty miles of open ocean that has always, during the span of human existence, separated Indonesia from the Bismarck Archipelago.

The Manuʻa Islands. Ofu is in the foreground, a glimpse of Olosega can be seen to the left of Ofu, with Taʻū in the distance. Geologically they are the oldest and socially the most traditional of the Sāmoan group.

The descendants of the earliest streams of New Guinea settlers eventually dispersed throughout New Guinea and into the Bismarck and Solomon archipelagos. For many millennia they continued to subsist by hunting, gathering and fishing. Then, about 9,000 years ago the revolutionary techniques of horticulture spread from the west into the settlements of New Guinea resulting in food growing largely replacing food hunting and gathering. At roughly the same time the raising of pigs, domesticated chickens and dogs became commonplace.

The descendants of these early New Guinea settlers most likely continued to drift into New Guinea from the west for thousands of years. But beginning about 5,000 years ago humans of a different physical type entered the islands, bearing a different type of language along with several other distinctive cultural traits. They differed from the New Guinea descendants in that they had straighter hair, lighter skin color, more rounded head shape and flatter faces. These people were members of the Mongoloid race, whose original domain extended throughout central and east Asia. These peoples spoke numerous languages which had originated in southeastern China or Formosa. Eventually the people speaking these languages migrated into the Philippines, Indonesia, Indochina and the Malay Peninsula, and ultimately into the Pacific Islands.

These people, which have been labeled Austronesians, entered the Pacific Islands by two separate routes. One group, most likely from the southern Philippines, eventually settled in the Mariana Islands and Yap. The other group, following a more southerly route, moved along New Guinea's northern coast through the Bismarck Archipelago, and down the island chains to New Caledonia. These groups most certainly migrated in waves over successive generations throughout the centuries, and although the northern group found the Marianas and Yap to be uninhabited, the southern group found their migratory routes

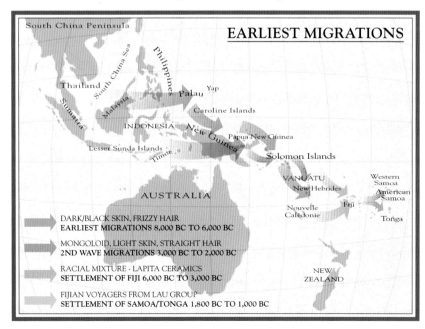

EARLIEST MIGRATIONS

DARK/BLACK SKIN, FRIZZY HAIR
EARLIEST MIGRATIONS 8,000 BC TO 6,000 BC

MONGOLOID, LIGHT SKIN, STRAIGHT HAIR
2ND WAVE MIGRATIONS 3,000 BC TO 2,000 BC

RACIAL MIXTURE - LAPITA CERAMICS
SETTLEMENT OF FIJI 6,000 BC TO 3,000 BC

FIJIAN VOYAGERS FROM LAU GROUP
SETTLEMENT OF SAMOA/TONGA 1,800 BC TO 1,000 BC

to be already inhabited by the descendants of the early New Guinea settlers.

Over the centuries certain groups retained both their Papuan-based languages and their New Guinean-type physical features, while others adopted the Austronesian traits into their languages and cultures. There were few, if any, Mongoloid genes mixed among certain groups, while others fused both their languages, other cultural traits and their genes with those of the newcomers.

While these movements and changes were taking place, other fleets of newcomers began to dare the unknown and sail further eastward. Eventually voyagers from the southeastern Solomon Islands settled in the islands of Fiji, where, over time, Fiji's distinct culture and language evolved. It is from Fiji that the story of Samoa, and eventually all of Polynesia, begins.

Those early settlers from the Solomon Islands brought with them a particular art form of ceramic decoration that spread throughout Fiji and ultimately became an established tradition within Fijian culture. This art form thrived in Fiji from the mid-third millennium B.C. through possibly the late first millennium A.D. This distinctive style of ceramic decoration eventually came to be known as "Lapita" style pottery, and would ultimately provide archaeologists with dramatic clues as to Polynesia's origins and earliest migrations.

▼ ▼ ▼

Fijian seafarers began sailing eastward into the unknown sometime around the mid-second millennium B.C. Archaeological discoveries of Lapita ceramics on the island of Lakeba in the Lau Group of Fiji and closely matching ceramics at Mulifanua on the western tip of 'Upolu Island in Sāmoa places settlers in Sāmoa back to the beginning of the first millennium B.C. These early settlers almost certainly had a direct connection to the people of Lakeba.

Discoveries of Lapita pottery in Tonga place the settlement of those islands at approximately the same time period as that of Sāmoa. The connection between Fiji, Tonga, and Sāmoa through Lapita ceramics has come to be known as the "Lapita cultural complex." This link between these three island groups not only involves the similarities in making and designing pottery, but also includes similarities in language, physical features, religious concepts and the structure of kinship units.

Once these ancestral Polynesians had become established in Sāmoa, how did their accomplishments compare with voyagers in other parts of the world?

In the Mediterranean, the Pharaohs ruled Egypt but their power was land-based and little thought was given to sea exploration. It would be nearly 200 years before the Phoenicians, the greatest seafaring nation the world had known up to that time, would even sail out of the trivial Mediterranean and into the Atlantic, all the while hugging coastal shores. Amazingly, more than 1,100 years would pass before the mighty Romans, in sophisticated ships of war, actually ventured out of sight of land.

Nowhere on earth did any human beings even remotely display the kind of bravery or deep understanding of astronomy as did the men of Polynesia. Nor would they for another 2,500 years. The few hundred who sailed from Lakeba to Sāmoa approximately 3,500 years ago discovered that the new islands were without question a more pleasant place to live. Of those who came to Sāmoa many would spread out, colonizing the easternmost islands in the chain in less than a generation. They became Sāmoa's earliest ancestors. In time they would forget Melanesia of the distant past and Fiji of the recent. The descen-

"*Lali*", wooden log drum used to call village councils, announce the start of church services, or notify fishermen a fishing expedition is to begin.

Coconut grove, Sa'ilele village.

**Seacoast near Vaitogi,
Tutuila.**

**Sāmoan fishhook
shaped from the
alili shell.**

**Octopus lure made
from whale ivory,
cowry shell, sennit
and rounded stone.**

dants of these earliest seafarers would, in about 1,800 years, become uniquely Sāmoan.

During this time period these people would thrive in the geographic area now known as the "western triangle." Among the islands of Sāmoa, Tonga and Fiji, the consistent contact over roughly a thousand years gave birth to a regional homeland of Polynesian culture. Scholars would find a common thread binding these islands together through a new and distinct language and reinforced with an amazing similarity in pottery ware which evolved and changed among the island groups with amazing consistency over the centuries. None of this could have happened by chance. The evidence of the relationship the islands had with one another is overwhelming.

These ancestral Polynesians were responsible for establishing the cultural foundation upon which later individual island groups would base their societies. For forty generations they were tied to each other by common physical similarities, linguistic dialects and the evolution and design of ceramics, fish hooks and adzes. They traveled between islands carrying their civilization with them to unpopulated lands which in time included the isolated islands of the Tokelau Group and Niue. They were in actuality purposeful pilgrims crossing the Pacific in a reasoned exodus, carrying provisional customs to be planted on awaiting shores. It is most certain that the ancestral Polynesians spread throughout the western triangle with every intention of colonizing new lands.

The people of Lakeba were most likely the first to sail east from Fiji and discover new land. Others most likely preceded them from surrounding islands over the decades, sailing toward the sunrise in their constant quest for adventure, or were blown off course by unexpected storms to happen upon uninhabited islands.

In the years that followed the initial voyage and discovery of Sāmoa, many sailed their

double-hulled canoes from Fiji east to Tonga or north to Sāmoa. Some made the journey to join relatives; others to establish new lives. Some went out of curiosity, liked what they found, and stayed. Some clashed with neighboring villages and sailed off to find a more peaceful life. And some were allured by the adventure of following the stars and discovering the numerous islands that awaited them. But it appears, so far as scholars can surmise, that very few sailed into unknown waters without a set purpose. They sailed with the conscious intention of settling new lands or finding undiscovered islands beyond the horizon.

Strangely, and for no set reasons that scholars can agree upon, once Sāmoa was settled the pattern of eastward migration which had brought the original seafarers to Sāmoa suddenly and curiously went into hibernation. A little over 1,000 years would pass before the descendants of these first seafarers would knowingly set out again to search for unknown islands to the east. When they did, the distances and impediments facing this new wave of adventurers would be much greater than those faced by the earliest voyagers.

▼ ▼ ▼

It appears that the millennium preceding the time of Christ was one of intense specialization and experimentation of open-ocean voyaging canoes by the earliest Sāmoan canoe-builders. These canoes ferried voyagers within the western triangle of Sāmoa in the north, Fiji to the west and Tonga to the south during this thousand-year period. Once the specific designs of these double-hulled canoes had been finely-shaped and proven seaworthy, the urge to set sail eastward in search of new lands most likely began to take hold.

The swift and capacious vessels of these Sāmoan navigators had become so specialized that once the migrations began that ultimately peopled

tradewinds. They accomplished this by tacking, coming about and changing the side of the sail presented to the wind.

It is believed that within the first century A.D. Sāmoan mariners spearheaded one of the greatest maritime ventures of all time–the exploration and settlement of Polynesia.

In their wooden double canoes stitched with coconut-fiber rope and rigged with sails of woven leaves, these mariners who knew nothing of instruments navigated 2,100 miles and made their landfall at Nuku Hiva in the Marquesas Islands. Aboard their canoe, or canoes, they may have

Polynesia, the vessels were probably little changed by the time Captain Cook arrived in the Pacific in 1769. Notes from his log on the *Endeavor* report that the Polynesian canoes were "much faster" than his own ship.

Most canoes were double-hulled 55-to-60-foot V-sectioned craft, built with wide planks lashed to the frames with sennit and caulked with sticky breadfruit sap. Hoisting their pandanus mat sails, the canoes could cover 100 to 150 miles a day in open-sea conditions. The canoes were constructed with adzes of basalt or clamshell and drills fashioned from sharks' teeth or shell.

As these earliest Sāmoans improved their sailing craft they also became specialized in the life-saving art of preserving food for long periods. This gave these great canoes a range of 5,000 miles in favorable conditions–more than enough for exploratory probes into the eastern Pacific.

Eastward explorations required that these early Sāmoans sail into the oncoming southeast

used Lapita-style pottery to hold water, food or living plants. For such pottery was discovered during excavations in Nuku Hiva in 1961.

Within a millennium the descendants of these first Sāmoan explorers–homing in on undiscovered islands revealed by such slight clues as the flight path of a bird or the formation of a cloud—had found every habitable speck of land in an area of the Pacific bigger than North America and Europe combined. From Nuku Hiva and neighbor island Hiva Oa these early Polynesians of Marquesan culture sailed away to find Easter Island 2,400 miles to the southeast, Hawai'i 2,200 miles to the north, and–via Tahiti–New Zealand 3,200 miles to the southwest.

It must have been these ancient Sāmoan explorers and their descendants who first perfected the skill of navigating by the stars. These master navigators developed the art of "steering down the star path." By picking a star that came up–or sank–in line with your island

Olosega Island, center, with Sunuʻitao Peak, Ofu, left. Asaga Strait separates the two islands. Taʻū island, approximately ten miles distant, can be seen at right.

15

Sāmoan fisherman in bonito canoe returns home following a day of fishing.

Streaks of sunlight shines on bird's nest ferns on the forest floor in the mountains behind Malaeloa, Tutuila.

target, then steering toward the star and its successors, the island destination could be found. This was known as the "compass" star—the star low on the horizon which navigators' steered by.

Today's master navigators know that the points of rise and set of stars do provide a directional compass every bit as accurate as a magnetic instrument. What must be remembered, however, is that Polynesian navigators had no instruments. They carried the map of the heavens in their heads.

A second skill these ancient navigators mastered was the incredible ability to steer their canoes by wave motion—that is, swells reflected from beyond the horizon. The skilled navigator taught himself to recognize the profile and characteristics of particular ocean swells as he would the faces of his own family, but he judged the swells more by feel than by sight.

By standing with feet firmly planted on the deck of his canoe, the navigator could sense the direction and movement of swells through his feet right up through his body. The complex patterns produced by swells that are reflected and refracted among the islands were understood by Polynesia's navigators. This unique knowledge was especially critical when canoes neared the vicinity of an island on a dark, moonless night, allowing the navigator to remain clear of surrounding reefs until daylight.

To successfully sail across the vast Pacific on journeys of a thousand miles or more demanded yet even more knowledge of the universe and its limitless diversity. Knowing the stars and the swells were not enough.

The navigators could read the clouds and knew the meaning of their formations. Clouds

"stuck" on the horizon in a certain way meant land stood beneath them. Cloud formations told of fair weather or approaching storm. Certain clouds could warn a navigator of an impending shift in the wind. Even the "color" of clouds could be read by these men, with subtle hues reflecting off the bottom of clouds indicating land, lagoon, or other physical features.

These men knew each species of ocean bird. They knew whether they were land-based or migratory. They knew each species' habits—how they fished and when they fished. They read and understood flight patterns and could identify each bird when it was only a mere speck in the distance. If the bird was migratory, such as the Pacific golden plover, a navigator could more precisely determine north and south, for he knew the plovers' migratory patterns and which direction they would be heading depending on the time of year.

If the bird was land-based, such as the terns, noddies and boobies, the direction of the nearest island could be determined by the direction those birds were flying at a certain time of day. The discovery of birds on the open ocean was especially critical after long open ocean voyages. A flock of boobies, spotted at mid-afternoon, would indicate land was near. The canoe would then keep the boobies in view for the remainder of the afternoon. At dusk the flock, returning to land, would lead the canoe unerringly toward it.

It was with these incredible navigational skills and a reservoir of immense knowledge of their ocean world that these ancient navigators discovered and peopled the islands of Polynesia. When the age of Polynesian exploration and discovery finally came to an end, sometime around 1000 A.D., regular contact between certain island groups continued for another 300 to 600 years. It was during this period that Sāmoan explorers or their direct descendants made their final—and one of their more spectacular—discoveries, the island of Kapingamarangi, a tiny speck of land on the southern reaches of Micronesia more than 2,000 miles northwest of Sāmoa.

▼ ▼ ▼

The original voyagers who sailed away from Sāmoa to discover the Marquesas Islands undoubtedly left many family members, friends and relatives behind. Of the people who remained, their descendants became uniquely Sāmoan. In time they remembered nothing but their beautiful islands; they forgot the migrations from the east and came to believe in Sāmoa as the center of the universe. As such they would pros-

per throughout the chain and positively thrive on the islands of Savai'i, 'Upolu, Tutuila, Aunu'u and the island group of Manu'a.

When Europeans finally arrived, three thousand years after the original discovery of Sāmoa and seventeen hundred years following the initial voyage from Sāmoa to the Marquesas, the apex of Polynesian exploration had long since passed. And finally, in 1492, when Christopher Columbus set sail on his remarkable voyage of discovery, Polynesia had been settled for nearly five centuries, illustrating how advanced Polynesian navigators truly were compared to the rest of the world.

Beach fale, Ofu, Manu'a.

Tagaloa – the Creator . . .

Flooded the lava rock and said to it

'Be blessed and enjoy the sea. . .

And the lava rock replied to Tagaloa

'Bless not me, for the sea will surround you also . . .

Chapter 1

The Islands

bout two hundred million years ago, when dinosaurs were becoming common upon the earth, an event of basic importance occurred below the surface of the sea 1,800 miles east of a great South Pacific land mass later to be known as Australia.

The crust of the earth was then, as now, a spherical shell of rock that consists of a few rigid plates. These tectonic plates move about continuously, shifting position and often colliding with one another.

Those features of the earth most common to us, the continents and oceans, rest on eleven giant plates – Australia is one, the Pacific Plate another – plus a number of smaller plates, each clearly defined, with their slow, almost imperceptible movement depending upon where and how the oceans and continents position themselves in relation to one another.

Through the millennia these wandering plates would collide then drift apart. These collisions and subsequent pulling apart resulted in the creation of volcanoes like Mt. Fuji in Japan, or huge seamounts which produced chains of islands like the Hawaiian or Tahitian. As the plates pulled apart, earthquakes occurred. This allowed upwelling magma – which accumulates deep within the earth's crust – to rise upward filling the cracks where the plates had drifted apart.

These plates moved far too slowly for events like Mt. Fuji to manifest themselves in a one-time cataclysm, although they could have. Rather, the movement of the plates continued over tens of millions of years. The rising heat has continued eon after eon, with the resulting replacement of old crust with new, continuing imperceptibly through today.

The movement of these tectonic plates from one location in the Pacific Ocean toward Eurasia or Australia presented impossible difficulties during the earth's history. But given enough time the plates could go just about anywhere – and they did.

tured, folded and deformed the seabed for tens of millions of years. When it was over, the Pacific Plate had gouged out a deep oceanic trench 1,500 miles long and 35,000 feet deep.

The plates collided with such titanic force that entirely new mountain ranges like the Himalayas were formed. As the plates continued to grind into one another they produced two of nature's most dramatic manifestations: earthquakes and volcanoes.

The same tectonic forces which create situations conducive to earthquake activity also produce volcanoes. As a result, this deep oceanic canyon, named the Tonga Trench by oceanographers, would become a contributing factor in the Ring of Fire, that unbroken chain of volcanoes which circles the Pacific Ocean wherever the Pacific Plate comes into contact with other plates.

While the many volcanoes comprising the Ring of Fire prove fascinating to study and offer compelling vistas, it was at the extreme north end of the Tonga Trench where the correct orientation existed 12 million years ago to generate dozens of volcanoes which would eventually produce a line of islands that would one day come to be known as Samoa.

From these eruptions great mountains would rise from far beneath the ocean's surface to become among the highest in the Pacific. In time, they would become home to the ancient mariners whose ancestors had originated in Indonesia, Melanesia and Southeast Asia.

It was during a period of time about 12 million years ago at a spot just over 100 miles from the northern end of the Tonga Trench that the rigid Pacific Plate, in its unending northwesterly drift, jerked sharply creating a rupture on the ocean floor 15,000 feet below the surface.

At the time the earth was still in the process of forming those basic features with which we are today familiar. The early Sierra Nevada and Rocky Mountains had already been built. The redwood tree was common in North America, a land then inhabited by camels and elephants.

The ocean floor, at the time the rupture occurred, stood at the moment of transformation. From deep within the earth's crust enormous concentrations of heat began to melt the previously solid rock below the rupture line. Slowly, but with irresistible power, the molten rock oozed through the rupture on the ocean floor. For the next 4,000 years the magma would pour through the fissure, spreading evenly over the ocean floor to a relatively insignificant height. As the liquid rock spread it solidified, and in time a small seamount began to develop.

▼ ▼ ▼

It was on a day approximately 200 million years ago that an event occurred which created an identifiable landmark on the ocean floor far below the waves that swept the surface of the empty sea. And with it the story of American Samoa begins.

Within the earth's crust, forces developed which caused the Pacific Plate to crash into the Australian. These great forces, awesome in the relentless power which manifested them, frac-

God visits man in this Sāmoan legend of Tagaloa and Pava. Tagaloa had descended to earth to pay Pava a visit. Pava's son, who was a disobedient boy, angered Tagaloa, who split the boy in half as a punishment. But when Tagaloa saw Pava's sadness at the loss of his son, he took pity on the grieving father and brought the boy back to life with a drop of *'ava*. Hence, the tradition of spilling a few drops of *'ava* before you drink. The *'ava* root symbolizes the *'ava* which Tagaloa brought from heaven. The gecko represents the delinquent son, kicked out of heaven, who landed in Manu'a. The swirling patterns symbolize the wind and waves; the centipede represents pain; the worm symbolizes life; the bamboo pillow represents peace between Tagaloa and Pava; and the *fuesaina* leaves symbolize medicine and healing.

Undersea volcanoes, building from depths of 15,000 feet over a period of 12 million years, formed great seamounts which in time built the islands of Sāmoa.

Within 300,000 years the seamount had become a remarkably smooth, simple cone that had been formed almost entirely by summit eruptions that flowed constantly for periods lasting thousands of years. In time, the great volcano forming this underwater mountain generated enough volumes of molten rock to build a massive surface platform, one layer of lava piling upon the other. The molten rock, building with infinite slowness, would ultimately stand 21,000 feet thick.

Within time the weight of this seamount became enormous and with this weight came an adjustment of the sea floor lasting many thousands of years. When the adjustment had ended, the sea floor had sunk nearly 2,000 feet.

Then one day, just over one million years after that first segment of molten rock poured through the original rupture on the sea floor, a continuous flow of lava pushed its way upward 15,000 feet. The lava that had climbed nearly three miles unexpectedly broached the ocean's surface. As the molten rock struck water and air together a mighty explosion resulted, sending clouds of powder-white steam rocketing skyward.

At long last an island had emerged above the mighty ocean. For the next two million years the island held tightly to its precarious existence. The violence of flaming growth, the tearing down of relentless waves, continued for another two or three million years, yet the island persevered. Finally, after about five million years, the island became secure in its existence. In time this island would take its historical place as the legendary homeland of the people of Polynesia. One day the island would be called Savai'i.

While Savai'i was rising to prominence, larval forms which traced their genesis back more than 300 million years drifted into the warm, nutritious waters that surrounded the island. In time coral polyps began to flourish, and slowly, over thousands of years, they built a reef which began to circle the island.

Two thousand miles to the west there existed an island of enormous size later to be called New Guinea. At this time New Guinea was home to a well-established plant and animal society composed of birds, trees and reptiles. These plants and animals, with millions of years of evolution behind them, had already begun to make exploratory journeys eastward through the Bismarck Archipelago, the Solomon Islands and New Hebrides. Slowly, with a patience that is difficult to comprehend, grasses and lizards and edible plants participated in this migration that would take millions of years to complete. Borne by storm and sea, assisted by cataclysm and the rise and fall of the world's oceans, these forms would eventually find their way to Savai'i as it rose to ever-increasing height.

In time airborne seeds of the most primitive mosses and other similar plants arrived on the island joined by larger seeds carried to the island by birds who came from islands to the west. With incredible tenacity these seeds established themselves by clinging to life on the barren, rocky surface. And in so doing began the process of breaking down the crusty surface rock, decomposing it into soil.

At some point in time a coconut, growing along the shoreline of a Melanesian island, dropped from beneath the tree's crown and plopped into a tidal lagoon. Kept afloat by its buoyant husk it eventually found its way into an equatorial current where it drifted due east for

over a thousand miles. There it was picked up by another subtropical current which swept it back toward the southwest. Once the coconut drifted into the waters surrounding Savai'i the ocean's swells swept the coconut ashore, possibly during an immense high tide agitated by a full moon. Protected by a small cove, the coconut found just enough soil to take root and prosper. In that moment Savai'i took a gigantic step in becoming a hospitable land, for the coconut was the one essential plant which Polynesian societies depended upon to sustain life and around which their cultures would develop.

Another hundred thousand years passed, then two hundred thousand. Then a cyclone swept out of Asia slamming into one of the larger islands west of Sāmoa such as Espiritu Santo or San Cristobal. After weeks of rain caused extensive flooding, a large tree, its roots exposed by the floodwaters along the banks of a river lost its grip and tumbled into the raging torrent. Bearing ants, insect larvae, a number of lizards and the seeds and roots of a half-dozen different tropical plants, the tree was swept down-river and into the sea where it was caught by the same current as the coconut countless centuries before.

Time passed. Long, long stretches of time. Through wind and rain and sun and the death and rotting of trees and plants the soil grew deep. New seashore plants like the pandanus and casuarina began to grow along the shoreline, their seeds having drifted ashore from far to the west.

More time passed. One hundred thousand years, or maybe five hundred thousand. Then one day a pair of fruit doves arrived on Savai'i. Blown far from their island home five hundred miles to the west by unseasonal winds, the pair had every chance of survival. But the female was too weak following her arduous journey and died, leaving her mate alone and unable to propagate their species. A thousand years passed, and no other birds arrived. Then one day a flock of shearwaters, a relatively small bird known for its fast flight and ability to glide long distances, spotted Savai'i from afar and landed there. The shearwaters made Savai'i their home. And as the eons passed, they would eventually be joined by dozens of other winged species who would thrive and populate every island in the Sāmoan chain.

Months passed. Many of the living things aboard the sea-soaked tree died. But many miraculously survived. When the tree finally washed ashore Savai'i had the ingredients for a forest with trees, flowers, insects and reptiles.

Fifty centuries came and went, then a hundred more. Only through the most remote accidents of natural history would life reach the island. Only through even more remote accidents could that life survive and propagate. Another hundred centuries passed, and by some accident equally preposterous, another log arrived bearing birds with deadened wings who otherwise could have never reached the island. In this accidental way, after a span of time so vast it is meaningless, living things eventually established themselves on Savai'i.

Nature was at work, as it is always at work, but it moved slowly. A million times through a million years, the irresistible combination of pure chance and pure will to survive gave Savai'i life. By chance living things arrived. And by chance they would prosper.

Rose Atoll, a wildlife preserve, lies approximately eighty miles east of Manu'a.

**Beach near To'aga,
Ofu, at sunset.**

▼ ▼ ▼

The rift created by the movement of the Pacific Plate which gave rise to the island stretched more than 300 miles along the ocean bottom. Along the entire length of the rift other would-be islands, reaching toward the east, also struggled to establish their own identities. Three other seamounts started their cycles within the same million years as did Savai'i. One seamount would eventually form the island of 'Upolu, the second largest island in the Sāmoan chain. The two remaining seamounts would form smaller islands in the group. Though smaller, these islands are considered by many to be the most visually spectacular.

One seamount, located near the center of the 300-mile-long rift, became Tutuila. The eastern-most seamount would give rise to the islands of Ofu, Olosega and Ta'ū – collectively known as Manu'a.

Tutuila is the largest of these five islands which were once known as Eastern Sāmoa. Located at 14 degrees south latitude, 170 degrees 40' W, Tutuila began its growth during the same million year cycle as did Savai'i. However, its rate and type of growth was entirely different than that of the larger island.

Tutuila's growth began as a series of five volcanoes punched their way above the ocean's surface at roughly the same time as Savai'i. These volcanoes had an extraordinary quantity of magma that was under great pressure within the earth's crust. As the volcanoes rose, molten rock poured through the vents with such great velocity that the lava flows built steep-sided cones which grew higher and higher over a period of nine million years.

These five volcanoes were especially violent, their eruptions causing great explosions of gaseous ash and clouds of steam that drifted westward across the sky for nearly a thousand miles. For nine million years the violent eruptions continued, though we know that there had to be long periods of latency. Four of the lava domes acted in concert, energized by the same fault zone deep within the earth's crust. This fault zone housed a tremendous reservoir of magma. The domes deposited an incredible amount of new lava which in time produced two giant calderas in the center of the island. Each caldera rose more than 4,000 feet in height, the external sides of the calderas falling steeply into the sea.

For eons the two massive volcanoes stood side by side as twin sisters embracing in fiery unison, until one day the building process was interrupted by a cataclysmic event. The entire portion of the 300-mile rupture line experienced a massive lurching in a northwesterly direction. Perhaps the Pacific Plate underwent some kind of adjustment, or there may have been a sizable flexing along the northern end of the Tonga Trench. At any rate, the movement from 18,000 feet below sponsored an earthquake of immense proportions causing whole sections of the two calderas to collapse.

When it was over the calderas had collapsed more than 4,000 feet. But all was not lost, for they left behind one spectacular caldera more than three miles wide and six miles long, a precursor of great beauty to come.

During this master cycle the two calderas, which had now become one, were joined on

either side, in a line running east to west, by dozens of smaller volcanoes. These volcanic cones poured layer upon endless layer of lava down their flanks, eventually creating steep ridges which plummeted into the sea. Whereas the twin calderas were born of exceptionally violent volcanoes, the eruptions which occurred along the ridgeline were quiet, slow, bubbling cauldrons that created a more solid, broad base on the floor of the ocean.

While these gigantic volcanic eruptions were in progress, the shore of Tutuila was alternately exposed to crashing waves or protected by an expanding coral reef. When the first condition prevailed, the south shore of the island was pummeled by incessant wind-driven waves which in time began to build sand and accumulate debris. Building quietly over a thousand centuries the coral erected a barrier between the crashing waves and the exposed shoreline giving the island critical protection from weathering by the sea.

Always, like everything to do with Tutuila throughout the early eons of its existence, the island stood poised between a promise of beautiful life or a sentence of death. At any given moment Tutuila was rising to ever increasing height, or it was sliding back into the sea, balancing between life and death.

Of course, there were periods of hundreds of thousands of years when it stood seemingly secure within that time period, followed by a million years when its demise seemed imminent. But Tutuila was not destined to die, but to live – and prosper. For if the island itself did not know its destiny, the forces driving the Pacific Plate knew, for these forces continued to build a tremendous reservoir of molten rock which would in time send the island new supplies of lava to replenish its ramparts and carry it through yet another cycle.

▼ ▼ ▼

As the master cycle came to an end about two million years ago, Tutuila – and its massive central caldera – stood poised to take the final steps that would decide its ultimate geologic form.

Plants and animals had long since reached the island from Savai'i and 'Upolu. The forests were thick and filled with birds. The coral reef was alive with sea life of every description. Lizards, snails, ants and spiders had established colonies, many species still in the process of evolutionary adjustments to the island environment.

When the island was well-formed the forces of nature began to apply their final touches. Out of the south and east winds howled down upon the mountain crests bringing with them rain in such quantities that in the space of an afternoon

flash-floods might carve away layers of lava rock that took ten thousand years to accumulate.

At various times during this cycle ice would collect at the poles in vast amounts. Accumulating and expanding for thousands of years the ice stole great quantities of ocean water causing a drop in the level of the world's oceans by as much as a hundred feet, exposing the coral reefs protecting the island and leaving them to die in the sun.

After twenty thousand years the polar ice melted causing the ocean to rise; then monstrous waves would beat down heavily on the shore for ten or twenty thousand years until the coral rebuilt along the shoreline many times; and each time the coral would rebound – rebuilding, dying, then building again.

For thousands of years powerful storms slammed into the steep mountain ridges that traversed the center of Tutuila. These rains produced unprecedented amounts of water creating floods of gigantic proportion. In the center of the island the massive caldera was exposed to fierce erosion that ripped at the caldera's interior walls. In time the caldera's south-facing wall eroded away, opening the southern rim to the sea.

A half-million years was required to re-shape the caldera and expose its southern flank. Then suddenly – that is, over a period of nearly a million years – another readjustment of the Pacific Plate occurred. The Pacific and Australian plates reacted to each other's immense, thrusting forces. During the same period another brief ice age was retreating, thereby flooding the world's oceans with unexpected water. When the adjustment had ended, Tutuila had sunk some 1,400 feet lower into the ocean.

This rapid submersion drowned the massive submarine shelf and accompanying coral reef which encircled the island, simultaneously flooding valley mouths and allowing the waves to attack the coast anew. During this cycle ice ages came and went, causing the great oceans to rise and sink, but always the coral persevered and built new reefs. Each time the coral rebounded,

"Sega'ula" (blue crowned lory).

Young man carries his canoe home to protect it from sun and rain.

In geologic time the Manu'a islands are quite young. Because of their youthful geologic-structure, they are characterized above all else by their steep, dramatic topography. As a result, the primary location of human habitation has been the narrow coastal plain. There has been little change in this pattern over the millennia. Today's village locations are in many respects a continuation of prehistoric settlement patterns.

The island of Ofu is the western-most island of Manu'a. Prior to human habitation the coastline of Ofu was much closer to the volcanic cliffs than it is today. The earliest occupation of Ofu was confined to a very narrow beach ridge along the south-east coast.

Along this coastline, just east of the present-day location of the airstrip, lies the site of an ancient settlement known as Toaga. The Toaga site has yielded one of the largest samples of Polynesian ceramics found in Sāmoa. Toaga has also provided archaeologists with one of the largest—and most ancient—finds associated with Sāmoa's oldest cultural materials—including fish-hooks, artifacts, ornaments and the vertebrate remains of birds and shellfish.

The ceramics found at Toaga date from 1307 to 907 B.C. The site contains a deeply stratified sequence of cultural occupation. Therefore, it is believed that Toaga was a permanent site which spanned the entire period of Sāmoan prehistory. The radiocarbon dates of the ceramics found at Toaga place human occupation of Ofu to possibly 1700 B.C. Archaeologists conclude that human colonization of Ofu had taken place by the mid-third millennium B.C. by a ceramic-producing population. This extends the boundary of the Lapita population in Sāmoa from 'Upolu to Manu'a. It also reinforces the theory that the dispersal and establishment of population centers throughout the Sāmoan chain was a very rapid phenomenon.

Archaeological and linguistic evidence strongly suggests that the islands of Eastern Polynesia, such as the Marquesas, Society and Cook Islands, were settled—at least to a certain degree – from Sāmoa. Using radiocarbon dating of cultural materials, the settlement of Eastern Polynesia took place from possibly as early as 200 B.C. to approximately 500 A.D. Since Sāmoa lies in an west-to-east configuration, and Manu'a is at

Freshwater stream, Vatia village, Tutuila.

Looking west at Tufu Point, Ta'ū, Manu'a.

Fishing lure made from cowry shell, sennit and feathers (top). Right, Flower Pot Rock–traditionally known as *"Fatu ma Futi."*

the eastern end of the chain, it would seem that the group would have provided the most likely point of departure for early voyaging canoes bound on eastward courses for discovery and colonization. Therefore, the timeless quest by these early Sāmoans to explore the ocean under the sunrise may have also played a significant role in the original settlement of Manu'a.

▼ ▼ ▼

Two possible clues that the islands of Manu'a provided the "sailing-off point" for voyages of exploration and discovery can be found in the ancient chant "Tui Manu'a lo'u ali'i e!" which means, "Tui Manu'a, thou art my lord!" This chant has been heard throughout numerous Polynesian island groups, including the Cook Islands, which lie approximately 650 miles southeast of Ta'ū.

There are also two islands, one in the Cook Islands group, the other in the Society Islands, whose names seem to originate in Manu'a. The name of these two islands is Manuae. The connection in the similarity of these names–and the importance of Manu'a as a sacred land–is too close to overlook.

It was then around the beginning of the Christian era that ancient Sāmoans pointed their canoes to the blue infinity of the Pacific and sailed eastward toward the sacred sunrise. These ancient

Sāmoans could not have known they were spearheading the greatest maritime venture of all time: the exploration and settlement of Polynesia. Sailing in wooden canoes stitched with coconut-fiber sennit and rigged with sails of woven leaves, and without the use of maps or metal instruments, the ancient mariners navigated 2,100 miles to discover the Marquesas Islands, the longest sea voyage the world had ever known.

Within a millennium the descendants of these early navigators – homing in on undiscovered islands revealed by such slight clues as the flight path of a bird – had found every habitable speck of land in an area of the Pacific larger than North America and Europe combined.

It was from these earliest Sāmoan navigators and explorers that the Polynesian descended. The first settlers in the Marquesas would within 500 years reach Tahiti where they developed the highly sophisticated culture of ancient Havai'i, which became the religious and cultural capital of the Society Islands. From these two island groups came the discovery of Hawai'i and New Zealand, and a truly remarkable feat – the 2,400 mile voyage against prevailing winds and currents to discover tiny Easter Island and establish an advanced society on the most isolated island in the Pacific.

The descendants left behind in Sāmoa would within a thousand years penetrate Micronesia and Melanesia to establish such isolated Sāmoan outposts as Kapingamarangi, Nukuoro, Nukumanu and others. Scholars would find the languages of these distant islands as close to Sāmoan as Spanish is to Portuguese. This could not have happened by chance.There had to have been contact between these islands.

Wherever Polynesians sailed in their quest for new land, they retained the memory of their ancestral homeland. Its ancient name, Havai'i, echoes in the names of two prominent islands in eastern Polynesia: Havai'i in Hawai'i and Havaiki in the Society Islands, now called Raiatea, both of which trace their origin back to Sāmoa's biggest island – Savai'i.

When Europeans finally arrived in the Pacific, 3,000 years after the discovery of Sāmoa and 1,700 years following the earliest voyages to Eastern Polynesia, the apex of Polynesian exploration had long since passed.

The first Europeans marveled at the design and seaworthiness of Polynesian canoes. One of Captain Cook's crewmen wrote in his diary, "These canoes run us nearly out of sight. They sail about three miles to our two."

A missionary stationed in Hawai'i observed, "One man will sometimes paddle a single (outrigger) canoe faster than a good boat's crew could row a whale-boat."

One of the earliest European buccaneers to enter the Pacific, Englishman William Dampier, wrote, "They sail the best of any boats in the world."

Polynesia had been settled for nearly five centuries when Christopher Columbus, sailing under the flag of Spain in three large ships, and

"Alia" -- double-hulled voyaging canoe. Circa 1890

supported by a society which had at its disposal maps, books, metals and sails of canvas, was the first to cross the Atlantic Ocean and discover the new world.

Without any of these advantages, the ancient Sāmoans and their descendants had been sailing on voyages nearly twice as far and ten times as dangerous for more than 1,500 years.

Turtle petroglyph, eastern Tutuila.

Ua tuʻu i tai le vaʻa tele

"The big vessel is launched."

Listen and consider the orator's words. — Proverb

Chapter 3

Fa'a Sāmoa
Sāmoan Life And Culture

From their heritage as the earliest Polynesians, the people of Sāmoa have devised a unique social organization which was admirably suited to their island and ocean environment.

There are two key units of social organization in Sāmoa: the 'āiga, a word which can be translated as "extended family," or "clan" and the nu'u, or village.

The 'āiga consists of a group of people related by blood, marriage or adoption. This family group can vary in size from eight or ten up to more than 100 individuals. At the head of an 'āiga, or a branch thereof, is the matai. The matai is an individual who holds a chiefly title. Depending upon the traditional nature of the chiefly title, a matai can either be an Ali'i (chief), or Tulafale (orator).

A *matai* is selected through a process in which all adult members of the *'āiga* have a voice. An elder matai may name his choice for a successor from his deathbed, and his wish requires consideration by members of the *'āiga*, but is not binding. Today, women are not excluded from this election process, and it is not uncommon for a capable woman to become a *matai*.

The word *matai* refers in general to all village chiefs. These include the *Fa'asuaga, Tamali'i, Ponao'o* and *Tulafale fa'a-vaipou*. The election process pertains only to the *matai* who is the *Sa'o* of the family. The *Sa'o* is legally defined as the senior *matai* of the family. All other lower matais in the family are appointed by the *Sa'o* and presented to the village council at his behest alone.

Family members cannot propose the seating of a lower *matai* in the village council without the consent of their *Sa'o*. This is an important aspect of being the *Matai Sa'o* of a family, coupled with the authority to control the communal family land uses.

When a death occurs and a family title vacated, members of the various branches of the *'āiga* come together to decide who will become the successor. The extended family will often produce several serious contenders for the title. When this is the case, deliberations over the successor can often be long and occasionally produce ill feeling among family members. A serious dispute can result in months, or even years, elapsing before the vacant title is filled.

Individuals are elected to hold *matai* titles based on numerous specific criteria. Traditionally, one of the most important requirements to be considered was service to the family, or *tautua*. Other criteria considered by family members are initiative and intelligence, age, and knowledge of ceremonial protocol. Since the 1950s the level of formal education has become an important factor. Other criteria include personal wealth and experience in either business or political affairs of government.

Once a *matai* title is conferred upon an individual, he or she assumes a wide range of authority and responsibility.

A matai, by virtue of the title, is the family patriarch. The title brings the family prestige, and the *matai* must uphold that prestige within the village and to a larger extent, the district and/or county. Within the extended family itself the *matai* is responsible for maintaining family unity and harmony, promoting participation in religious or church-related activities, and insuring the family's children are educated. The *matai* serves as the family spokesman in the village council of chiefs, or *fono*, thereby providing the family a voice in all village matters and public affairs.

One of the most important responsibilities of any *matai* is serving as trustee of family land.

Most land in American Sāmoa falls under one of two categories: 1) family land; or,2) village land. All land not designated "village" land belongs to one extended family or another, with

Vaitogi village, home of the legend "Shark and the Turtle." circa 1920

Sāmoan village by Reggie Meredith Malala.

the exception being "freehold" land, which can be privately owned. Village and family land in American Sāmoa make up more than 98% of all land in the territory.

As trustee of family land, the *matai* does not own the land, nor does he have the authority to alienate the family from their land through sale or gifts. The *matai* does, however, have the authority to determine the use of family land. Individual family units may use a piece of land upon which to build a house or cultivate crops, as well as other ways to put the land to use. Actual sale of family land, to the government, for example, must be agreed upon by all members of the extended family. Such agreement is often difficult to obtain, for Sāmoans, as a rule, are quite reluctant to be permanently separated from landholdings.

▼ ▼ ▼

As stated earlier, *matai* titles fall into one of two categories: *Ali'i* and *Tulafale*. There are two stations within the *ali'i*, or chief, category. The highest station is the *ali'i sili*, or high chief. The second category is the *ali'i*, or chief. The ranks of chiefs are: *Fa'asuaga* — the *Ali'ita'i* of each village; and *Tamali'i* — the high chiefs, most of whom are the *Sa'o* of each family.

High chiefs often hold a paramount rank in a village, or in certain cases, within a county. High chief titles are always very old and carry a great deal of tradition and history that is associated with them. Traditionally, when Sāmoan *fales* were in use, high chiefs took their seats at certain posts which designated their rank. This tradition is still carried on through today, with the *ali'i* sitting at the *matua tala* of the *faletalimalo*.

Next in order of rank are the chiefs. Chiefs are also heads of extended families, but the rank of their titles does not carry sufficient prestige or status to warrant special attention in the power structure of the village. In village council meetings, they sit on the flanks of the high chiefs.

43

Taupou mixes *ava* as attendant fills *ava* cup in preparation to serve attending chiefs.

Tulafale, or talking chiefs, are the orators of the village. There are three ranks of orators: The *Tama Matua* (in certain villages only); the *To‘oto‘o* (in all villages of Manu‘a); and the *Ponao‘o* (in all villages of American Sāmoa). There are also the *Tulafale Fa‘a-vaipou*. This last rank does not have a *pou* (post, or seat) in the *fale*, and therefore sits in the space available only in between posts in the back of the *fale*.

The *Ponao‘o* are usually the main orators of the village councils. *Tama Matua*, which are found only in certain counties (Sua and Vaifanua in the east; Fofo and Aitulagi in the west) usually function only at the county level during certain important occasions. Otherwise, the *Ponao‘o* are the main drivers of village politics, while the *To‘oto‘o* functions at all levels.

The *To‘oto‘o*, or orator chiefs, are often the chiefs for high chiefs and usually serve as the spokesman for the entire village in inter-village ceremonies or negotiations. Their seating positions withing the *fale* are the posts at the front and back (each side) of the council house. They are flanked in council meetings by talking chiefs of secondary rank.

The roles of chiefs and orators varies within the village according to the rank of each individual chief. In most villages there is only one high chief. However, in other villages there may be a group of chiefs who hold high chief rank. High

Members of village ‘aumāga uncover ground oven.

Taupou in formal sitting position (top) wearing a necklace of "*lopā*" seeds and holding the "nifo oti"— a war-knife called the "tooth of death." Below, artist's rendering of Sāmoan maiden drawn from historical photograph. Circa 1890

chiefs preside over village council meetings and represent their village at the district or county level. A high chief is by virtue of his title a village leader. However, his individual personality, strength and intelligence are very important to the degree in which a high chief can exert his authority.

One of the more prestigious rights a high chief maintains is the appointment of his daughter or close relative to the position of *taupou*, or ceremonial village maiden. The high chief's son is also qualified to serve as the *manaia*, which is the leader of the village society of untitled men. Both the *taupou* and *manaia* are titled positions, and carry with them much prestige and status in traditional ceremonies.

The *tulafale*, referred to as either orators or talking chiefs, is a group or society of specialized chiefs that is intertwined into the hierarchy of chiefs at the village, county and district levels. The relationship between a high chief and talking chief has been compared to that between a sovereign and his premier.

High Talking Chiefs have special advantages over high chiefs, which include the opportunity to gain wealth and public acclaim. There is much history, legend and myth surrounding the ancient beginning of this particular class of chiefs in Sāmoa. Whatever their beginning, High Talking Chiefs can become well known and highly respected for their artistry with words and knowledge of protocol. Their ability to persuade, cajole and otherwise impose their will upon others through their mastery of language is cultural fact and a source of pride among this elite group of men.

Among *tulafale* there are highly prescribed procedures which tradition demands be followed during formal ceremonies. There are elaborate structures for speeches, ancient references and numerous proverbs that must be committed to memory.

Most important of these references is the *fa'alupega*. The *fa'alupega* is the official list of names and relative ranks of each village's chiefs and talking chiefs. This list also includes the specific esoteric and symbolic references which identify—historically and politically—the basic structure or hierarchy of a village. Most, if not all, important ceremonial occasions require the recital of a village *fa'alupega* by a talking chief.

High Talking Chiefs are recognizable during important ceremonies. Their titles give them the right to carry a large *fue* (sennit whisk) and staff, the two symbols of their position in this elite fraternity of men. The *fue 'afa* of second or third-ranking talking chiefs do not match those of the high talking chiefs in size, thus providing observers with an opportunity to recognize the individual talking chief with the highest rank.

▼ ▼ ▼

The 'Aumāga and Aualuma

Within the village structure there is a group of untitled men called the *'aumāga*. The *'aumāga* represents the village's main labor force in both the individual household unit and the village as a whole.

The untitled men in the *'aumāga* are known as *taule'ale'a*, which translates loosely into English as "young man." The young men of the *'aumāga* are very important to the overall operation of the village. They play an important role in ceremonial functions and serve the village council. In ancient days they served as the warrior class during times of war.

The *'aumāga* has often been referred to as "the strength of the village." The group assists the chiefs in numerous capacities, is held responsible for successfully

Sāmoan *taupou* is featured in this painting by Janet Stewart. The *taupou* wears a *tuiga*, a headdress made of bleached ancestors' hair. The headband is comprised of seashells, above which are mother of pearl shells, *tifa*. She wears a whale's tooth necklace and a feathered necklace, *Ula*. Around her waist is wrapped a fine mat, *'ie toga*, over which she wears a kilt of feathers, *titi*. The little girl wears flowers over her ear, *sei*, and a flower *ula*. The flowers are from the plumeria tree, *pua*. Behind the *taupou* coconut palms grow at the water's edge. A collared lory and blue-crowned lory, *sega vao* and *sega 'ula*, rest on the coconut trunk. A *fale* stands in the background; the foundation made of river washed stones. Above the *taupou* grows the *moso'oi* tree — with its scented flowers blooming a bright greenish-yellow.

An orator, *tulafale*, stands with the symbols of his rank and title. Over his left shoulder is draped the sennit whisk, *fue*, made of braided coconut-fiber strands lashed to a hardwood handle. In the orator's right hand is the staff, *to'oto'o*. The orator wears a bark cloth wrap-around, *siapo*, which is tied at the waist by a belt, *fusi*. Above the orator glisten the leaves of the breadfruit tree, *'ulu*, with the round fruits ripening on the branches. Behind him are coconut-shell water containers. To his right an *'ava* bowl, *tanoa*. Beside the *tanoa* are a carving adze, *to'i*, and hardwood war club, *uatogi*. A voyaging canoe, *alia*, sails across the lagoon. Between the *alia* and the beach, warriors paddle a war canoe.

'Ava roots, "*tugase*," are gathered in preparation for a formal presentation.

'Ava bowl with coconut-shell water containers.

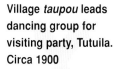

Village *taupou* leads dancing group for visiting party, Tutuila. Circa 1900

completing mandated village projects, and plans and carries out such activities as group fishing, harvesting and constructing or repairing church buildings.

The 'aumāga prepares and serves food for the village council during fono gatherings and ceremonial occasions. They play the major role in the presentation and serving of 'ava. They also serve as the village police force, enforcing village rules and regulations as determined by the village council.

The female counterpart to the 'aumāga is the aualuma. This is the village organization of unmarried women and normally represents all village household units. The function of the aualuma, like the 'aumāga, is to contribute and promote the general welfare of the village.

The aualuma, unlike the aumaga, has changed in its traditional role over the years. While the duties and responsibilities of the 'aumāga has remained much the same, even in modern times, the role of the aualuma has changed considerably.

Traditionally the role of the aualuma, which was originally comprised of a select, handpicked group of women, was to serve the taupou–the village ceremonial princess. They served the taupou as handmaidens and chaperones. They were constantly in her attendance, sleeping beside her and caring for all her needs.

By the early to middle part of the 1900s the ancient traditions of the institution of the taupou had, for the most part, changed dramatically or disappeared all together. Therefore, there was no need for the aualuma to serve the taupou.

Today the aualuma serves a very different function. The group is composed primarily of unmarried girls and widows, but is also part of a greater women's organization known as the Women's Committee. This committee includes the wives of untitled men as well as the wives of chiefs and talking chiefs. Together the two groups are responsible for a wide range of responsibilities and activities–from working with the government's Department of Public Health to promote and improve the systems involving the health of village residents, to dancing in festivals such as Flag Day.

The leadership of the Women's Committee, and by extension the aualuma, comes from the wives of high chiefs and high talking chiefs. These women rule the organization by virtue of their husband's titles in the village hierarchy. In modern times the Women's Committee has grown increasingly powerful and influential within the village structure.

Its importance to the overall well-being of the village cannot be understated. The Women's

An *'ava* bowl stands in foreground as village matters are discussed among family *matais*.

Committee has become a very important part of village life.

▼ ▼ ▼

The **'Ava** Ceremony

The *'ava* ceremony is considered to be the most significant traditional event within Sāmoan culture. All important ceremonies, from the village level to the county and district levels, to ceremonial government proceedings, are begun with the formal serving of *'ava*.

The origin of the drinking of *'ava*, and the formal ceremony surrounding the *'ava*'s presentation, date back to the most distant of Sāmoa's earliest ancestors. Much myth, legend and history surround this ceremony and its hallowed place in Sāmoan society.

Over the past two or three centuries, through the early part of the 20th century, the *'ava* ceremony's basic tenets changed very little. From Ta'ū island in the east to Savai'i in the west, the various rituals involved in the formal presentation of *'ava* were very much the same. Within a particular village or district there may be subtle differences in a particular aspect of a certain ritual, or in a sequence of events, but overall the *'ava* ceremony has remained quite consistent from one village and one island to the next.

In modern times, however, certain aspects of the ceremony have been modified or shortened to fit time constraints. Throughout earlier history, time was not an issue in Sāmoa. The elaborate rituals were detailed and time-consuming. Speeches were long and filled with references to myths,

legends, history, and, after the mid-1800s, amply supplied with Biblical phrases and allusions.

The *'ava* ceremony involves numerous formal rituals. The rituals, or order of certain rituals, may vary depending on the reason the ceremony is held. For example, an *'ava* ceremony held on an important occasion only among a village council itself, may be somewhat different from an *'ava* ceremony in which a village council was hosting a visiting council of chiefs from another village.

Today the formal role and ritualistic serving of *'ava* retains the importance it has always had. Whether within a village or district setting, or in the Executive or Legislative branches of the American Sāmoa Government, *'ava* maintains its significance.

▼ ▼ ▼

Daily Life

Traditional life in a Sāmoan village was centered around essential daily activities involving each individual family, such as food gathering and cooking, plantation work and fishing, the construction of a family *fale* or other similar project. There was a time in Sāmoa when every man could plant and harvest his taro and banana plantations, shape the hull for a canoe out of a log then fashion it into an outrigger canoe, go fishing on the open ocean in his canoe using hooks he had carved himself, build his own house, trap pigeons in the forest and braid sennit from the fibers of a coconut husk.

Women were skilled in dozens of tasks beyond the raising of children, caring for basic family needs and everyday preparation of meals.

Village "*manaia*" (left) with *taupou*. Circa 1890

Coconut-husk fiber is pounded to prepare the fiber to be braided into sennit.

Most women were expert weavers, adept at creating numerous kinds of mats, including the highly valuable "fine mat," which involved at least a dozen different steps and took months to complete. The fine mat was, and still is, an integral part of many of Sāmoa's most formal ceremonies.

Women knew the art of *siapo* making. The process of creating bark cloth, making dyes from forest plants, and decorating the cloth with colors and designs required a broad variety of skills and knowledge, as well as an inherent talent for art and design. Women were skilled at reef fishing, and knew the habits of shellfish, octopus and other animals who inhabited the coral reefs. They worked in plantations beside their men, though it was not common for women to do strenuous work such as clearing and planting. Women most often weeded and helped in harvest activities. They were not shy, however, in joining the men in carrying heavy loads of bananas or taro home from the plantations in woven coconut leaf baskets placed on the ends of a wooden carrying pole which served as a yoke.

While much of the work was shared by most village or family members, there was also a recognizable division of labor between men and women, the young and old, and the everyday worker and the specialist.

In every Sāmoan village there were a number of *tufuga*, which means a "specialist" or "expert." The Sāmoan *tufuga* might be an expert canoe builder, house builder or tattooer. In most instances, a *tufuga* used his skill to supplement his income, whether in the traditional form of

"payment" in fine mats, kegs of salt beef or tinned corned beef, or in actual payment of money.

Sāmoans divided much of their time between subsistence agriculture and fishing. Prior to 1900, before European or canned food was readily available, villagers spent roughly equal amounts of time on the land or harvesting the resources of the sea. As imported goods increased in the islands throughout the early to mid-1900s, with a dramatic surge during World War II, a shift occurred in which more time became devoted to farming and the land than to the sea. After World War II, it was easier to send someone to the bush store for a tin of sardines than to spend hours trying to catch fresh fish.

The *matai* is the authority over family lands. This means he has administrative control over family land and its uses. While the *matai* maintains authority over this land, he does not have the power to negotiate any transaction that would permanently alienate a family from their land. In modern times it has become the practice for a matai to allocate portions of family land for personal use and profit, though in a permanent sense all lands remain the property of the 'āiga.

The pattern of land ownership and utilization remains much the same today as it has for centuries. This pattern involves plantation plots, village land, lots adjacent to family houses and family "reserve" lands.

Plantation plots are those most commonly used for the cultivation of banana, taro, yam, *ta'amu*,

Bolts of material are presented to guests of honor during village celebration.

breadfruit and other food staples. They are found outside the village on the lower slopes of hills extending inland toward mountainous regions.

Village land lies farthest inland from the village and is cultivated only on occasion by those villagers who have received permission of the village council. An individual with the initiative, strength and energy to clear densely covered land and make it productive is usually allowed to keep the majority of produce and profit derived from his labors.

Lots adjacent to family houses are within village boundaries and are used primarily as the location for family housing and associated traditional-use structures like the *umu*. The graves of deceased family members are located here, along with some food plants such as papaya, breadfruit or small bunches of banana trees.

Family reserve lands belong to the families within each village. The boundaries of these lands are well-known. They are not used as commonly as plantation lands, but can still be used to grow taro or bananas. It is not uncommon for reserve lands to be loaned to friends or neighbors to grow a few crops, though it is rarely loaned on a long-term basis.

Agriculture is a very labor-intensive activity. The land is lush and thickly forested. Clearing land is very difficult and requires very hard work. The bushknife, axe and pointed hardwood digging stick, called *'oso*, are the primary tools of the Sāmoan farmer. Axes are used to fell large trees and bushes, the bushknife for clearing and removing weeds, ferns and scrub vegetation, and the *'oso* for creating holes to plant seedlings or prying rocks from the soil. Until recently no fertilizers were used. However, farmers allowed the leaves from certain trees to fall and rot on plantation lands to improve soil productivity.

The coconut has always been the most useful, if not the most important, agricultural product in Sāmoa–as throughout Polynesia. Over the centuries Sāmoans devised literally dozens of uses and useful products from this plant. The leaves alone are woven into many important and necessary components such as baskets, sections of thatch, house blinds, food trays, floor and sleeping mats, fans, hats and various kinds of decorations. Coconut fiber is used to braid sennit, the indispensable cord which is used for lashing in both housing and canoe construction, and weaving ropes used for *lepaga*, or shark fishing.

The meat of the immature–or green–coconut is very valuable as a food source. The meat of the green nut, or *niu*, is especially good eaten raw. It is both tasty and nutritious.

Taken together with the sweet water of the immature nut, the meat and liquid combined provide quick energy to the fisherman at sea in his canoe, or to the farmer laboring in his plantation. The hard meat of the mature coconut, or *popo*, can be grated and strained into a whitish liquid called "coconut cream." This liquid, when baked in taro leaves, combines to make one of Sāmoa's most popular food dishes called *palusami*. The meat and spongy core of the *popo* have many different uses for humans. The meat and core of the *popo* are also commonly used as feed for the family pigs.

The art of traditional basket-weaving lives on in American Sāmoa.

The elderly never out-live their importance in the Sāmoan family. A great grandmother works on a floor mat, while her great grand-child looks on.

While the coconut is usually considered Sāmoa's most valuable and useful agricultural product, the most popular foodstuff is *talo*. *Talo* is a starchy grey tuber which serves the same dietary role as do potatoes in the United States or Great Britain. *Talo* is prepared by baking in the *umu* or boiling, and is oftentimes served covered in coconut cream. Green bananas are also boiled or baked, and also can be served in coconut cream. It is more common for bananas to be cooked and eaten while green, though ripe bananas are eaten as a snack, especially the tiny banana known as *misiluki*.

Breadfruit is a third staple of the Sāmoan diet which is especially abundant at family meals during the three breadfruit bearing seasons when the trees produce the fruit. It is cooked and served much the same way as taro and bananas. In ancient times breadfruit helped sustain villagers during periods of famine which resulted from hurricanes or drought. Following a natural disaster breadfruit was buried in pits and stored for long periods of time. When the storage pits are

uncovered the breadfruit will have decomposed into a rancid smelling mass somewhat like very old cheese. This rare food was called *masi*. When *masi* was removed from the pit, it was cured in baskets, mixed with *peʻepeʻe* and *penu* (ground coconut meat), wrapped in banana leaves, then baked in the *umu*. Many Sāmoans consider this food to be a delicacy.

Agriculture and the land are at the heart of Sāmoan life. Everyone is tied to the land, even if they are specialists in some other activity such as house-building or tattooing. Even today, most people spend some of their time on their agricultural lands. The one exception being those living in the urban areas or who have adopted a more "American" or non-traditional Sāmoan lifestyle. Traditionally it was everyone's job, men and women, both children and adults, to carry out assigned tasks on family land. Around these activities much of Sāmoan village and family life revolved.

▼ ▼ ▼

The term *faʻa Sāmoa* means "the Sāmoan way of life" or "Sāmoan custom." The *faʻa Sāmoa* has been especially resilient since the arrival of LMS missionary John Williams at Savaiʻi in 1830. The 19th century was an especially turbulent time in Sāmoa. The islands of ʻUpolu, Savaiʻi and Tutuila were all affected by the arrival of whalers,

A rare aerial view of Vaitogi, Tutuila. circa 1939

nearly sixty years of civil war, international intrigue and colonial power struggles. All the islands of Sāmoa experienced profound change as a result of Christian missionaries. Yet, the *fa'a Sāmoa* survived. It held the Sāmoan people and ancient Sāmoan traditions together. While it is true that numerous aspects of Sāmoan life and tradition were erased by Christian missionaries, and other ancient aspects faded away with the passage of time, the basic tenets of the *fa'a Sāmoa* remained, providing the people of Sāmoa with a clear and unmistakable identity.

The arrival of European and American influence in the Pacific during the 19th century had a devastating effect on the Polynesian cultures of Hawai'i, Tahiti, the Marquesas and other island groups. While ancient ways of life and culture disappeared throughout much of Polynesia, the *fa'a Sāmoa* proved to be both resilient and accommodating to the onslaught of overwhelming forces brought to the islands by the outside world. Through it all, the *fa'a Sāmoa* survived. Village life continued as it always had, the ancient ebb and flow uninterrupted with but a few alterations.

Cooking and food preparation, especially ceremonial cooking, has remained an important aspect of village life.

The traditional art of Sāmoan food preparation has always been the special preserve of the men. Among the many duties of the *aumaga* is serving village chiefs. Ceremonial cooking is one

of the *aumaga*'s more important duties. It is the responsibility of the *'aumāga* to prepare and cook traditional foods for their chiefs.

The division of labor at one time was very strict, though in recent decades has been fading away. Traditionally, the *taule'ale'a* were the singular preparers of food, even within a household. This has changed significantly over the past two or three generations. The pattern today seems to be that men still prepare and cook more traditional foods–those cooked in the *umu*—while the women prepare newer "foreign" foods. Food that is cooked on stoves, requires frying, or comes out of a box, such as cake, or out of a can, like *pisupo*, are now prepared by women, as are food items like potato salad and chop suey.

The traditional form of Sāmoan cooking takes place in the *umu*. The *umu* is an earthen oven, where a fire is built over a pile of cooking stones on a level floor inside the *fale umu*, or cooking hut. When the fire is burning very hot, more fist-sized stones are placed on top. Within an hour the fiery embers and pieces of charcoal are removed from the white-hot stones with wooden tongs, and the stones are spread out in an oval shape roughly three feet across. Now the food, which has been prepared earlier, is placed near the center of the hot stones. This food is usually taro or breadfruit, green bananas, and dishes such as fish wrapped in breadfruit leaves, or *palusami*–coconut cream wrapped in taro leaves. Sometimes a layer of banana leaves are placed over the food to prevent charring, on top of which are placed another layer of stones. Finally, a thick covering of banana leaves completes the *umu* preparation–the function of the leaves being to hold in the heat.

The most important ceremonial food cooked in the *umu* is the pig. The presentation of cooked pigs during important ceremonies is essential, with the number of pigs being presented serving as documentation of the degree of importance of a particular ceremony.

After a pig is slaughtered and its outer skin and insides are properly prepared, the carcass is placed on the heated cooking stones with the feet tucked underneath. Hot stones are built up around the lower part of the pig, which is then covered with banana leaves and damp burlap bags producing a kind of steaming effect. If the ceremony is an especially important one, only the largest pigs will be cooked. In most instances, the pigs will not be cooked in the *umu* long enough to cook the carcass thoroughly. This allows for enough to be eaten during the ceremonial feast; and the meat can be easily divided without falling

"Taule'ale'a" prepares food for the *"umu."*

"Pe'epe'e" (coconut cream) is poured into *talo* leaf (left) to make *"palusami."*

Talo and other food crops are for sale at the market in Fagatogo.

Roofing spars, purlins, ribs and rafters are bound by sennit in the construction of a *fale* (right).

plan placed the guest houses of chiefs in two parallel lines with the *malae*, or village green, in the middle, between the two rows of houses. The alternate plan was the semi-circle, in which the chiefs' houses were constructed in a wide circular fashion, again with the malae in the middle.

Geography was an important indicator of which plan might be used. If the village was situated on a thin strip of sand between the ocean and a steep ridge or mountain, like the village of Olosega on Olosega Island, the chiefs' guest houses would be constructed in a long neat row. When a village was built on a wide area of flat land, the semi-circular plan might be used. This plan is more commonly seen in 'Upolu and Savai'i than in the islands of American Sāmoa. Population growth throughout Sāmoa, especially following World War II, resulted in the eventual disappearance of these orderly and attractive plans as many villages abandoned this form of master-planning.

Chiefs' guest houses are placed upon elevated stone platforms, called *tia*, the height of the *tia* coinciding with rank of the chiefly title of the occupant. The height of the apex of the *fale* roof also served as an indicator of the rank of a particular title. Large black lava stones were the most common material used to build the platform. White coral rubble was a much-used floor covering which gave the inside of the *fale* a bright, clean appearance.

The *fale* roof of the round *fale tele* is supported by one, two, or even three huge center columns, called *poutu*. These are massive columns cut from huge trees, sometimes far inland from the village, which are anchored in the ground and supported by large lava boulders. Gables, *tala*, together with a center section, *itu*, form the *fale* roof. Columns, rafters, purlins and ribs form the roof superstructure. The crisscrossing pieces of wood form an intricate pattern, their various shapes, lengths and sizes creating a mosaic that is very pleasing to the eye. The entire roofing structure is held together by hundreds of lashings of

apart. The ceremonial division of the cooked pig among the chiefs and guests attending the event is an important part of every ceremony, and must be done according to a strict system of distribution. In the most traditional ceremonies, similar–and precise–divisions are also made of sharks, bonito, turtle, chicken and other large fish.

▼ ▼ ▼

The Sāmoan Fale

There are two distinct kinds of Sāmoan *fale*–the round or "guest" *fale*, known as *fale tali malo*; and the oblong *fale*, called *fale afolau*. The *fale tele* served as the *faletalimalo* of the high chief; the *fale atolau* signified the *faletalimalo* of the high talking chief.

It was customary at one time that villages be laid out according to one of two basic plans. One

Sun shines on a *fale* nestled among tropical foliage. *Pola* can be lowered to shield inhabitants from the sun's rays.

strong, pliable sennit braid. Many of the lashings are done in decorative, sometimes geometric, patterns.

Sugar cane leaves are used to make three-foot sections of thatch which are twisted around a rod and attached to roofing spars with sennit. Though Sāmoan houses have no walls and are open on all sides, woven coconut frond blinds, *pola*, are tucked underneath the eaves similar to venetian blinds and may be lowered to provide protection from the sun or inclement weather.

Carpenters built these large *fales* without blueprints or written plans of any kind. The entire construction of the fale was based on the "eye" of the master-carpenter. The fact that Sāmoan houses were round or elliptical, with semi-circular or oval-shaped roofs, is an indication that Sāmoan master-builders were extremely talented individuals with an inherent understanding of mathematics, physics and geometric design. It was not uncommon for a Sāmoan *fale* to stand for seventy or eighty years and withstand as many as two or three hurricanes, with only the thatch and occasional lashings replaced over that time.

▼ ▼ ▼

Fishing and the Sea

In May, 1768, French navigator Louis-Antoine de Bougainville sighted the Sāmoan islands. Impressed with the Sāmoans' canoe-handling skills, he named the archipelago the "Navigator Islands," and they were known by that name for over a century.

It is reported that Bougainville spotted Sāmoan fishermen far at sea in their large sailing canoes, out of sight of land, and he marveled at their apparent knowledge of the sea and ability to navigate so far from their home islands.

In pre-European Sāmoa fishermen most probably spent significant amounts of time at sea. This pattern must have continued throughout the 1800s. By the early 1900s, with Sāmoa divided into the two political spheres of German and American Sāmoa, the time spent fishing on the open ocean most likely began to decline. This was due to numerous factors brought upon Sāmoa by the colonial governments as well as the overall influence of Western culture.

Fishermen encounter waves as they head to sea in their bonito canoes.

The two teachers traveled to Aunu'u to wait for favorable sea conditions for the 60-mile crossing. There they found a group of travelers from Manu'a with their canoe, also waiting for the right weather conditions to return home.

When the weather appeared good for a crossing, the three vessels set out for Ta'ū. They may have covered less than half the distance when a storm struck, and the passengers on all three craft found themselves hanging on for their lives. When the storm finally cleared, the Manu'an vessel was lost with all passengers. The other two vessels with Raki and U'ea aboard had survived the storm and reached Ta'ū together. There, in November, 1837, the two teachers officially established the first LMS mission in Manu'a. Within three years LMS missionaries characterized the islands of Manu'a as one of the mission's strongest settlements.

In 1839 the LMS held its first church conference on the island of Manono. All English missionaries and their teachers attended. When the ship carrying the missionaries and teachers dropped anchor off the reef between 'Upolu and Manono, they were surprised to see many dozens of canoes stretched in a line from shore to the ship. Seeing their warm reception, the English missionaries believed their work to be making an impression on the Sāmoans.

The missionaries and teachers were welcomed to the island by Malietoa Vai'inupo. His encouraging words at the beginning of the conference gave the missionaries hope that their mission would ultimately succeed.

Presentation of fine mats and sleeping mats from bride's family to groom's family following a wedding in Fagatogo, Tutuila.

However, the values held by these early English missionaries in Sāmoa were in conflict with the life and culture of Sāmoa. They could not separate their religious beliefs from their own personal values. Within a few years their adherence to English cultural values and other personal viewpoints would seriously damage the LMS Church in Sāmoa, resulting in an ever-decreasing number of Church converts.

Atauloma Girls School, completed in 1900– by the London Missionary Society, Afao, Tutuila.

Sunset behind Ofu as seen from the beach at Olosega, Manu'a.

The Church conference in Manono began with a letter to the missionaries from the LMS Board of Directors in London. The letter said in part: ". . . Your charge is to institutionalize the laws of the Church of Sāmoa. Your mission must be to prescribe the ethics and conventions of puritanism . . . profound, lasting change will only emanate from conversion of the heathen heart to that of a true Christian . . . once that is attained, the exercise of discipline becomes a most solemn office of the Church . . ."

The first English missionaries to Sāmoa, who had arrived aboard the *Dunottar Castle* in 1836, were joined at the conference by newly-arrived missionaries James Pratt and Charles Hardie. The pattern of the conference was set following the letter from the LMS Board of Directors. One of the new missionaries said in part, ". . . For the sake of Godliness and decency the Sāmoans will have to mend their ways. . . the Church must eradicate divination and magic. . . insist that the Sabbath

be strictly kept . . . the habits of industry be encouraged. The dignity of work must be enforced . . . our congregations will learn to clothe and house themselves properly. We must convey our Christian sense of propriety and shame, thereby teaching our society's more appropriate manner of living. . ."

Another missionary stated, " . . . We labor among a people who from infancy know only the vices and abominations of heathenism . . . abominations which we, as Christians, cannot even name. We labor among a people who have grown up destitute of a standard of right and wrong . . . who know not how to distinguish between truth and falsehood . . . a great paucity of living examples of moral and religious character exists . . . thereby delaying the eventual success of our mission by many, many years . . ."

Originally, the LMS Board of Directors in London instructed their missionaries to "bring the Sāmoan to the pulpit" as soon as possible.

Beach and old church structure at Ta'ū village, Manu'a.

The issue of Sāmoans preaching the word of God as official members of the ministry was brought before the missionaries at the conference. Nearly every conference delegate disagreed with the concept of Sāmoans preaching God's word. Said one missionary, ". . . those men in London have never been to Sāmoa. We must change their view and rectify their error. How can one preach what he'll never be able to understand?"

The values of these early missionaries were apparent by their statements at the Manono conference. Clearly such values came into conflict with ancient Sāmoan traditions and beliefs. Many of the early missionaries who held to these views failed to realize that Sāmoans welcomed the Church and wanted to accommodate these new beliefs into their lives.

Following nearly a week of debate and discussion among the missionaries, the conference produced the official rules for the LMS Church in Sāmoa. The rules stated in part:

On sex and family relations: The abolition of polygamy and in most cases, divorce.

Prohibition of adultry, fornication and prostitution; the prohibition of obscenity in word and action.

On marriage: No celebration of monogamous marriages in church. Prohibition of certain customary rites, including the exchange of goods and public test of virginity; the prevention of marriages between Christians and non Christians.

On the Sāmoan house: Internal partitioning of houses into rooms. More liberal use of external blinds to increase personal privacy.

On dress and grooming: The imposition of new standards of dress, including 'full coverage' for women and, when at worship, shirts or coats for men. The adoption of hair styles appropriate to the individual's sex, meaning long for women and short for men.

On certain Sāmoan traditions: The abolition of tattooing, mediumship, and the treatment of illness by divination and magic. The prohibition of funeral feasts; the enforcement of burial in the ground of all dead without delay and abolishment of the practice of dispatching corpses to sea in canoes. The prohibition of drinking kava and accompanying ceremonies including the siva and similar dances.

On Christian ethics and values: The Sabbath will be strictly kept. Habits of industry are to be encouraged and the dignity of work enshrined. People must adopt the goal of clothing and housing themselves in a civilized manner. The Christian sense of propriety and shame will be taught in Church schools.

In spite of the missionaries' apparent disdain for Sāmoan traditions and way of life, the Sāmoans themselves were quick to appreciate the new Christian beliefs taught by the missionaries. The islanders enjoyed the sermons and the ceremonies attached to the Christian religion. In time Bible stories were added to the speeches made by talking chiefs, who were among the first to serve as deacons or elders within the village church organization. Other aspects of Sāmoan culture found easy assimilation into church tradition. Generosity in gift exchange had always been a prevalent Sāmoan practice. Christianity provided

the people a new avenue to gain respect by fellow villagers by giving lavishly to the church.

The church brought many positive changes to Sāmoan life, and the Sāmoans themselves recognized the good these changes brought. Despite the many new church rules and regulations imposed on the Christian converts, the new church members in turn received numerous benefits. Christians learned to read and write, and gained spiritual reward for their hard work. They found great joy in church ceremonies, such as baptism, weddings and communion. Church hymns, once translated into Sāmoan, gave rise to church choirs who sang in wonderful new harmonies. Through the church there was easier access to the implements of the outside world such as cotton cloth, metal knives, axes and pots.

In 1845 the LMS established a theological college at Malua on the island of 'Upolu. Though some missionaries persisted in thinking that Sāmoans should not be trained in the ministry,

Rare photograph of village woman with short hair wearing a leaf skirt. Early female converts to Christianity were encouraged by the missionaries to grow their hair long in the European style and to wear cotton clothing. This photo suggests the woman may not have yet joined the Christian church. Circa 1880

Bible in hand, a worshipper waits for church services to begin.

numerous forces outside Sāmoa which affected LMS activities around the world gave the Sāmoan mission no choice. For the Church of Sāmoa to continue, Sāmoans themselves would have to become an integral part of church ministry.

Once Sāmoan teachers and village pastors were assigned to villages it became apparent that they could not be supported by the Sāmoan church. Unknown to the Sāmoans, all monies collected in Sāmoa were sent to LMS headquarters in London. The Sāmoan church was then reimbursed from London according to certain criteria. This proved an unworkable situation and would eventually cause numerous economic difficulties within the Sāmoan church. In time village donations would be kept within the village. Each individual village was then made responsible for the support of their own pastor. This system established in the 1840s still prevails to this day.

▼ ▼ ▼

The missionaries saw numerous conflicts between their beliefs and values and the beliefs and values of the Sāmoan people. Conversely, Sāmoans saw little of this conflict.

Sāmoans, practically from the very beginning in their religious education, found it relatively easy to compartmentalize their traditional beliefs with that of Christianity. What the missionaries found to be in contradiction in the two systems, the Sāmoans found very little to worry about.

Europeans living in Sāmoa through the mid 19th century found the true acceptance of Christianity by Sāmoans to be questionable. One missionary during these years was quoted as saying: ". . . I am afraid that from the Christian viewpoint the missions have not been entirely successful. Instead of accepting Christianity and allowing it to remold their lives, the Sāmoans have taken religious practices taught to them and fitted them inside Sāmoan custom, making them a part of native culture. Christianity has changed Sāmoan theology a little, that is all. There is no religious questioning or conflict – things remain easy-going. Christianity, instead of bursting the bonds of the old life, has been eaten up by it."

The London Missionary Society was not alone in Sāmoa. Approximately one year before the *Dunottar Castle* arrived with the first LMS missionaries in 1836, the Wesleyan Mission, known in Sāmoa as the Lotu Toga – the Tongan Church – had been established by Peter Turner. Wesleyan missionaries began working in Manu'a in 1928, but their efforts were not well received. The Wesleyan Mission achieved substantial growth in 'Upolu during the middle decades of the 1800s. At one point the Wesleyan mission joined with the LMS in a coordinated effort to increase converts and limit church competition between villages, but that union lasted less than a decade.

Marist missionaries of the Roman Catholic Church arrived in Sāmoa in 1845. The Marist mission was headquartered in Apia, with outlying church centers in Savai'i and Tutuila. The Marists found fertile ground among those Sāmoans who had already been converted to the Christian Church and were members of either the LMS or Wesleyan missions. Catholic ceremony such as the Mass and Stations of the Cross, as well as the numerous statues, vestments of priests and other Catholic paraphernalia, were very attractive to Sāmoans, providing the Marist mission with many converts from the LMS church. Manu'a, however, was an exception. The people remained fiercely loyal to the London Missionary Society. As a result, Catholic priests were never allowed to gain a permanent foothold in these three islands.

Missionaries from the Mormon Church began working in Tutuila in 1888. Mormon missionaries attempted to find converts in Ta'ū in 1904, but after three months realized that they faced opposition to their church by village chiefs as well as the Tui Manu'a. Despite efforts in Fitiuta and other Manu'an villages, the Mormons met with little success.

By the early 1900s other denominations were sending missionaries to Sāmoa. The arrival of Christian missionaries continues in the islands through today. Seventh Day Adventist and several varieties of the Pentecostal Church have made inroads in American Sāmoa and have built sizable memberships.

Since the 1980s there has been a rise in the establishment of interdenominational churches in American Sāmoa, as well as growth in popularity of the Bahai faith. However, the work begun by the early LMS missionaries in Sāmoa established a strong foundation. Today, the LMS Church remains the predominant religion in American Sāmoa. The Roman Catholics, Mormons and Methodists also maintain substantial church membership.

The church begun by the London Missionary Society in the 1830s came to be known as the Congregational Christian Church of Sāmoa. Originally the Congregational Christian Church of Sāmoa was headquartered in (Western) Sāmoa. American Sāmoa was one of eight districts within the church. In the 1970s a

By 1982 the CCCAS had become a financially sound and progressively-operated church organization. Plans were made to construct a church center in Tafuna to be named Kanana Fou. By 1984 the church center had completed the first phase of construction, including church offices and housing for pastors. Construction on the cathedral began and plans were begun to build housing and classrooms for a seminary. In 1997 a multi-million dollar gymnasium and athletic facility were completed. Kanana Fou had become a true religious center for seminarians, church conferences, retired and elderly pastors, athletic and youth activities and a wide range of community uses.

Tafuna also became the central location for the operation of the territory's Catholic Church. In the late 1980s and early 1990s planning and construction began on the cathedral, church hall, dormitories, and other support buildings. Construction of the new complex, named Fatu O Aiga, was completed at a cost of more than $3,000,000.

Congregational Christian Church, Leone, Tutuila.

division arose between the American Sāmoa district and church officials in (Western) Sāmoa over the distribution of church monies raised in American Sāmoa. The result was a declaration by the American Sāmoa branch to become an independent church entity. This proved to be a very successful organizational move for the American Sāmoa church, who took the official name Congregational Christian Church of American Sāmoa (CCCAS).

'They appeared very knowing merchants . . . lively with all, which is indeed their natural disposition.'

— Missionary John Williams

Chapter 5

Colonists And Commerce

The traditional dress of Sāmoan men prior to the arrival of Europeans was a small circle of ti leaves around the waist. Men also wore a loin cloth made of tapa called a malo. Women wore a slightly larger, thicker skirt of leaves around their waists which extended to their knees. On formal occasions both men and women wore skirts fashioned from a "fine mat," as well as wrap-around skirts of tapa cloth which were known as lavalava.

The ti leaf skirts were hot, heavy and not especially comfortable, and the tapa lavalava could not be washed. Once Europeans began to arrive in Sāmoa the islanders quickly understood the benefits of cotton cloth. And, being men of the sea themselves, Sāmoans immediately determined that European ships, after long months at sea, needed to be re-provisioned. By 1836 commerce in the Sāmoan islands had begun.

Southwest coastline near Vaitogi.

Women wanted not only cotton cloth, but needles and thread. They quickly acquired an interest in mirrors, certain musical instruments, metal pots and utensils. By the 1840s a demand for manufactured articles had been created. Villagers quickly adapted to this demand and adjusted certain aspects of their daily lives in order to provide the trade goods necessary to "purchase" the articles they wanted.

Barter became the medium of exchange for imported items. In 1839, Commodore Charles Wilkes of the United States Navy sailed into Pago Pago aboard the USS Vincennes. The first Sāmoan chief that Commodore Wilkes met asked for his uniform coat.

Wilkes offered the chief a fine metal hatchet, which the chief gladly accepted.

Wilkes was in Sāmoa as commander of the Wilkes Expedition to chart and survey the Sāmoan Islands. He anchored the Vincennes off the island of *Ta'ū* during the course of his expedition and found that the islanders were interested in trading for metal fishhooks and tobacco. Not long after Wilkes left Sāmoa to return to the United States, Sāmoan chiefs began bartering for guns to supply their armies. The demand for guns would last the remainder of the century, as Sāmoa fought one civil war after another.

Commodore Wilkes named money as a medium of exchange in Sāmoa in 1839, though barter was the most common means by which Sāmoans acquired imported products. By 1842 Sāmoans had learned that coconut oil was needed in Europe to make candles and soap. Coconuts quickly became a form of currency, for access to this tree was available to every Sāmoan who had the motivation to harvest the nuts.

Crude presses were used at first to crush the oil from the coconut meat. The oil was then stored in barrels to wait for shipment. This process proved wasteful and difficult, and was soon abandoned once a better system was devised. The most convenient and economical way to process coconut oil and ship it to Europe was the use of the mature coconut, called copra. The dried meat of the nut was cut into pieces by the villagers, who then set the pieces out in the sun to dry. This natural process evaporated the water content and shrunk the meat from the shell. The bits of dried coconut meat were then collected and taken to a central location to be weighed, bagged, then stored to await the arrival of a vessel.

John Williams, Jr., son of the LMS missionary, was the first person to begin a copra trading operation in Sāmoa. Williams exported six tons of copra in 1842. Williams conducted much of his business with Sydney, Australia, which was regularly served by ships traveling to and from Europe. Williams exported copra to Sydney, and in return imported those items which were in demand, which were then called "trade goods."

The LMS church was drawn into the trade business by the early 1840s, the reasons being both spiritual and practical. From the spiritual standpoint, missionaries in Sāmoa believed that the slow pace of island life was not conducive to good Christian living. They believed that idle time gave rise to certain activities which they hoped to eradicate. It made sense to church leaders to encourage villagers to become engaged in copra trading for they believed it kept church members "busy." From the practical standpoint, copra trading afforded church members the opportunity to acquire trade goods which the LMS believed church members should have, such as cotton cloth, which could be made into clothing to wear to church.

The harbor of Pago Pago is far superior to the harbor at Apia, both in size and the protection it offered to ships at anchor. Apia, however,

Looking east from Coconut Point. Rainmaker Mountain is visible center right with Flower Pot Rock below.

was by far a more active port through the middle decades of the 19th century. 'Upolu was a more productive island than Tutuila due to its much larger size, thick soil and gradual slopes. The copra trade grew rapidly in 'Upolu, and by 1850 Apia harbor was crowded with both trading and whaling ships. Apia itself was growing rapidly, as numerous businesses, shops and trading establishments were springing up along Beach Road.

Outside Apia merchants were assisted by traders who served as agents in outlying districts. Villagers took their copra to the agents who usually worked from a small "bush" store. The villagers were paid mostly by credit, which they in turn used to buy their cotton cloth and needed metal items.

In 1854 commerce took a great leap forward in the Sāmoan islands. Herr August Unshelm of the large German firm, J.C. Godeffroy and Company of Hamburg, determined that Sāmoa was the best island group in the southwest Pacific in which to establish the production of coconut oil on a large scale. Godeffroy had the financial resources, outstanding management and the determination to expand the company. In 1857 Godeffroy opened their first company store at Matafele fronting Apia harbor. Unshelm moved quickly. He bought two pieces of property at the west end of Beach Road. Here he built company housing for his staff, a massive warehouse and the first of three wharves to serve company ships.

The first German consul, Herr Gunter Preuss, arrived in 1861. Preuss began immediately to establish Germany as the premier political force in Sāmoa, replacing Great Britain and the United States. Unshelm turned his energies

Fagatogo village near site of present-day market. Circa 1900

Three youths on a fishing expedition carry their hand-made outrigger canoe to the lagoon. Sa'ilele, Tutuila.

to German control of Sāmoa and company expansion. He built a two-story building on the most prominent corner of what would later become the center of Apia. The building housed the German consulate on the first floor, and J.C. Godeffroy staff on the second. With that important building complete, he designed the company treasury building, company stores, and Apia's first hotel–to be owned and operated by the company. Plans were made to build a second, larger wharf, a German hospital, and a half-dozen other necessary buildings for the overhaul of company ships putting into Apia.

When construction of these necessary elements to Godeffroy's operation were completed, Unshelm began to extend his company's reach throughout the South Pacific. Coconut oil, turtle shell, pearl and copra were obtained in the Marquesas, Fiji, Tonga, Tahiti and the Gilbert Islands, transported to Apia on company ships and stored in company warehouses until shipment back to Hamburg.

August Unshelm was lost at sea in 1864. It would be his successor, Herr Theodore Weber,

who made J.C. Godeffroy the most powerful trading company of its time in the southwest Pacific. At Godeffroy headquarters in Apia, Weber presided over a corps of German clerks and young executives. He operated the company like an army general, using military-style discipline throughout all levels of company operation. His approach to business in Sāmoa was simple: Control everything.

Weber devised the concept of permanent coconut plantations, where coconut trees were planted in perfectly straight lines with proper separation between them, to insure maximum yield. He planted cotton between the rows of coconut trees, which proved to be very successful and profitable. To keep weeds from his plantations, he imported cattle. When it became obvious to Weber that Sāmoans would not work for wages in his plantations, he imported indentured laborers from Micronesia and the Solomon Islands.

The copra trade, and its by-product coconut oil, proved to be very profitable, as did the export of cotton. Shipping lanes from Sāmoa to Europe were busy with traffic from ships laden

with products from the Godeffroy plantations. Even with the success of his exports, Weber continued to experiment with other products such as coffee, chinchona, tobacco, jute and sugar cane.

Godeffroy expanded beyond 'Upolu to Savai'i and Tutuila. Weber himself traveled to Pago Pago on numerous occasions to meet with Paramount Chief Mauga, though his reasons in meeting with Mauga were more political than to expand business operations. Tutuila was too small and mountainous to establish coconut plantations on a large scale.

The Polynesian Land Company was the first large American business to operate in Sāmoa. The firm was organized to speculate in real estate. James Stewart, the company agent, was especially interested in Pago Pago harbor. From the beginning he believed Pago Pago was the best harbor in the South Pacific and would be an ideal place to establish a commercial depot. Stewart apparently persuaded a number of chiefs to seek American annexation of Tutuila. He also hoped for more active American intervention regarding Pago Pago harbor. But he was unable to garner any American political interest. When it became clear the U.S. government was not interested in Pago Pago harbor, the Polynesian Land Company collapsed and the land it had acquired was sold at auction.

The Union Pacific Railroad was completed in the United States in 1869. Travel and shipment from England to the American east coast and across the North American continent to the Pacific was greatly reduced in both time and expense. This one event had unexpected repercussions that would eventually be felt on the island of Tutuila.

By 1871 both Australia and New Zealand had become important British colonial outposts in the Pacific. The colonial governments in both Sydney and Auckland sought to open regular shipping lanes to San Francisco in order to expand trade not only to the United States, but also to faraway England. The two colonies offered a subsidy to Mr. W.H. Webb of New York, who had proposed a similar plan to the U.S. government to open shipping lanes to Australia and New Zealand. When he realized there was no government interest in his plan, he accepted the offer from Australia and New Zealand. His shipping line at first provided service with side-wheel steamers which had been used during the Civil War. By 1875 more modern ships of the Pacific Mail Steamship Company were traversing the Pacific from San Francisco to Auckland and Sydney.

The major problems facing the steamers of the day were limited fuel capacity and a lack of coaling stations along their routes. Webb knew of Pago Pago as a potential site to establish a coaling station. He sent Captain E. Wakeman to Tutuila in 1871 to look over Pago Pago and report on its suitability. Wakeman reported that Pago Pago was the best harbor in the south Pacific, and that the Sāmoans were a ". . . fine race." Wakeman also informed the United States Navy that Pago Pago harbor was about to fall into German hands due to a lack of U.S. interest in the Sāmoan Islands.

That same year the New Zealand government recommended to London that the Sāmoan Islands should be brought "in some form under the protection or guidance of Great Britain or a British colony." Government leaders in Auckland were also growing nervous about expanding German influence.

On February 14, 1872, a number of months after Wakeman had provided his findings to the U.S. Navy, Commander Richard W. Meade, USN, in command of the USS *Narragansett*, sailed into Pago Pago harbor. Meade had been sent to Sāmoa at the request of Henry A. Pierce, U.S. Minister to Hawai'i, to make a treaty with Sāmoan chiefs in the hope of establishing some sort of official American interest in the islands.

While the *Narragansett* remained off shore charting the waters and reefs at the entrance of Pago Pago harbor, Commander Meade met with Paramount Chief Mauga to discuss the possibility of renting land in the harbor area for a U.S. Naval station. Chief Mauga, as the highest ranking chief of the area, granted the United States the exclusive right to build and maintain a naval station in the harbor area in return for the "friendship and protection of the great government of the United States."

'Afa--sennit braid plaited from the strands of coconut-husk fiber.

Sennit lashings hold cross-beams of *fale* roof support structure (left). Beginning stages of *fale* construction (top).

Once the agreement was reached, Commander Meade established a set of commercial regulations for the port and named a board to insure port regulations were enforced. Meade

Europeans began entering the Pacific in large numbers during the middle decades of the 1800s.

appointed Mauga to the board, the agent of the California and Australian Steamship Company, as well as the foreign consuls assigned there. Meade then entered into an agreement with the chiefs of Tutuila's eastern district, in which they promised to uphold the agreement Mauga had signed with Meade.

The "treaty" signed between Commander Meade and the chiefs of Tutuila was never officially approved by the United States Senate. Nevertheless, Mauga and the other signatories considered it binding.

▼ ▼ ▼

Mauga's treaty with Commander Meade did not go unnoticed by the Germans in Apia. Theodore Weber hurried to Pago Pago to meet with Mauga. He warned the paramount chief that the treaty he had signed with Meade was not official and that German rights in Tutuila must be upheld.

Though he could not have known it at the time, Herr Weber's meeting with Mauga set the stage for the next decade of Sāmoan history, in which the colonial powers would position themselves to further their own country's interests in the islands.

Civil war broke out in 'Upolu when Malietoa Laupepa and Malietoa Talavou fought over the proper succession and right to be the true holder of the

Paramount Chief Mauga Moimoi of Pago Pago (right), one of the signatories of the Deed of Cession.

Malietoa title. The war between the two Malietoa factions provided Theodore Weber and the Germans with a golden opportunity—and they seized upon that opportunity quickly. Trading guns for land the Germans positioned themselves to acquire even more political power than they already possessed.

In August, 1873, Colonel Albert B. Steinberger arrived in Pago Pago. Steinberger would become one of the more remarkable figures in Sāmoa's history. Steinberger, a friend of American President Ulysses S. Grant, arrived in Sāmoa as Grant's personal emissary as well as "special agent" of Secretary of State Hamilton Fish.

Fish appointed Steinberger to study and report on the people, products and harbors of the Sāmoan Islands. Fish also told Steinberger to express his views on the protection of the islanders in his report and to warn them not to sell their land to foreigners.

When Steinberger met with Paramount Chief Mauga in Pago Pago he found the chief already considered the harbor, if not all of Tutuila, to be under the protection of the United States by virtue of his treaty with Commander Meade. Steinberger noticed, however, that certain aspects of the treaty had been disregarded, especially those that concerned themselves with shipping and anchorage. It became clear to Steinberger that Mauga could not maintain the harbor facilities by himself, as the other members of the board were eighty miles away in Apia.

Steinberger sailed on to Apia where he found a Fono serving as a semi-official assembly. With his commission from Secretary of State Fish and his association with President Grant, Colonel Steinberger was warmly welcomed by the majority of Sāmoan leaders in 'Upolu. Steinberger moved quickly to advise the Sāmoans to protect their land. The Sāmoans themselves correctly deduced that Steinberger was a sincere man with Sāmoan interests at heart. Within a few short months Sāmoan leadership presented Steinberger with the symbols of a talking chief – the flywhisk and staff – as well as

the fine mat of the Tui Atua, and informed him that Sāmoa desired to become a protectorate of the United States. He was also given a letter signed by Malietoa Laupepa which was to be given personally to "The Chief Who Rules America." The letter stated that Malietoa Laupepa hoped the "American Chief" would appoint Steinberger to assist Sāmoa in planning a future government.

Soon thereafter the Fono, which now consisted of two governing bodies – the upper house, or *Ta'imua*; and a lower house, the *Faipule* –passed a new constitution. The new *Ta'imua* gave Steinberger a letter addressed to President Grant asking for his personal guidance as well as expressing their concern over German influence in the islands. The letter was drafted with the assistance, or advice, of certain LMS missionaries, the Roman Catholic Bishop and the Reverend George Brown of the Wesleyan mission. These church representatives believed this letter to be a reasonably valid expression of the will of Sāmoa's leaders at the time.

Steinberger returned to Tutuila, landing at the village of Leone. There he found that High Chiefs Satele and Tuitele endorsed the *Ta'imua*'s letter to President Grant. He then traveled over-land to Pago Pago – a one-day trip – and was again cordially received by Mauga, who also added his strong support for United States protec-tion. Following his meetings with Mauga, Steinberger then sailed to Manu'a to discuss the *Ta'imua*'s letter with the Tui Manu'a. However, Steinberger was saddened when he found the Tui Manu'a incapacitated by blindness and old age. Tui Manu'a's advisors, however, did express to

Steinberger that they were entirely satisfied with things as they were in their islands and showed little interest in getting involved with political activities in Tutuila and 'Upolu.

Steinberger returned to Washington, D.C. and presented the letter to President Grant along with the flywhisk, staff, and fine mat of Tui Atua. At the time, Grant was faced with numerous political problems, many of them from within his own Republican party. He was not enthusiastic about the idea of taking on some form of respon-sibility for the Sāmoan Islands, which at the time seemed to be at the far end of the globe. Facing such problems as reconstruction in the South, and

Family members working together in this traditional Sāmoan scene. The woman is weaving coconut leaves into "pola" – which can be seen hanging from under the thatch. The men are breaking coconuts to make coconut cream which will be squeezed into bowl.

Ofu and Olosega in the distance as seen from Ta'ū, Manu'a.

Tutuila as seen in this military photograph taken in 1939. Pago Pago bay is visible, center, with the Pola rocks-- "Cockscomb"--jutting out from Vatia village, right. Faga'itua bay is in foreground.

Ulysses S. Grant, 18th President of the United States, 1869-1877. Grant was the first American president to officially send an emissary to Sāmoa.

Indian wars in the West, Grant knew Congress would not be interested in Sāmoa. But Steinberger presented a good case for official recognition of the new Sāmoan government in Apia, stressing the geographic importance Sāmoa held to future American shipping in the Pacific.

President Grant forwarded Steinberger's report to the Senate. Steinberger understood that it would take some time for the Senate to act upon his report. He took advantage of the available time by sailing to Hamburg, the results of which would become apparent in the ensuing months.

When Steinberger returned to Washington he met with members of Congress. He soon realized that Congress showed little interest in Sāmoa and was therefore unwilling to act upon his recommendations. It became disappointingly clear to Steinberger that Congress would not consider the annexation or protection of Sāmoa regardless of growing German influence. Steinberger was further disappointed when President Grant could not offer him an official position as government agent to Sāmoa. Grant did ask Steinberger to return to Sāmoa on Grant's behalf – with neither salary nor expense money – in order to deliver a letter to the Sāmoans thanking them for their gifts and expressing his interest and support for the new Sāmoan government.

Steinberger returned to Apia on April 1, 1875 aboard the USS *Tuscarora*. The Constitution the Sāmoans had devised in 1873 had already been revised, allowing for two "kings" at the head of government: Malietoa Laupepa and Pule Pule of A'ana. Steinberger presented Grant's letter to the Sāmoan leadership, who, it appears, were further impressed with Steinberger's relationship with the President of the United States as well as the fact he had returned to Sāmoa aboard a warship of the U.S. Navy. This opened the door for Steinberger to become actively involved in the political affairs of Sāmoa's young government, which he was eager to accept. Within a very short period of time A.B. Steinberger took charge of the Sāmoan government.

Steinberger's first act was to abolish the offices of the two Sāmoan "kings," and in so doing proved he understood much of the subtleties of Sāmoan culture as they related to the royal chiefly titles. He devised a plan preserving the "royal honor" between the Malietoa and Tupua families by establishing a "royal term of office" to each titleholder for a four-year period. The *Ta'imua* selected Malietoa Laupepa to serve the first four-year term. Steinberger placed Malietoa Laupepa in residence at Mulinu'u and deemed that he be crowned with the title, "King Malietoa I." He then increased the membership of the *Ta'imua* to fourteen and entrusted it with the responsibility to select the judiciary. He next increased the membership of the *Faipule* to forty, giving that body the authority to elect the king. These two acts completed, Steinberger then moved on to the most important act of all: he created the Office of Prime Minister.

The Office of Prime Minister established, he initiated the enactment whereby the king could take no action without the prior knowledge of

the Prime Minister and that the Prime Minister had the right to address both houses of the legislature. Sāmoan leadership gave Steinberger himself the position of Prime Minister on July 4, 1875. He immediately wrote a letter to the Department of State notifying Secretary Fish of his appointment, adding that he would not accept any salary until he was assured that the State Department approved of his new status.

With Steinberger as Prime Minister, the Sāmoan government had a strong advocate who stood for Sāmoan rights against the self-serving interests of both the European consuls and foreign companies. It did not take long before foreigners in Apia became disgruntled with the fact that Sāmoa, for the first time, had a legitimate government. They did not like the idea of being restricted in their business practices by new laws and regulations.

United States Consul, Steven Foster, was also unhappy with the fact that Steinberger had assumed a position superior to his own. Even the leadership of the LMS mission questioned Steinberger's position as Prime Minister. Foster wrote his superiors at the State Department asking them if Steinberger's position in the government indicated an American protectorate over Sāmoa. In his response, Secretary Fish indicated there was no such protectorate and that Steinberger was simply an emissary whose mission to Sāmoa had been fulfilled. Foster, who had developed a personal dislike for Steinberger, used Fish's letter to undermine Steinberger's authority within the foreign community. It did not take long before everyone who was unhappy with the new government held Steinberger responsible and pointed their attacks at him. With Foster's urging, the British consul, S.F. Williams, and the LMS mission soon opposed the Prime Minister.

Steinberger held office for only five months. On December 12, 1875, the HMS *Barracouta*, commanded by Captain Stevens of the Royal Navy, dropped anchor in Apia harbor. U.S. Consul Foster and British Consul Williams hurried aboard ship and complained to Stevens to the effect that Steinberger held his office under false pretenses and that Sāmoan leadership had been misled about his association with the American government. Based on both Foster's and Williams' testimony, Captain Stevens landed British bluejackets at Mulinu'u who seized Malietoa and brought him aboard the *Barracouta*. The warship then put to sea for several days during which time they convinced the King that Steinberger was a usurper who should have never been given his position as Prime Minister. Upon

his return Malietoa dismissed Steinberger, only to realize that he himself had been deposed as King by the *Ta'imua* and the *Faipule*.

At the same time Consul Foster became suspicious of German support for Steinberger. While Malietoa was aboard the *Barracouta*, Foster boarded the yacht Peerless, which had been given to the Prime Minster by the Godeffroy Company. There he discovered papers that Steinberger had met with Godeffroy officials in Hamburg, where

Tranquil waters near Afono village on Tutuila's north shore.

he had negotiated a preferred position for the company in the field of commerce in return for German support of his political ambitions. Foster had found the evidence he needed to destroy Steinberger's credibility. He took the papers to Captain Stevens, who ordered Steinberger be arrested and held as a prisoner until the *Barracouta* sailed for Fiji.

Once Steinberger arrived in Fiji a series of political repercussions began that would be felt from London to Washington. Sir Arthur Gordon, Governor of Fiji, found Steinberger's incarceration to be illegal and ordered him released. Steinberger sailed to New Zealand where he protested his arrest by the British Navy and demanded damages. Once the U.S. State Department learned what had transpired in Apia, they

Orator, Ta'ū, Manu'a. Circa 1938

investigated the matter by sending an official to London to determine the British understanding of the events that had occurred. As a result of the investigation the State Department dismissed Foster for having entered into an illegal conspiracy with a military officer of a foreign warship against a fellow U.S. citizen. In London, Her Majesty's government was quite displeased with the role

factions who sought power and from Theodore Weber, who wanted it dissolved altogether.

Threatened by German authority and facing rebellion by the rival faction known as the *Puletua*, the *Ta'imua* and *Faipule* decided that continuance of their government could be found only under the protection of either Britain or the United States. They sent emissaries to Fiji and

Sunu'itao Peak, Ofu, Manu'a. The strait between Ofu and Olosega is just beyond the base of the peak, lower right.

Consul Williams had played in the conspiracy and relieved him of his post. Captain Stevens was tried by court martial for actions grossly exceeding his authority.

Steinberger, though somewhat absolved by the actions taken against Foster and Williams, never returned to Sāmoa. His efforts to build a viable Sāmoan government did prove, however, to have been founded on solid footing. Even without him the "Steinberger government," as it was called, continued for a number of years. As time passed, the government faced numerous challenges to its authority, from both rival Sāmoan

Washington to find out whether either government would intervene on their behalf.

The Sāmoan delegates to Fiji were warmly received by Sir Arthur Gordon and Fijian King Cacobau, but Sir Gordon could give the delegates nothing but his personal support for their government. The delegate to Washington, Mamea, however, fared much better. He received considerable – and very favorable – press upon arrival in San Francisco. Once in Washington, Mamea was received by both President Rutherford B. Hayes and the Secretary of State. Although Mamea could not convince government officials to

Looking west from Si'u Point, Ta'ū. In the distance Si'ufa'alele Point.

assume an American protectorate over his islands, he did succeed in negotiating a treaty between the United States and Sāmoa. The treaty was ratified by the Senate on February 13, 1878. It provided for mutual peace and friendship between the two countries for a period of ten years and included the following articles: the treaty was renewable; it confirmed the right of the United States to establish a naval station at Pago Pago (although the right was not exclusive); it empowered the consul of the United States in Apia to settle disputes arising between Sāmoans and Americans. Most importantly, the treaty bound the United States to use its consular offices in the event that Sāmoa should become engaged in a dispute with any third nation.

While Mamea was away on his mission, the *Puletua* revolted against the *Ta'imua* and *Faipule*. They were quickly suppressed in 'Upolu, but the fighting grew serious in Tutuila. Mauga of Pago Pago supported the *Puletua* in their revolt. He assembled troops that had been armed by ex-consul Foster, who had settled in Pago Pago after his dismissal. The government forces, based at Leone, attacked Pago Pago and set fire to every building, forcing the *Puletua* warriors to escape to the islet of Aunu'u. From their stronghold on Aunu'u, *Puletua* forces attacked villages who supported the government, but their revolt had been doomed from the start. Facing certain defeat they escaped Aunu'u for villages on the northeast coast of Tutuila where they hoped to establish a solid defensive position. LMS pastor Charles Phillips then persuaded Mauga that his cause was lost and that he should surrender. Mauga finally agreed and surrendered his warriors at Leone. A trial was held and the warriors were released after a payment of fines. As reparation for his role in the revolt, Mauga was forced to yield a fine mat which was considered to be extremely valuable.

When Mamea returned to Apia with his treaty he was accompanied by U.S. Commissioner G.W. Goward. The American Commissioner had been appointed to ensure the new treaty was properly executed. The *Ta'imua* and *Faipule* accepted the treaty with enthusiasm and gave Mamea a hero's welcome. As a symbol of their appreciation, they presented Goward with the fine mat that had been given by Mauga as his reparation. Goward then sailed to Tutuila where, on August 5, 1878, he signed agreements with

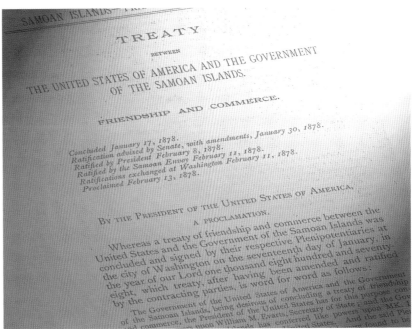

land-owners which transferred certain lands to the U.S. Navy for use as a coaling depot. Goward then instructed that the United States flag be raised on Goat Island in Pago Pago bay.

▼ ▼ ▼

The treaty of 1878 proved to be an especially important document in terms of the political and economic forces at play in 19th century

Treaty of Friendship between Sāmoa and the United States, 1878. The treaty confirmed the right of the United States to establish a naval station at Pago Pago.

Sāmoa. The treaty accomplished two major steps: first, it recognized Sāmoa as an independent nation; and second, it gave the United States an official foothold in Pago Pago harbor. At the same time, however, it entangled the United States in Sāmoa's political affairs which were to become extremely sticky in the months and years ahead.

The Germans were not happy with the treaty Mamea had negotiated in Washington and in turn made a treaty with the Sāmoan government themselves. The treaty protected German lands acquired earlier; exempted German ship-

Bananas and coconuts for sale, Fagatogo Market, Tutuila.

ping from the payment of tonnage dues; granted German citizens the right to be tried according to German law; and accorded the German Navy the right to build a naval station at Saluafata in Savai'i to counteract the American naval presence at Pago Pago.

Although the Sāmoan government had now been officially recognized by the United States and Germany, Malietoa Talavou soon stepped forward to challenge its authority by seizing Mulinu'u by force, proclaiming himself "King of Sāmoa." When the USS *Lackawanna* arrived in Apia, her commanding officer did not know which government to recognize, the "old" government which had signed the treaties, or the government now headed by Malietoa Talavou. The commander compromised and invited the *Ta'imua* and *Faipule* to his ship, where he honored them with a salute from his guns. At the recommendation of the American, British and German consuls, he gave Malietoa Talavou the same honor.

When Sir Arthur Gordon arrived in Apia to make a treaty on behalf of Great Britain, he faced the same quandary as had the *Lackawanna's* commander. Again at the advice of the three consuls, he decided to conduct the treaty with Malietoa Talavou, who was seated at Mulinu'u, while the *Ta'imua* and *Faipule* were dispersed outside Apia. After signing the treaty Sir Arthur was surprised when Talavou offered Sāmoa as an outright gift to Britain. The British envoy explained he had no authority to accept such a proposal. Talavou then asked instead that Sāmoa be given joint protection by Great Britain, Germany and the United States.

Meanwhile the foreigners living in Apia were unhappy with any form of Sāmoan government, regardless of who was officially in power. While Sir Arthur was in Apia the foreigners took advantage of his presence and convinced him that serious changes needed to be made to protect their interests. In conjunction with Sir Arthur and the three consuls a municipal convention was drafted declaring Apia as a separate entity from the surrounding environs. The convention also placed Apia under the authority of a municipal board composed of the three consuls. The new municipal board was given the responsibility to maintain a police force, license businesses, issue sanitary ordinances and levy taxes.

Sāmoans were in actuality excluded from the creation of the new municipal organization. They were, however, allowed to fly their flag above the building where the board held its meetings and were granted a guarantee that the convention could be renewed, altered or abolished after a period of four years depending on the circumstances that existed at that time. When the convention was signed on September 2, 1879, the American signers indicated their signatures were subject to approval by the U.S. State Department. In time the State Department notified American officials in Apia that the department regarded the convention as a necessary arrangement, but that it did not have the force or effect of a treaty.

The rivalry between Malietoa Talavou, who was himself a forceful leader who demanded the respect of all who knew him, and the "old" government" continued, leaving the stability of Sāmoa's government in question. In late 1879 the German warship SMS *Bismarck* arrived in Apia, and the timing of her arrival couldn't have been better, as Talavou's warriors and the warriors of the *Ta'imua* and *Faipule* were poised for battle.

The *Bismarck's* commanding officer, Captain Deinhart, called upon the opposing

factions to meet aboard his ship. On December 15, 1879 Deinhart secured an agreement in which both factions would support previous treaties and abide by the municipal convention. Under Deinhart's direction a new constitution was drafted which made Malietoa Talavou "king for life." In keeping with the spirit of compromise, *Malietoa Laupepa* was given the title of "regent." The membership of both the *Ta'imua* and *Faipule* were changed, with the two houses basing membership on the population of each representative district. A standing committee of the *Ta'imua* would remain permanently in session, with both houses meeting on an annual basis. Any disagreements between the *Ta'imua* and *Faipule* would be settled by the king.

The primary weakness of the "Bismarck Constitution" was that it had been conducted entirely by German authorities to the exclusion of both the British and Americans. Three months later, in March, 1880, the document was succeeded by a new agreement in which the Americans and British participated. The new agreement contained a preamble in which Talavou's desire for Sāmoa to be protected under the authority of the three powers was clarified, along with his wishes that all issues of general concern be discussed by the three consuls. It was clear to all that Talavou wanted joint protection by the three powers over Sāmoa and that as long as he was king, he would willingly support that arrangement.

Eight months later, on November 8, 1880, Talavou suddenly and unexpectedly died, leaving Sāmoa without the one powerful leader around which the new government had been organized. However, it was the view of many Sāmoans, regardless of Talavou's many qualities, that the new agreement had put the Malietoa lineage in a special class above other titles. Members of the *Faipule* began to search for a new leader around whom they could cast their support. They found that Tui A'ana Tamasese was the man they were looking for, for in his veins flowed another line of "royal" blood. When Malietoa Laupepa was crowned to succeed Talavou, the *Faipule* rejected Laupepa's succession and claimed Tamasese as their "king."

The USS *Lackawanna* returned to Sāmoa in the middle months of 1881. With Sāmoa's government split in two, the foreigners requested Captain Gillis, commander of the ship, to try to solve the situation. The result was the "Lackawanna Agreement," signed on July 12, 1881, which once again divided kingly authority between *Malietoa Laupepa* and Tamasese. The former was named king, and Tamasese, vice-king.

For the moment the agreement satisfied all of Sāmoa's rival factions, but it recreated the impossible arrangement of two kings. Further, it failed to determine the time frame of the two positions or how their successions would occur.

Although little thought was given to America's involvement in the Lackawanna Treaty at the time, the treaty would become yet one more affair which would draw the United States progressively deeper into the entanglement of Sāmoan affairs.

Curios and handicrafts for sale to passengers arriving in Pago Pago harbor aboard a Matson liner, Fagatogo *malae.* **Circa 1930**

Rutherford B. Hayes, 19th President of the United States, 1877-1881. Hayes was the first American president to receive an official delegate from Sāmoa.

"In no place have I landed where better arrangements were made or greater order preserved."
— Missionary John Williams

Chapter 6

American Interest
In Sāmoa Grows

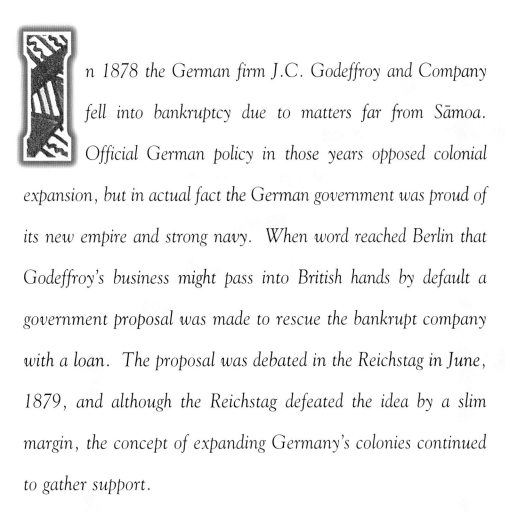

n 1878 the German firm J.C. Godeffroy and Company fell into bankruptcy due to matters far from Sāmoa. Official German policy in those years opposed colonial expansion, but in actual fact the German government was proud of its new empire and strong navy. When word reached Berlin that Godeffroy's business might pass into British hands by default a government proposal was made to rescue the bankrupt company with a loan. The proposal was debated in the Reichstag in June, 1879, and although the Reichstag defeated the idea by a slim margin, the concept of expanding Germany's colonies continued to gather support.

Vatia Bay, Tutuila.

German interests in Sāmoa were too big — and too important – to be allowed to fall under British or American influence. The number of Germans in Sāmoa was greater than that of all other foreigners combined. Since Germans controlled four-fifths of the islands' business, it was natural for the Germans to take management of Sāmoa's affairs into their own hands. And since the largest German interest had been J.C. Godeffroy and Company, it only made sense that Godeffroy led the Germans.

Political leaders in Berlin insisted that Germans overseas be officially supported. The end result of that policy was the rescue of the Godeffroy firm, which emerged from its financial troubles with the name "Deutsche Handels und Plantagen Gesellschaft der Sudsee zu Hamburg," or, German Commercial and Plantation Company, which was commonly shortened to "The D.H. & P.G.," or simply, "The Firm." As far as Sāmoa's political affairs were concerned, the

Western tip of Tutuila near Poloa.

name change meant nothing. Theodore Weber continued to direct The Firm's operations while at the same time assumed the role, in the opinion of many, as the most powerful man in Sāmoa.

In 1875 Weber's operations were joined by a second German firm, Hedemann, Ruge and Company. Between the two German companies the entire Apia waterfront was dominated by German buildings and agriculture-based operations. "The moment you enter the harbor," wrote a German official in the 1880s, "your eye rests upon the great warehouses and business premises of the German firms Hedeman, Ruge and Company and the German Commercial and Plantation Company, especially the establishment for the cleaning of cotton and for the processing of coconuts by steam. The extensive buildings and stately row of houses occupied by employees of the company are conspicuous objects, while you perceive clearly on the green hills that come down close to the harbor the extensive German plantations of Vaitele, Moto'otua, Vailele, and especially the coffee plantations of Utumapu lying above the rest."

Political affairs in Sāmoa remained relatively quiet through the early 1880s. The two German companies continued to expand, German influence continued to grow, and Theodore Weber continued to wield tremendous power in all affairs affecting the islands.

In 1884 the German consul, Dr. Stuebel, imposed a new agreement on Malietoa Laupepa. Stuebel was relatively new to Sāmoa, and as such was a man many considered to be under the complete influence of Theodore Weber. Stuebel's agreement established a council consisting of himself, two other Germans and two Sāmoans. The council was charged with the authority to draft laws for the mutual benefit of their two peoples. It further provided that Malietoa should appoint a German secretary to advise on all matters concerning German interests and to act as judge in the event of a dispute.

The British and American consuls immediately saw Stuebel's move for what it was – an attempt by Theodore Weber to further extend Germany's control over Sāmoan leadership with the eventual goal of officially making Sāmoa a German colony. In response to the American and British concerns, Stuebel claimed, with backing from the German government, that this new agreement was only an implementation of the earlier German-Sāmoan Treaty. Malietoa Laupepa clearly saw the new agreement would result in a government by and for the Germans.

Unwilling to oppose the Germans publicly, Malietoa signed a petition addressed to Great Britain which implored that Sāmoa be annexed outright to the British Empire. Vice-King Tamasese and other Sāmoan chiefs also signed the petition. The petition was delivered only days before the new agreement was to take effect. On November 10, 1884, the date the agreement was to take effect, Malietoa notified the American consul he had signed the German agreement under duress.

Dr. Steubel was incensed that Malietoa had gone to the British and Americans pleading his case against the agreement. Steubel was further angered over the petition which had been given to the British. Wasting little time, Steubel directed the commanding officer of a German warship to land a party of sailors to detain Malietoa until the German flag could be raised over Mulinu'u. The British and American consuls were outraged, but were powerless to act. Unconcerned with their protests, Steubel resigned from Apia's Municipal Board, thereby ceasing the Board's operations.

With Malietoa detained by the German navy, Steubel knew he needed a Sāmoan of "royal" stature to replace Malietoa – also someone he could control. Steubel approached Vice King Tui A'ana Tamasese. Due to the probability that Tamasese was unhappy with his secondary status, he listened to Steubel's proposal. Tamasese withdrew to Leulumoega where, after meeting with the *Ta'imua* and *Faipule*, he proclaimed himself "King of Sāmoa." Even though Tamasese had signed the petition to Great Britain, Steubel believed he had a strong claimant to Sāmoa's highest position. On behalf of the German government, Steubel announced that his country recognized Tamasese as "King."

In spite of Tamasese's claim that he was Sāmoa's King, Malietoa Laupepa still considered the title to be his. As a result, there were now two governments in Sāmoa: that of Malietoa Laupepa, recognized by the United States and Britain; and that of Tamasese, recognized by Germany. Malietoa now called upon the treaty Mamea had signed with the United States in 1878, claiming that a serious dispute existed between Sāmoa and Germany. Political wheels in Washington began to turn.

American Secretary of State Bayard requested a statement from the German minister in Washington, von Alvensleben, as to German intentions in Sāmoa. Von Alvensleben gave Bayard a reassuring reply, backed by a statement from Berlin. Unfortunately, Secretary Bayard was not completely sure of all the facts due to time and distance from Sāmoa. He could not be sure as to the exact approach the U.S. government should take. He appointed a new consul to Sāmoa, Berchtold Greenebaum, telling him he would be faced with a serious – and delicate – situation. Bayard took the position that the U.S. had not officially recognized the municipal convention regarding Apia, so therefore, could not object to German moves within town. He did instruct Greenebaum that if proof existed that Germany used the convention as a means to establish a protectorate over Sāmoa, that the U.S. would find such a move "distasteful" and would then take a position in favor of the tripartite protection the Sāmoans desired. Bayard further stated, ". . . the moral interests of the United States would counsel us to look with concern on any movement by which the independence of those South Pacific nationalities might be extinguished." He instructed Greenebaum to maintain a position of strict neutrality between dynasties and to work to promote harmony and good will.

In December, 1885, German sailors from the SMS *Albatross* came ashore in Apia and tore down the Sāmoan flag from the Municipal Building, where it flew in accordance with the Municipal Convention. When Secretary of State Bayard learned of this offensive act he realized a new, more aggressive approach towards Sāmoa

Tilly's letter to Washington, D.C., April 18, 1900.

Olosega Island in foreground with Ta'ū looming in the distance.

was needed. Bayard called upon Germany to live up to its earlier assurances. The German Foreign Minister only replied that he was uninformed as to the alleged events and in any case, Germany was going to let things stand as they were. It was evident to the American Secretary of State that events in Sāmoa were escalating and that an international conference would be required to find a solution. Bayard invited Britain and Germany to hold such a meeting in Washington. At the same time he learned that Consul Greenebaum had declared an American protectorate over Sāmoa in response to the aggressive German moves in Apia.

The three powers agreed the only way to correctly discern all the facts was to send a fact-finding and advisory commission to Apia. The United States was represented by George Bates; Britain by John Thurston, Governor of Fiji; and Germany by Herr Travers, the Consul General in Sydney. The three commissioners arrived separately in August, 1886. Upon his arrival, Bates immediately disavowed Greenebaum's "protectorate." He was also relieved to learn that the contentious Dr. Stuebel had been recalled to Berlin.

The commissioners were determined to find a workable solution to the complex problems facing Sāmoa. They sought to work without discord and seek consensus on the issues before the commission. There was no disagreement as to the facts causing the dissension, and the commissioners agreed in the view that Sāmoa was incapable of self-government. They also agreed that claims by foreigners over title to Sāmoan land would have to be settled by an international land claims commission. The most important point they could not agree upon: The future government of Sāmoa.

In simple terms, George Bates stated that since Sāmoa was already recognized by international treaties, that the three powers should manage Sāmoa in a tripartite arrangement. Governor Thurston stated that Britain favored a plan which borrowed ideas from Colonel Steinberger's government. He proposed a Sāmoan king with two elected councils that included a foreign representative chosen by the three powers. For Germany, Travers expressed the view that a tripartite government was unworkable. He recommended that one of the three powers assume total control. Since German interests in Sāmoa far exceeded those of the United States or Britain, it was only logical that Germany assume sole responsibility, with the king of Sāmoa relegated to the status of advisor.

Once the commission completed its recommendations it would take time for the three governments to study them in detail. In January, 1887, while the commission reports were under review, Consul Greenebaum reported that a German military officer, Captain Brandeis, was training an army for Tamasese. When Secretary Bayard inquired as to whether this was true he was informed by Germany's Foreign Ministry that they were "uninformed" of any military activities by Captain Brandeis. Bayard was also concerned over the continuing rivalry between Malietoa and Tamasese. When he expressed his concern, the German government took the position that Malietoa had no special rights regarding his claim to be king. The questions as to whether Brandeis was building an army, and whether he was under the employ of the German government or D.H. & P.G., were left unanswered.

On February 17, 1887 Malietoa Laupepa, still claiming himself to be "King of Sāmoa," signed an alliance with Hawai'i. The Hawaiian monarch, King Kalakaua, had dreams of creating a United Polynesia, with himself and his kingdom as the nucleus of the island empire. Malietoa met with Kalakaua's minister in Apia and asked that Hawai'i's representative to Washington act as Malietoa's representative also.

From Malietoa's point of view there was more to the Hawai'ian mission and its dealing with Sāmoa than met the eye. Malietoa was well aware of the growing interest of Americans in Hawai'i, and he most likely hoped that by allying himself with Hawai'i he might quietly bring Sāmoa under the wing of the United States government. The Germans, however, had no intention of recognizing Hawai'i as a legitimate power. The negotiations between Malietoa and Hawai'i only angered them further. They became more determined than ever to remove Malietoa from any claim of leadership.

On June 25, 1887, the representatives of the United States, Great Britain and Germany met in Washington, D.C., but could not agree on the future course of the Sāmoan government. Secretary of State Bayard stuck to his position that Malietoa Laupepa was Sāmoa's legitimate ruler and that the islands should be governed by a tripartite arrangement. The Germans were adamant that Malietoa had no claim as king. They insisted that a tripartite government would

not work and that management of Sāmoa be assigned to one of the three powers. Surprisingly, Britain supported the German position, much to Secretary Bayard's dismay. After a month of debate, the conference adjourned to permit the three representatives to confer with their governments.

One month later, in August, 1887, German consul Ralph Becker in Apia presented Malietoa Laupepa with an ultimatum. Using a fight that had broken out on the Kaiser's birthday as an excuse, Becker demanded a $1,000 fine and a public apology from Malietoa, stating his warriors had caused the fight to start. Further, Becker demanded $12,000 as compensation for damages to German property he said had been committed over the preceding four years, again alleging that Malietoa's supporters had committed the crimes.

Malietoa was stunned by the demand for $12,000, an astronomical amount for the time. He requested three days in which to consider Becker's demands. Becker was not interested in giving Malietoa any leeway and declared war upon him. German sailors immediately came ashore in Apia and raised the German flag over the Municipal Building. The following day Becker dispatched a German warship to Leulumoega in which to bring Tamasese back to Apia as Germany's choice to be Sāmoa's "king."

Upon learning that Germany had installed Tamasese and believing that the United States would not intervene, Malietoa escaped into the bush. From there he sent his emissaries to ask Mata'afa for his help. Mata'afa personally went to Tamasese to determine his intentions. Tamasese, however, would not, or could not, do anything to

"Uatogi" coconut stalk war club (above). Pago Pago Bay as seen from top of Rainmaker mountain. (below)

Bilateral toothed warclub called *fa'alaufa'i*. **(left) Paddle-shaped war club. (right) Samoan war clubs were traditionally made from very hard wood and were quite heavy.**

change the present state of affairs. Malietoa had no choice but to remain hidden in the forest while German search parties were sent out to capture him.

When word reached Malietoa that German warships had given Tamasese a 21-gun salute and that Tamasese had installed Viktor Brandeis as his premier, Malietoa realized further resistance was useless. He made the decision to surrender to German forces.

Malietoa Laupepa presented himself to German Consul Becker and Commodore Heusner of the German navy, who were backed by a large contingent of German marines. In a display lacking any form of decency or respect, Malietoa Laupepa left Sāmoa a prisoner aboard a German warship, which wandered across the Pacific to the Indian Ocean, and then up the west coast of Africa to the unlikely spot of Cameroon. There, in one of the hottest, most feverish outposts in Africa, he was kept penned up aboard ship, where he grew increasingly weak as the months passed. Finally, fearing the exiled king might soon die, German authorities ordered the warship to Hamburg. Malietoa Laupepa was now to be imprisoned in the country that he believed had imprisoned Sāmoa.

▼ ▼ ▼

Repercussions of Malietoa's deportation overflowed to Tutuila. Before surrendering to the Germans, Malietoa entrusted his people to the care of Mata'afa. Sāmoan chiefs who were suspected of supporting Mata'afa were rounded up by Premier Brandeis and exiled. Among one of the chiefs was Mauga of Pago Pago, who was an outward opponent of the Germans and very pro-American in his stance.

Brandeis was determined to maintain strict German control of the Pago Pago bay area. When the villages of Fagatogo and Aua fell behind in paying their taxes under the new tax laws that Brandeis had imposed, he demanded the two villages pay a fine of $300. He then issued a threat to the two villages that failure to pay the tax would result in war being declared against them and that their chiefs would be exiled to distant islands. The threat must have been taken seriously, for the fine was paid and village taxes from Tutuila flowed into the German treasury in Apia.

The United States consul to Apia, Harold M. Sewall, found himself in constant conflict with German Consul Becker. When Tamasese's forces occupied Mulinu'u, which had been declared neutral territory within the Municipality of Apia, Sewall strongly protested. Becker responded by declaring Mulinu'u, and by extension the Apia municipality, under German control. Consul Sewall, in an attempt to mediate the matter, invited Becker to join him in meetings with the British consul. Becker refused. Then to make his position clear, he reappointed the Apia magistrate on his own authority – though the appointment required the approval of the American and British consuls – and claimed that the convention establishing the municipality was nullified due to the actions of the Americans and British.

Consul Sewall proved to be an American who could not be intimidated by the outward show of German force. He was backed by another American, H.J. Moors, a successful trader and businessman who was The Firm's leading business rival. The two men were joined by another American, William Blacklock, Moors' business associate and acting consul in Sewall's absence. When the conflict over German control of the Apia municipality reached its peak, the three Americans asserted their leadership of the non-German foreigners and called a tax-payers strike. The strike proved successful. Within a few short months revenues plummeted and Becker was left without the funds to operate the government.

American consul Sewall kept Washington well informed of the events unfolding in 'Upolu and Tutuila. At the same time H.J. Moors, working in unison with the American and British consuls, became quietly involved in supplying the military forces of Mata'afa with weapons. Moors, along with Blacklock and Sewall saw the outbreak of war almost inevitable. As the American consul, Sewall was required to remain outwardly neutral. But he, along with his British counterpart, knew that political compromise with the Germans was at best, quite remote. They also knew that Mata'afa, a devout nationalist and charismatic leader, was not only the one man who should be "king," but also the one who had the overwhelming support of his people with the ability to defeat Germany on the battlefield.

It did not take long for Brandeis to learn that Mata'afa was building his army. What Brandeis did not know was that many of Mata'afa's warriors were equipped with new rifles smuggled to them by American warships. In late August, 1888, Mata'afa felt the time was right to test his army against the forces of Tamasese, who

ment" of Sāmoa, calling Malietoa Laupepa's European advisors "incapable mischief-makers." His book, *A Footnote to History*, was very critical of European intervention in Sāmoa, and angered both the Germans and the British. Though Stevenson was an outspoken supporter of Mata'afa, whom he considered the natural leader of Sāmoa, he personally liked Malietoa Laupepa, but thought him incapable of dealing with the difficult problems with which he was faced.

Stevenson joined American, H.J. Moors, in publicly supporting Mata'afa. But the tripartite administrators clearly saw Mata'afa as a rebel, and were determined to squash his rebellion. Stevenson made numerous attempts to induce Mata'afa to meet with Laupepa, but was unsuccessful. In June, 1893, Mata'afa's warriors were gathering near Malie, and the government feared an attack was imminent. The government forces, comprised of warriors loyal to Malietoa Laupepa, marched out toward Malie to attack Mata'afa's army. The battle was a bloody affair, costing many lives on both sides. Mata'afa's army, undermanned and lacking modern rifles, suffered a bitter defeat. Mata'afa fled to Savai'i, where a month later, he again lost a major battle, this time to be captured. The government in Apia swiftly exiled him to Jaluit in the Marshall Islands.

With Mata'afa and a number of supporting chiefs expelled, Malietoa Laupepa turned his attention to Tutuila. He considered Le'iato and the other high chiefs to be a threat to his personal authority, as well as to the government in Apia. Recognizing that Le'iato and the other chiefs were a sizable group, he asked the American, British and German consuls for assistance.

The consuls, who were now the acting authority in Apia following von Pilsach's resignation, complied with his request and sent three warships to Tutuila. The British ship, HMS *Katoomba*, anchored in Pago Pago harbor. The presence of her guns sent a clear message to the followers of Mata'afa. The German ship SMS *Bussard* rescued the Malietoa supporters living on Aunu'u, while the SMS *Sperber* neutralized Mata'afa supporters in eastern Tutuila.

By 1894 dissension in both Tutuila and 'Upolu had died down, but again civil war flared when a new Tui A'ana Tamasese gathered enough support to launch a short, and futile, civil war. Throughout the year the government maintained no authority beyond the confines of the Apia township. In a report to the State Department acting Consul Blacklock wrote, ". . . the Sāmoans enjoy the existing state of affairs; it is like a festival to them. No taxes; no laws; no order; every-

thing is free for the taking . . . Foreigners may complain, and do, but that is the end of it."

Despite the overwhelming problems, the American, British and German consuls were determined to establish and maintain a good working government. They succeeded well enough to feel secure in allowing Mata'afa and his fellow chiefs to return from exile. But, the stability that had finally been achieved, was undermined once again when Malietoa Laupepa died on August 22, 1898.

As a young man Laupepa had been chosen by the LMS church to accede to the Malietoa title, though his wish had been to enter the ministry. He was thrust into the arena of international politics and caught in a difficult civil war. His personality and temperament were not suited to deal with the complex difficulties that faced Sāmoa throughout the entire second half of the 19th century. No one doubted his sincerity to serve his people in the best way he knew how, but his detractors only saw him as a puppet of

Europeans whose actions were not in the best interest of Sāmoa.

Despite the problems and injustice that faced Malietoa Laupepa throughout his life, he nevertheless represented Sāmoa's only hope for independence from foreign domination. When he died, the dream of Sāmoan independence died with him.

▼ ▼ ▼

Under the terms of the Berlin Act of 1889, Sāmoans were now entrusted with the responsibility to elect a "king" to succeed Malietoa Laupepa. Once a new king was chosen, the powers were to recognize their new choice. The fact that Sāmoan custom and tradition had no precedent in this regard now became clearly evident.

Village of Alao with Aunu'u visible across the strait. Circa 1950.

Coconut leaves glisten in the tropical sunlight.

Sunset on Tutuila.

The selection of the new Malietoa repeated, in a similar fashion, the selection of Laupepa decades earlier. The Malietoa clan selected Tanumafili as the new title-holder. Like Laupepa before him, Tanumafili hoped to become an LMS pastor and serve his people through the church. When Tanumafili was named the new "king of Sāmoa," the supporters of Mata'afa reacted by naming Mata'afa to the same position. Since the *fa'a Sāmoa* had no precedent to elect a "king," the two sides could only settle the question by resorting to the force of arms, and a new civil war broke out.

The dissension worsened when the tripartite administrators disagreed on whom to support. The Chief Justice supported Tanumafili, while the President of the Apia Municipal Council supported Mata'afa, going so far as to call Mata'afa's regime a "provisional government," and closed the Chief Justice's court. This action angered the American and British consuls, who requested military intervention by the American and British navies. American and British warships shelled Apia and jointly landed a party of sailors, who fought a gun battle with Mata'afa forces. Several officers and men were killed, but the Mata'afa forces lost the skirmish and his government was deposed. A few days later, on March 23, 1899, Tanumafili was installed as "king", but the following week Mata'afa defeated his army in battle. Once again Sāmoa was thrust into civil war.

The Germans had never truly supported the idea of international control of Sāmoa. They argued it could never work, and the last three decades had proven them right. Once Malietoa Laupepa had died, the Germans began a series of diplomatic overtures intended to eliminate the tripartite setup altogether. Germany understood America's interest in their naval station at Pago Pago, and recognized that Britain's interest in Sāmoa had declined. The German government first proposed that Sāmoa be divided between Germany and the United States, and that Britain be compensated by the relinquishment of all German claims in Tonga. Although Britain rejected the plan, the outbreak of new civil war in Sāmoa made them receptive to further discussions on the Sāmoan issue. The Germans then proposed a new international commission be sent to Sāmoa. The idea was gladly approved by both the United States and Britain.

The commission of 1899 differed from the commission of 1886 in that it was given the specific mission by the three powers to take control of Sāmoa and establish a government in Apia. The three delegates, Bartlett Tripp of the United States, C.E.N. Elliot of Britain, and F.S.

von Sternberg of Germany, met in San Francisco and sailed to Sāmoa together aboard the USS *Badger*. The vessel was equipped with two modern conveniences especially installed for the occasion – electric fans and an ice machine. While en route to Sāmoa, the three commissioners prepared for the task ahead. Their first decision was to stay removed from local squabbles and politics by remaining aboard ship, where they would conduct all business.

Upon arriving in Apia the commissioners summoned the three consuls and most influential foreigners aboard the *Badger*. After lengthy discussions the commissioners found the group in agreement on two fundamental issues: first, that the concept of a "kingship" in Sāmoa was entirely foreign to Sāmoan tradition, and that it could therefore be abolished with the support of Sāmoans themselves; and second, that as long as the Sāmoans remained armed, they could expect fighting to continue. The three commissioners decided to make disarmament their first objective and the abolishment of the "kingship" their second.

The commissioners invited Mata'afa aboard the *Badger* the first day, and Malietoa Tanumafili the second. The commissioners read a prepared statement to each man stating that the United States, Great Britain and Germany were "very strong and very good" countries, but that they were "much grieved when they learned that the Sāmoans were making war upon and killing each other." The statement concluded that if the Sāmoans did not give up their arms and stop fighting, they would be bombed by the great

warships which "could throw shells twelve miles." Mataʻafa promised to surrender his arms if Malietoa would do the same. Malietoa did agree, and the commissioners set May 31, 1899, for disarmament to begin.

Both Mataʻafa and Malietoa kept their word, and within a short period of time 4,000 guns had been collected aboard the *Badger*. The commissioners concluded their first goal had been reasonably successful. They now turned their attention to the termination of the "kingship."

The commission's first step was to accept the decision by Chief Justice Chambers that Malietoa Tanumafili was "King of Sāmoa." As soon as they made this announcement, the commission then persuaded the young Malietoa to resign his position. Malietoa, who Tripp described as a "young and unambitious boy," was glad to divest himself from a position which he did not want. On June 10, 1899, the "kingship" of Sāmoa was abolished. In its place the commission installed a provisional government composed of the three consuls. Dr. Heinrich Solf, the German consul, was chosen to be the new President of the Municipality of Apia and serve as the executive officer.

American delegate, Bartlett Tripp, wrote in his report, "Our work was now accomplished. The natives were disarmed, their guns in the hold of the *Badger*, the King had resigned, the office was abolished, and a white man's government substituted in its place, leaving the chief of each tribe to control affairs in his own locality in accordance with the customs of Sāmoa."

On the same day the first of the firearms were being delivered to the Badger, the German Minister in Washington proposed to the State Department that the Sāmoan Islands be divided among the three powers. The proposal recommended that Tutuila, with its islet, Aunuʻu, and the three islands of Manuʻa group be apportioned to the United States, Savaiʻi to Great Britain and ʻUpolu to Germany. The Americans liked the idea, but the British hesitated, and further discussions were required.

On November 9, 1899, a formula was agreed upon which satisfied all three powers. The United States accepted Tutuila, Aunuʻu and Manuʻa. All remaining islands in the Sāmoa group were to come under German control. Great Britain relinquished all official claims to Sāmoa, and accepted in return Germany's rights in Tonga, as well as other disputed areas in the Solomon Islands and West Africa.

The three powers signed an agreement to this effect on November 14, 1899. The following

month a tripartite convention was held in Washington, D.C., finalizing the entire matter.

Eighty years of turbulence had finally come to an end. The people of Sāmoa, united as a culture for a millennia, now found themselves politically divided. For a brief period they had precariously held on to their political independence, but the international pressures of the 19th century made such independence impossible to maintain. The division of Sāmoa on the eve of the new century would have far reaching implications for both the people and the islands themselves. It would be an arrangement, however, that would prove to be a successful one as the people of each Sāmoa stepped into the 20th century.

Looking east, Olosega Island, Manuʻa.

Talanoa atu, 'ae le talanoa manu

'The bonitos swim about thoughtlessly, but the seagalls are on the alert.'
An incautious person will be surprised by his enemy. — Proverb

Chapter 8

The United States
Naval Station, Tutuila

n August 13, 1899, Commander B.F. Tilley, USN, age 51, entered Pago Pago bay aboard the USS Abarenda, a 4,000-ton naval auxiliary freighter. Tilley had sailed from Norfolk, Virginia, to deliver a cargo of coal and structural steel to be used to complete the United States Naval Station which was already under construction. Upon arrival Commander Tilley became the Officer in Charge of the United States Naval Station, Tutuila. He was joined in this mission by officers Lt. Commander Edward J. Dorn, Ensign Louis C. Richardson, and Assistant Surgeon Lt. Commander Edward M. Blackwell.

USS "Abarenda" fires a military salute in Pago Pago harbor as the first American flag is raised on Sogelau Ridge the morning of April 17, 1900.

Commander Benjamin Franklin Tilley, first U.S. Naval Governor of American Sāmoa, and the person to whom the Deed of Cession is addressed.

The United States had rented a few pieces of land in Fagatogo a few years following the American-Sāmoan Treaty of 1878, as the first step in establishing a coal depot in Pago Pago Bay. Matthew Hunkin, an early assistant to the LMS missionaries, was assigned by the U.S. consul in Apia to oversee the coaling station and serve as the U.S. consular agent for Tutuila. However, during the time Hunkin held these positions, virtually nothing was done to actually construct any kind of coaling station. In 1888, Consul Sewall recommended that the consular agency in Tutuila be discontinued and suggested that the U.S. Navy become directly involved in the management of the coal depot.

The U.S. Navy clearly recognized the value of Pago Pago Bay and began taking steps to secure a coal depot in 1889 following the great hurricane of 1889 in Apia. Following the loss of his squadron in the hurricane, Admiral Kimberly traveled to Tutuila aboard a schooner to survey the bay and choose a site for the depot. He selected a tract of land on the southern shore of the inner part of the bay which stretched from Goat Island to a spot known as "Swimming Bay," which was completely protected from the sea and well-sheltered from storm winds. "Swimming Bay" is today the area near the inter-island ferry dock. Kimberly noted that flat land along this area

could be provided by shaving off part of the hillsides and reclaiming land over the narrow reef between the shoreline and deep water. There a dock, capable of taking large seagoing vessels alongside, could easily be constructed.

The Navy also considered the possibility of an attack on the coaling station once it had been constructed, and made an attempt to purchase the two headlands fronting the entrance to the bay. Breakers Point is a rocky promontory on the eastern side of the entrance to the bay. Blunts Point stands on the western side. In 1893 Acting Consul Blacklock went to Tutuila to determine if these two pieces of land could be bought. When he arrived he found that a war between Mauga of Pago Pago and Le'iato of the eastern village of Faga'itua was being fought, which made it impossible to conclude any binding agreements regarding the purchase of the land. Blacklock had to be content with an option to buy the land at some later date.

The title to the property for the Naval station had to pass the strict analysis of the International Land Claims Commission in 1894. Once that requirement had been cleared the Navy was free to begin operations. Four years passed before the Navy signed a contract with Healy, Tibbetts, and Company of San Francisco to construct a wooden-floored steel dock, a corrugated iron coal shed, a stonehouse, a residence for the coal depot manager, and a water reservoir on the hill above the coal station.

When Commander Tilley arrived he found a naval civil engineer, W.I. Chambers, already at work with two assistants, along with Mr. Tibbetts, who was assisted by thirty laborers. Ten days later, on August 23rd, the U.S. Government

purchased unnumbered parcels of land for the U.S. Naval Station which were listed as "Acquisition of Water Rights: Reservoir, pipeline, etc." from "Mauga, Lutu, Tiamalu, Faanate, Mailo, Tamuu, Taesali, Isoa, chief talking men of Fagatogo, Mailo, Afoa, Samia, Tamuu, Fagini, and Ifupo, owners of certain lands in and around Fagatogo" for $300.00.

Tilley unloaded the steel and building materials upon arrival, then made plans to proceed to Auckland, New Zealand. Before departure, on December 6, 1899, he learned that the United States, together with Great Britain and Germany, had agreed to divide the Sāmoan Islands. Unable to delay his trip, he wrote a letter to Mauga Moimoi informing him of the partition of Sāmoa by the three powers and asked him to disseminate the news. He then charged him to keep order in the bay, promising that the authority of Sāmoan chiefs, ". . . when properly exercised, will be upheld."

On February 17, 1900, Commander Tilley became American Sāmoa's first naval governor, a post he would hold until November 27, 1901. His first official designation was "Commandant, U.S. Naval Station Tutuila." Two days later, February 19th, President William McKinley placed Tutuila and "all the Sāmoan Islands east of 171 degrees west longitude" under the authority of the U.S. Navy. On the same day, Secretary of the Navy, John D. Long, named these islands "U.S. Naval Station Tutuila."

Looking westward at the beach near To'aga. Ofu, Manu'a.

Navy Officer's Club, Goat Island, Pago Pago Harbor. Circa 1930

The following week, on February 23rd, Commander Tilley wrote to the Navy Department regarding his position as Commandant of the U.S. Naval Station Tutuila, saying that it would be better "if the officer charged with this responsibility has the explicit authority of this Government and knows its wishes." Unbeknown to Tilley, President McKinley had already signed the executive order giving him the authority that he wanted. Tilley did not receive his orders, and a copy of the executive order, until April 4, 1900.

In the letter naming Tilley Commandant, Assistant Secretary of the Navy Charles H. Allen wrote, "While your position as commandant will invest you with authority over the islands embraced within the limits of the station, you will at all times exercise care to conciliate and cultivate friendly relations with the natives. A simple,

Fita Fita Barracks, U.S. Naval Station, Tutuila. Circa 1910

straightforward method of administration, such as to win and hold the confidence of the people, is expected of you."

The partition of Sāmoa provided the United States with the authority to establish a naval station on Tutuila, and in that regard the Tripartite Agreement signed aboard the USS *Badger* could be termed a success. The United States, however, had worked for many years to have Sāmoa one day emerge as a small, independent nation, free of colonial interference. Therefore, once the Tripartite Agreement was concluded, the United States suddenly found itself responsible for an island dependency, a responsibility for which it was significantly unprepared. In Washington there was no officially designated office to oversee the management of "eastern" Sāmoa, so plans had to be improvised. The

result of this improvisation was President McKinley's directive of February 19th, 1900, placing the newly-acquired islands under the U.S. Navy.

With the islands of Tutuila and Aunu'u now under American authority, Tilley deemed it imperative that he meet with the Tui Manu'a to discuss the cession of those three islands to the United States. Tilley noted that "centuries of isolation" had made Manu'ans ". . . very shy, and somewhat averse to any change in their government. They seemed to think," he continued, "they formed an independent nation which was quite able to take care of itself." In order to insure that diplomacy be properly conducted, Tilley took Luther Osborn, the American Consul General in Apia, and High Chiefs Mauga and Tuitele, and Tiamalu of Fagatogo, to meet with the Tui Manu'a. All three chiefs were strong proponents of the American cession, and Tilley relied upon them to serve as his ambassadors.

Anchoring offshore Ta'ū aboard the *Abarenda* on the afternoon of March 11, 1900, Commander Tilley invited Tui Manu'a Eliasara to sign the Deed of Cession, thus ceding Manu'a to the United States. The Tui Manu'a replied that he was not yet prepared to make a decision, but he invited Tilley to meet with him the next day to discuss the matter further.

The next morning, March 12th, Commander Tilley went ashore accompanied by Consul Osborn, Assistant Surgeon Blackwell and the Tutuila chiefs. A fringing reef fronts the village of Ta'ū, and, depending on the wind and surf conditions, going ashore can be treacherous due to large, pounding waves. There are two narrow channels in the reef which provide access to and from shore, and even when the sea is calm, the currents and jagged coral can make passage difficult. The boats used to ferry people ashore are built to be swift and maneuverable so the steersman and rowers can negotiate the channel safely. The most skillful steersman of his day was High Chief Tufele, and on the morning of March 12th he commanded the longboat which came out to the *Abarenda* to bring the guests to shore. As the boat neared the channel Tufele kept his eye seaward and waited for the right wave to carry the longboat into the channel and the safety of the inside reef. At just the right moment he shouted to his rowers to paddle. His men pulled on their oars and the wave lifted the boat cleanly into the channel.

A two-hour 'ava ceremony was conducted which was highlighted by the arrival of the Tui Manu'a. When the ceremony concluded, the morning was nearly over. A large luncheon followed, after which Tilley again met with the Tui Manu'a and his chiefs.

Tilley reported that "Tui Manu'a addressed me very courteously, giving me a hearty welcome to Manu'a, but at the same time giving me plainly to understand that he did not wish any interference with his 'kingdom' by any outside power." The *fono* lasted "until 3 p.m., without much result." Tilley further reported that "I was asked many questions by the Tui Manu'a and other chiefs . . . They seemed suspicious and somewhat sullen. (I learned afterward that they feared that I would take away their lands and their property. They had been told this by some of the mischievous and dissolute white men, who are the curse of these islands.)" Upon rejoining his hosts in the evening, Tilley "found them in a very different frame of mind." After the evening session was "opened with prayers and singing," the Tui Manu'a handed Tilley a letter, ". . . accepting gracefully for himself, the chiefs, and the people the sovereignty and protection of the United States of America, for the island(s) of Manu'a. I felt much gratified with the result of the day's work."

Tilley invited the Tui Manu'a to travel back with him to join with Tutuilans in signing the pending Deed of Cession. The Tui Manu'a agreed to permit some of his people to go to Tutuila as observers, but in the matter of the islands of Manu'a, he remained adamant, and would not consider cession.

▼ ▼ ▼

On April 1, 1900, twenty of Tutuila's highest chiefs wrote to Governor Tilley, expressing

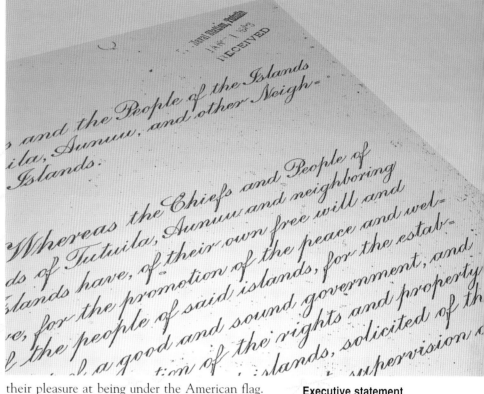

their pleasure at being under the American flag. Their letter promised they would "obey all laws and statutes made by the government or those appointed by the government to legislate and govern."

April 17, 1900 was selected to be the day the United States flag would be formally raised on Tutuila. The place chosen for the flag-raising ceremony was a bluff known as Sogelau which stood above the new coal shed and dock area, which at the time was under construction. The Governor of German Sāmoa, Heinrich Solf, came to Pago Pago aboard the SMS *Cormoran*, to join in the ceremonies. The *Cormoran* joined the USS *Abarenda* in the harbor along with several island schooners to both witness and participate in the event.

In the early morning hours of April 17th, it seemed that the entire population of Tutuila converged on the newly-excavated land below Sogelau. The area was filled with hundreds of Sāmoans dressed in their formal white attire normally reserved for church and only the most solemn events. Many people shielded themselves with umbrellas and carried printed programs in their hands. The programs officially referred to Tilley – for the first time – as the "Governor" of American Sāmoa.

German visitors from Apia joined the crowd as everyone waited for the arrival of Governor Tilley and other naval officials. Tilley began the ceremonies by reading the Proclamation of the President of the United States, which asserted sovereignty over the islands,

Executive statement signed by President Theodore Roosevelt on July 21, 1902, officially recognizing the Deed of Cession.

Celebrants gather atop Sogelau Ridge the morning of April 17, 1900, to witness the raising of the first United States flag in American Sāmoa. Construction of the new docking facilities are in the foreground.

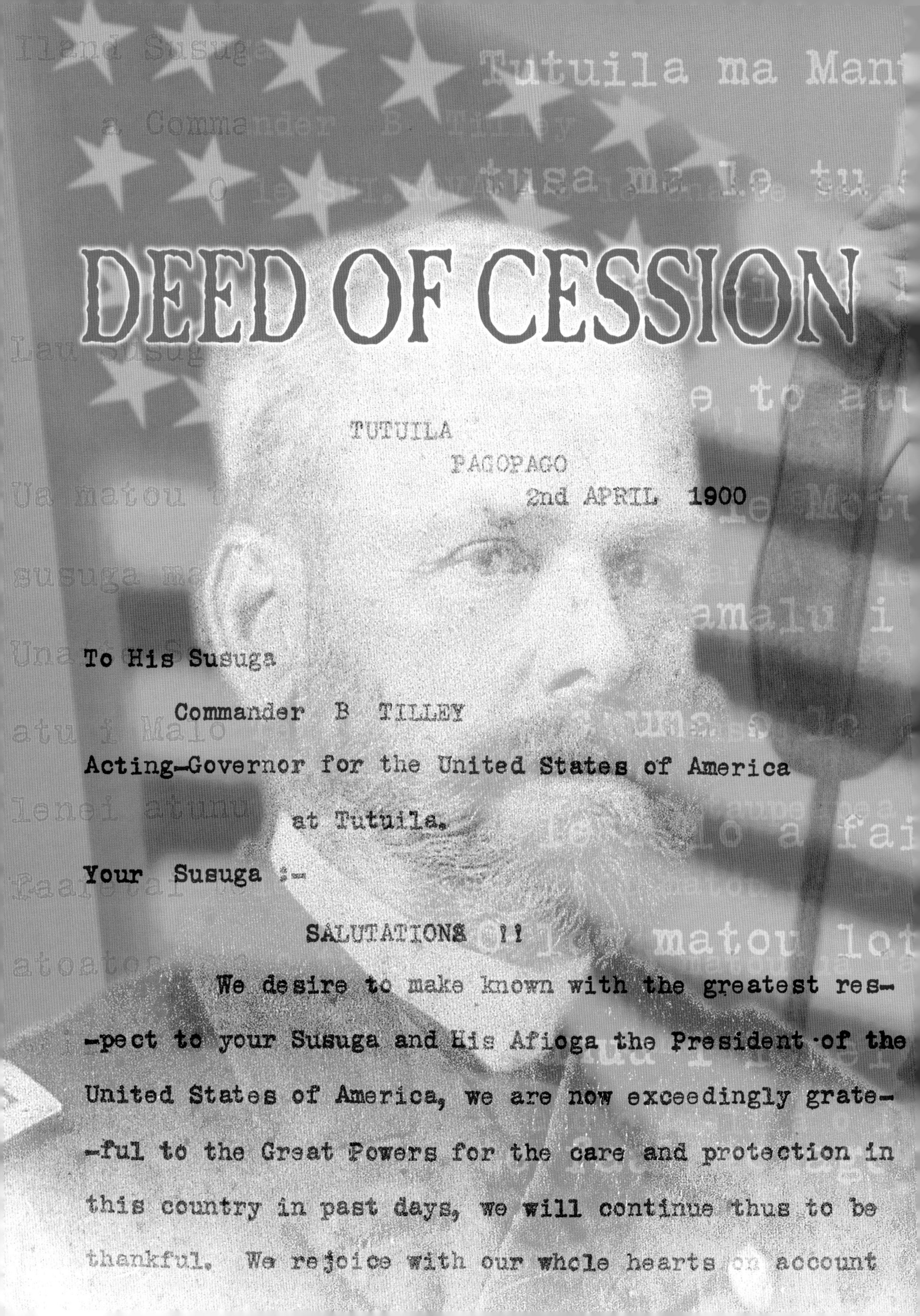

DEED OF CESSION

TUTUILA

PAGOPAGO

2nd APRIL 1900

To His Susuga

Commander B TILLEY

Acting-Governor for the United States of America

at Tutuila.

Your Susuga :-

SALUTATIONS !!

We desire to make known with the greatest res-

-pect to your Susuga and His Afioga the President of the

United States of America, we are now exceedingly grate-

-ful to the Great Powers for the care and protection in

this country in past days, we will continue thus to be

thankful. We rejoice with our whole hearts on account

AMERIKA SAMOA

of the tidings we have received, the Conventions of the
Great Powers concerning Samoa are ended, their Declara-
-tions are thus :- " Only the Government of the United
States of America shall rule in Tutuila and Manua, other
foreign Governments shall not again have authority there."
We give great thanks to the Great Powers for that result
that Declaration is accepted by us with glad hearts.
NOW THEREFORE , LET YOUR SUSUGA KNOWX, AND LET ALSO HIS
AFIOGA THE PRESIDENT OF THE UNITED STATES OF AMERICA
KNOW, AND LET ALL THE NATIONS OF THE EARTH KNOW AND ALL
PEOPLE DWELLING THEREIN , that in order to set aside all
possible doubts in the future concerning our true desire
at this time on account of the Rule of the United States
of America in Tutuila and Manua, We now, rightly appoin-
-ted according to the customs of Samoa to be the repre-
-sentatives of all the different districts in Tutuila
we do confirm all the things done by the Great Powers
for Tutuila, we do also cede and transfer to the Govern-
-ment of the United States of America the Island of
Tutuila and all things there to rule and to protect it.
We will obey all laws and statutes made by that Govern-
-ment or by those appointed by the Government to legis-
-late and to govern.
Our whole desire is to obey the laws that honor and dwe-
-lling in peace may come to pass in this country.
We depend on the Government and we hope that we indeed

and the Government will be prosperous, that the Govern-

-ment will correctly guide and advise us in order that

we may be able to care for and guard well and uprightly

our different villages and also our districts.

Let good and useful laws be made, let the foundations

of the Government stand firm for ever.

May your Susuga, the Acting-Governor live!

May His Afioga the President of the Government of Amer-

-ca live, and all the Government also !

We are, your humble servants

        I am Mauga   of Pagopago
              Leiato   of Fagaitua
              Faumuina   of Aunuu
              Pere   of   Laulii
              Masani   of   Vatia
              Tupuola   of   Fagasa
              Soliai   of   Nuuuli
              Mauga (2) of Pagopago
        THE   SUA   AND   THE   VAIFANUA.

(note.   The Sua ma le Vaifanua is the term applied to
    and embracing the whole of the eastern district of
    Tutuila.)

FOFO and AITULAGI (Term applied to and embracing the
                    whole of the western district)
Tuitele of Leone
Faiivae of Leone
Letuli of Iliili
Fuimaono of Vailoa
Satele of   Vailoa
Leoso of Leone
Olo of Leone
Namoa of Malaeola
Malota of Malaeloa
Tunaitaui of Pavaiai
Lulemana of Asu
Amituanai Ituau

William McKi...

...dent of the United States ...

...ll to whom these Presents ...

...now Ye that whereas ...

...ited States of ...

... Brit...

...have ...

...oan ...

...misu...

...sever...

...diction ...

...their ...

TUTUILA
PAGOPAGO
2nd APRIL 1900

To His Exunga
Commander B. TILLEY
Acting-Governor for the United States of America
at Tutuila.

Your Exunga :—

SALUTATIONS !!

—pect to your Exunga and His Afioga the ...
United States of America, we are now exceedingly grate...
—ful to the Great Powers for the care and protection in ...
this country in past days. We will continue thus to be ...
thankful. We rejoice with our whole hearts on account ...

[112]

MEMORANDUM FOR THE S...

SAMOA.

In 1889, the Sam...
...he United States, Germany and ...
...tripartite protectorate, which was ...

The first article of the treaty between the ...
...vided as follows:

"It is declared that the islands of Samoa are neutr...
territory in which the citizens and subjects of the Three
Signatory Powers have equal rights of residence, trade and
personal protection. The Three Powers recognize the independence of the Samoan Government and the free right of
the natives to elect their own Chief or King and choose
their form of Government according to their own laws and
customs".

This arrangement continued until 1899, when by ...
treaty between the Three Powers, Great Britain and Germany
...drew from all that territory east of longitude 171 de-
...anty providing:

WASHINGTON, D. C.

Feb. 6, 1900.

MEMORANDUM ON THE SAMOAN ISLANDS.

...NDS UNDER THE JURISDICTION OF THE UNITED
STATES.

...are such of the group as lie to the East of
...f West longitude. The main islands (see
..."Tutuila", "Tau" or "Manua", "Ofoo" and
...miles North of Manua is an atoll called

...AND OF TUTUILA.

COAL DEPOT FOR THE UNITED STATES NAVY.

The Coal Depot is located on Swimming Point in the harbor ...

SAMOA

...ge
...te
...
...w
...t
...ee
...nik
...k
...Tage Page
...Vaifanua

...lagi
...Leone
...Leone
...Hila
...Aoloau
...Vaitoa
...Lyone
...Leone
...Malaeloa
...Malaeloa
...Pavaiai
...Aoe
...Ituau

[117]

115

and the Order of the Secretary of the Navy creating the United States Naval Station, Tutuila.

Sāmoan chiefs responded by reading the Deed of Cession, which said in part, ". . . We give thanks to the Great Powers for that result that Declaration is accepted by us with glad hearts. Now therefore, let your Susuga know, and let also his Afioga the President of the United States know, and let all the nations of the earth know and all people dwelling therein, that in order to set aside all possible doubts in the future concerning our true desire at this time on account of the Rule of the United States of America in Tutuila and Manu'a, We now, rightly appointed according to the customs of Sāmoa to be the representatives of all the different districts in Tutuila we do

Cover of the official program containing the schedule of events for April 17, 1900.

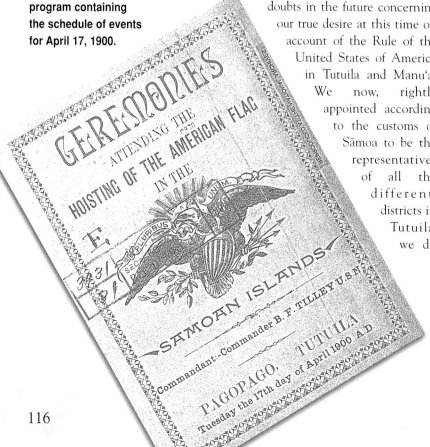

confirm all the things done by the Great Powers for Tutuila, we do also cede and transfer to the Government of the United States of America the Island of Tutuila and all things there to rule and to protect it. We will obey all laws and statutes made by that Government or by those appointed by the Government to legislate and to govern. Our whole desire is to obey the laws that honor and dwelling in peace may come to pass in this country. . ."

When the chiefs finished their address and it was duly acknowledged, the Reverend E.V. Cooper of the London Missionary Society and the Reverend Father Meinaidier of the Roman Catholic Mission offered prayers. When the prayers concluded, Governor Tilley raised the American flag, saying, "Acting with this (Presidential) authority, I hereby declare the islands I have named, Tutuila and all east of the 171st parallel of longitude, to be under the sovereignty of the United States, and I hoist this flag as a sign that these islands now form part of the territory of the United States."

With the hoisting of the American flag a specially-trained group of students from the LMS school at Fagalele sang "America" in English, and the USS *Abarenda* and SMS *Cormoran* fired their guns in national salutes – the gunfire echoing off the bay's surrounding mountains numerous times. When the naval salute quieted, Talking Chief Pele, representing the Eastern half of Tutuila, affixed the final signature to the Deed of Cession, formally concluding the flag-raising ceremony. Officials and guests then proceeded to Fagatogo to enjoy a huge banquet prepared for the occasion.

▼ ▼ ▼

Now that the cession of the islands of "eastern" Sāmoa to the United States was official, B.F. Tilley faced the daunting task of governing the islands. As commander of the naval station, Tilley's responsibilities were military in nature. As governor of American Sāmoa, Tilley's authority was both civilian and administrative, as an operational government needed to be established.

Tilley decided to divide his approach to governing into two areas: he would use existing – and traditional – Sāmoan authority at the village level; and save regulatory power for the commandant of the naval station. "The government I wish to establish," he wrote, "is a government of the chiefs who are to receive additional appointments by the commandant." Tilley was determined to govern the territory humanely and justly, but within a military structure. The responsibility of the Commandant of the U.S. Naval Station, Tutuila, must certainly have been unique within the Navy's sphere of operations.

On April 24th Tilley announced that official notification of government and naval station policies and activities would be accomplished by posting notices on the naval station bulletin board in Fagatogo. The first two regulations posted were: "No. 1: Regulation for Promulgation of Laws for Tutuila and Manu'a," and "No. 2: Notice Concerning Temporary Customs Regulations." The same day Tilley appointed Chief Boatswain Henry Hudson, USN, as customs officer for the U.S. Naval Station, Tutuila, including the islands of the Manu'a Group. Pago Pago was made the only port of entry.

On April 25th Tilley paid another visit to Manu'a. "The Manu'ans", Tilley wrote, "had expressed to me a strong desire to have the American flag hoisted over their island." Tilley presented the chiefs with their own flag, "which they wished to hoist themselves."

The new governor's third regulation forbade the sale of liquor to Sāmoans. This ordinance reflected Tilley's belief that Sāmoans and their lands "must be protected from the harmful elements" of western civilization.

Tilley's fourth regulation, released on April 30th, was known as the Native Lands Ordinance. The following day, May 1st, Tilley issued regulation Number 5, called the Declaration of the Form of Government. Regulations 4 and 5 are considered to be the two most important regulations that Tilley issued during his tenure as Governor/Commandant of the Naval Station.

The Native Lands Ordinance forbade the alienation of Sāmoan land. Tilley was very concerned that Sāmoans were easily misled by the

Looking toward Fagatogo from Pago Pago. Circa 1905

No.144

Sir!
1. I have the
American fl
Station, Pa
10 o'clock

whites into selling their land for nearly nothing, and that it would only be a matter of time before their land would be gone. Tilley resolved he would not let this happen in American Sāmoa. The Navy had already acquired much of the land previously owned by outsiders, and Tilley moved quickly to acquire the remaining land ahead of white speculators to insure such land would at least remain with the government. The Native Lands Ordinance would insure that in Tutuila and Manuʻa land ownership would remain exclusively in the hands of Sāmoans or their government.

districts, with Manuʻa to constitute the third. To the governorship of each district he appointed the then leading authority, and in so doing, set a precedent which has been generally followed through today. The declaration stated that "the governor, for the time being, of American Sāmoa, is the head of the government. He is the maker of all laws, and he shall make and control all appointments." The subsequent sections of the Declaration dealt with districts, district governors, *pulenuʻu*, judicial administration, village and district courts, the High Court, civil and

Commander B.F. Tilley (center) holding court in Fagatogo, Tutuila. Circa 1900

The Declaration of the Form of Government proclaimed that the laws of the United States were in force in the territory, and that Sāmoan laws and customs not in conflict with the laws of the United States would be preserved. Under the declaration, traditional Sāmoan forms of political/authoritative structures, such as village, county and district councils, would "retain their own form or forms of meeting together to discuss affairs of the village, county or district according to their own Sāmoan custom." Tilley recognized the ancient division of Tutuila by dividing the island into two administrative

criminal procedure, the Secretary of Native Affairs, and the Departments of Public Health and Public Works.

It was obvious to Governor Tilley that he knew very little of the *faʻa Sāmoa*. He knew he needed a civilian assistant on native affairs who would be capable of advising him in these matters. Tilley had no appropriated funds for such a post but used his discretionary powers to hire an interpreter at a salary of $150 a month. He had two possible choices for the post, William Blacklock, the former acting U.S. Consul in Apia, and E.W. Gurr, a New

Station. His successor, Commander C.B.T. Moore arrived in Pago Pago on January 28, 1905, and officially assumed command of the Naval Station two days later, on January 30th. Commander Moore became the fifth naval governor of American Sāmoa. He was the first to receive a formal presidential appointment as "Governor of Tutuila" from President Theodore Roosevelt.

President Roosevelt's appointment of a "governor" for the territory was pleasing to the islands' traditional leaders, who clearly understood the difference between a "commandant" and a "governor." To Sāmoans, the title of "governor" conferred a standing upon the incumbent in the executive department of the United States government apart from his position in the military. With his presidential appointment, Moore began to devote more of his time to the civil administration of the islands, looking to nearby German Sāmoa as a model which could serve as a blueprint for developing an administrative plan for Tutuila and Manuʻa.

Governor Moore visited ʻUpolu to study Germany's administration of their islands under the leadership of Dr. Heinrich Solf. Moore recognized immediately the emphasis placed on agriculture by the Germans, as well as their persistence in preventing beachcombers and drifters from staying permanently in the islands. To Moore, however, the biggest asset in Germany's administration of ʻUpolu and Savaiʻi was the length of Dr. Solf's assignment. When Moore arrived in Tutuila, Solf had already been governing in Apia for six years, during which time three American governors had come and gone. Moore saw the benefit of a longer tour of duty to establish continuity, as well as learn the necessary components of the *faʻa Sāmoa*, about which Moore considered himself completely unknowledgeable. He had witnessed first hand Dr. Solf's able administration, as well as his understanding of Sāmoan custom and history, and recognized such knowledge was necessary in order to run an effective administration in the American islands.

Governor Moore may have been the first naval administrator to recognize the problems encountered in administering American Sāmoa under the navy policy of two-year assignments.

It was a policy that would be criticized continually for the next four decades. Moore recommended to the Secretary of the Navy that the American governors' tours of duty be extended from two to four years. The Navy Department, however, was not willing to permit the administration of Sāmoa to interfere with the normal rotation of Navy officers. The Navy Secretary replied that Moore's proposal to extend the terms would not ". . . conserve the best interests of the Navy."

On May 3, 1905, Commander Moore issued Regulation, No. 3-1905, clarifying the term "legal tender" within the Naval Station. One month later, on June 6th, Commander Moore was informed by Secretary of the Navy Charles J. Bonaparte, that the Commission which appointed Moore Governor of Tutuila gave him jurisdiction over all United States possessions in (Eastern) Sāmoa.

Meanwhile in Apia, Dr. Heinrich Solf continued to face opposition to Germany's administration of Sāmoa's western islands. The concept of a Sāmoan "king" had been abolished in 1899, but talk of reestablishing a Sāmoan king still lingered. Solf eliminated this possibility by proclaiming Kaiser Wilhelm II as "Chief King of Sāmoa," thereby removing any possible contenders.

With the "kingship" of German Sāmoa in Berlin, Solf believed only two possible sources of opposition remained to his authority, the Taʻimua and Faipule – the governing body established during the Steinberger government – and the unofficial but influential bodies of talking chiefs, the Tumua and Pule, as the orators from ʻUpolu and Savaiʻi were known. When the Taʻimua and Pule interfered with his administration, Solf dismissed the two groups and established, on the 14th of August, the Fono a Faipule in their place, giving this new council advisory power only.

By coincidence Commander Moore was visiting Apia as these events were unfolding. Solf's actions, plus the concept of a Sāmoan assembly, must have made an impression on Commander Moore. Soon after his return to Tutuila Moore revived an idea set forth earlier by E.W. Gurr to establish an assembly of Sāmoan "representatives." He directed that an assembly convene on October 20th, with each of the

Eli Jennings with wife Margaret. Circa 1935.

Commander Charles B.T. Moore, 5th Naval Governor, 1905-1908.

Village *Taupou* with Fita Fita guard. Circa 1940.

A father attends to a *tanoa* used for food preparation with his wife and children gathered beside him. Circa 1940.

three districts to be represented by eight delegates. The delegates were to submit in writing in advance all topics they wished to discuss, excluding only those matters pertaining to the Naval Station. Moore reserved veto power for himself.

The first Fono of American Sāmoa was more successful than Commander Moore had thought possible. For the first time, the gathering brought together the *matais* of Tutuila and Manu'a, which had long been divided by history and geography. By bringing the two groups together, Commander Moore created a consciousness within these traditional leaders of "American Sāmoa" as its own unique political entity. Further, the American Sāmoan Fono formed, for the first time, the concept of political separation from "German Sāmoa," a concept which would continue to evolve for the ensuing six decades.

The Fono delegates addressed such topics as the production and sale of copra under the government's monopoly, but directed most of their attention to ancient Sāmoan custom as it pertained to births, marriages and deaths.

One matter of concern to Fono delegates concerned the *fa'amasei'au* – the public defloration of the bride during marriage ceremonies. This was an ancient custom, but one which had become unacceptable once Sāmoans had embraced Christianity. Despite the objection to the ceremony from the Christian viewpoint, *fa'amasei'au* was still practiced during marriages involving a taupou or high chief.

Also discussed were the cultural obligations placed upon families to conduct burdensome celebrations with the birth of a first-born child, as well as the ceremonial mourning required following the death of a high chief.

The *auosoga*, as practiced within the *fa'a Sāmoa*, demanded that following a certain high chief's death, large displays of shouting, the killing of domestic animals and the destruction of property, such as the cutting down of coconut and breadfruit trees near the deceased chief's house, must be done to express village and family grief. To the delegates of the Fono, such displays had become senselessly destructive.

The first Fono of American Sāmoa resulted in numerous ordinances that affected Sāmoa custom. The *auosoga* was banned on December 6th, under Regulation No. 8-1905, "Auosoga Prohibited," which stated "The word 'auosoga' in this regulation shall mean and include the willful damaging or destroying of trees or property . . . or any indecent conduct upon the death of a person of rank or during the ceremony known as the 'lagi.'"

The *fa'amasei'au* was also prohibited, but this custom continued for nearly four decades, with the last known ceremony of its kind occurring in the 1940s. The Fono also taught Commander Moore how deeply embedded the "matai system" was in Sāmoan life and custom. Moore had earlier thought of *matais* as a caste within Sāmoan society, not realizing they were titled heads elected by their family groups to represent them in public affairs. Once Moore understood the importance of the *matai* in Sāmoan life, he concluded it necessary they be accorded legal status. He subsequently drafted an ordinance establishing the rules of succession for *matai* titles, called for the registration of these titles, and enabled rival claimants for a title to go to court to settle the issue in the event they could not reach agreement within the *fa'a Sāmoa*.

▼ ▼ ▼

The year 1907 brought a number of regulations by Commander Moore which he hoped would clarify and solve a number of issues affecting daily life.

On January 7th Moore issued Regulation No. 1-1907, "Cricket Games," which stated that "the game of cricket and other games, when played between persons of one village against persons of another village, or between the people of one county against any other county, are prohibited, unless written permission of the governor be first obtained." Regulation No. 2, issued in February, dealt with "Customs Duties," Regulation No. 5, the "Adoption of Children," and Regulation No. 7, "Trespass on Native Lands."

In March, 1907, Rear Admiral B.F. Tilley died on active duty at the Philadelphia Naval Yard at age 59 and was buried at Annapolis, Maryland. His death reminded American Sāmoa's chiefs of the many positive steps in strengthening the relationship with the United States that had been made under Tilley's leadership. Within a year following Tilley's death, the chiefs of Tutuila and Manu'a drafted a statement acknowledging their satisfaction with the state of affairs between American Sāmoa and the United States. The statement said in part ". . . that the naval administration . . . be continued until such time as a majority of the Sāmoan people can understand and realize the system of government in vogue in the United States of America." A few months earlier, the Secretary of the Navy, in his annual report for 1907, stated, "the people of the United States having assumed control of the islands, it is earnestly recommended that Congress give consideration to this matter."

Captain John F. Parker, USN, relieved Commander Moore on May 21, 1908, becoming the territory's sixth naval governor. Nearly one year later, on April 2, 1909, Tui Manu'a Elisara died. Captain Parker's official statement on the death of the last of Sāmoa's true kings, said, "Tui Manu'a was the last of a line of kings in the Manu'a Group, his title being changed to District Governor from the date of the hoisting of the American flag in those islands. He was a devout Christian and a faithful supporter of government, and his loss . . . is keenly felt."

It is not known whether Parker's statement was naive or intentional, for few would have believed that Tui Manu'a Elisara would have accepted the position of District Governor if it was perceived as a "demotion," or that the position of District Governor would have been equal to that of the Tui Manu'a. Most likely, Elisara considered that he occupied both positions simultaneously, not separately as Parker's statement seemed to have suggested.

The death of Tui Manu'a Elisara was yet another consequential event that had far-reaching affect on the most ancient and honored aspects of the *fa'a Sāmoa*. For unknown reasons, Manu'a's traditional leaders made no immediate attempt to name a new successor as the Tui Manu'a. Nearly seventeen years later, however, talking chiefs Tauanu'u, Tulifua and Ti'a explained the reason for the inactivity had been a lack of a suitable candidate, especially in light of the fact that Elisara had been the most effective and forceful Tui Manu'a in modern times. Captain Edward S. Kellogg, naval governor from 1923 to 1925, took the position that the naval governors preceding him had "abolished" the

kingly title due to the fact it was royal in nature and therefore unallowable under the Constitution of the United States.

In actuality, there is probably some truth in both reasons. Within Manu'a itself, the fact there was not a reigning Tui Manu'a gave certain talking chiefs — who were endowed with the authority to elect the Tui Manu'a — more power among themselves, therefore leaving the election of a suitable Tui Manu'a open to endless debate. From the Navy's point of view, the memory of the case of the "Ipu of the Tui Manu'a" remained fresh, and their view that the Tui Manu'a title was royal in nature may have been guided by the recent history of the kingly titles of Hawai'i.

Following the death of Tui Manu'a Elisara, Governor Parker appointed Tufele Timiali as district governor. When he died in 1925, the district governorship passed to

Hand-driven sewing machines were a family's prize possession throughout most of the century. Circa 1927.

Commander William M. Crose, 7th Naval Governor, 1910-1913.

Tufele Faʻatoia, considered by many to be a very able and adept individual.

From the time Manuʻa was ceded to the United States, the designation "U.S. Naval Station, Tutuila" had been inappropriate. Numerous attempts were made to change the name but for one reason or another each attempt failed.

On May 15, 1911 Naval governor Commander William M. Crose made an issue of the matter. He wrote a two-page letter to Secretary of the Navy George von L. Meyer stating that the designation "U.S. Naval Station Tutuila" was inadequate and incorrect, as it did not include the eastern Sāmoa islands. He said that "The people of Manuʻa resent their being classed as part of 'Tutuila,' as Manuʻa has always been independent, prosperous and of great pride of race." He noted that the western islands were called "German Sāmoa," and suggested that America's Sāmoan territory be called either "American Sāmoa" or "Eastern Sāmoa."

On July 7, 1911, the Solicitor of the Navy Department stated there was no reason why the name should not be changed in accordance with the wishes of the Naval Governor and the people of the islands. On that date the islands of Tutuila, Aunuʻu and Manuʻa were officially designated "American Sāmoa," though the actual Naval Station in Fagatogo and Utulei continued to be called "U.S. Naval Station Tutuila."

On July 11th the Solicitor authorized Commander Crose, who was both Commandant, U.S. Naval Station Tutuila, and Governor of Tutuila, to use the designation "American Sāmoa." Thus, Crose was the first person to be designated as "Governor of American Sāmoa" rather than "Governor of Tutuila," although he, and all succeeding naval governors continued also to be designated as "Commandant, U.S. Naval Station Tutuila."

On July 17, 1911, Governor Crose, in his Annual Report to the Secretary of the Navy, reported on the Fita Fita Guard. His report on the Guard stated, in part, as follows: "A noticeable improvement has been affected in the teaching of the English language to the members of the Native Guard. The instruction has been, and is, in charge of the Chaplain. He now holds two instruction periods daily, of one hour each, and more interest is shown by the fitafitas than formerly. An attempt has been made to have a limited conversational knowledge of English a requirement for reenlistment, but it seems next to impossible for some of the fitafi-

Captain John F. Parker, 6th Naval Governor, 1908-1910.

tas to learn English . . . Instruction in wig-wag signaling has begun, and some of the Guard are able to send and receive messages, signaling slowly. Signal parties are today on two mountain peaks – Matafao and Tuaolo – signaling each other. Practice marches have been instituted, and the fitafitas are gaining much more extended knowledge of the trails on the island. Small-arm target practice will be taken up during this year. The Band plays very well, considering the material from which it is made. Sāmoans do not play any musical instruments except harmonica, and have no knowledge of written music, so the difficulties confronting a bandmaster may be appreciated . . . There is great demand for duty in the fitafitas, and we have no trouble in getting the best of the young men of the Island to enlist."

In the 1890s, the Oceanic Steamship Company of San Francisco and the Union Steamship Company of New Zealand jointly maintained a service between California and New Zealand and Australia. Ships called first at Honolulu, then Suva, and later added Apia to their route. In 1900 the Union Company was forced to back out when Honolulu became an American port. As a foreign company, Union was prevented by law from competing for mail and traffic between Hawaiʻi and California.

The cross-Pacific route was thus left to the Oceanic Steamship Company, whose steamers *Sierra*, *Ventura* and *Sonoma* began to call in Pago Pago – instead of Apia – in 1900. Within seven years, however, it became apparent that calling at

Pago Pago was unprofitable, and in 1907 the Oceanic liners abandoned their stop at the port. The loss of regular steamship service was a serious blow to the island economy, as the Island Government suffered a loss of revenue when the collection of customs duties fell in proportion to the decrease in imports. Commander Moore urged that the Oceanic company be subsidized due to the fact that the islands depended on customs revenues for its public services. In response, the Comptroller of the U.S. Treasury stated, "I am not aware of any law that expressly or implicitly makes it the duty of the Navy Department to make improvements in the islands outside the Naval Station proper . . ." The statement was clear: any desire of the Governor or of the Navy Department to improve living conditions among the Sāmoans was purely voluntary on their part, and in the absence of legislation by Congress, there was no way in which the United States government or its agents could make a financial contribution to their welfare.

The problem created by the abrupt halt in the mail service could not be overlooked. Commander Moore provided documentation that registered U.S. mail outbound from Pago Pago was sitting in port for three months before moving, and this forced the Postmaster General to join the Germans in subsidizing the transport of mail between Sāmoa and Fiji, the port of call of the Canadian-Australasian Royal Mail Line. After years of effort by succeeding Naval governors and local businessmen, the Oceanic Steamship Company finally resumed voyages between San Francisco and Sydney in July, 1912, calling at Pago Pago every twenty-eight days.

▼ ▼ ▼

On September 1, 1912, the first Sāmoan Hospital was completed at Malaloa. The buildings were constructed on the hillside next to the present-day location of the Sadie Thompson building . The new facility consisted of a wooden central administration building which contained an examination room, dispensary, lavatory and dressing room. There were outbuildings for a kitchen, baths, a storeroom and latrine. A windmill was erected near the beach to pump water to a 10,000-gallon tank located sixty feet above the level of the main building.

Twelve years earlier when the United States flag was raised on Tutuila, there were no public health services on the island. The necessity to improve health services to the general population was recognized by Naval governors very early, and their administrations spent considerable effort in

Fita Fita band at flag-raising ceremony, Swains Island. Circa 1940.

coping with the problems that resulted from a lack of these modern services.

With the arrival of Europeans in the previous century, most of the world's illnesses and diseases had found their way to Sāmoa. By 1900 such ailments as the common cold, pneumonia, typhoid, the various dysenteries, diphtheria, tuberculosis and leprosy were found in the islands, as well as the endemic diseases such as filariasis, intestinal parasites, trachoma-like disease of the eyes, tropical ulcers and fungus diseases of the skin. Islanders suffered from occasional epidemics of influenza, measles, mumps and chicken pox, oftentimes with very serious results. Early surveys showed the rate of infant mortality to be shockingly high, reaching possibly two-thirds of all children born.

On April 18, 1900, the day following the first raising of the United States flag, Navy surgeon Dr. Blackwell recommended that a dispensary be built and staffed by the *Abarenda*'s medical officer. Dr. Blackwell set up the first regular clinic for Sāmoans in Fagatogo, and after some months reported formally that ". . . coughs, catarrhal troubles, rheumatism, disorders of digestion, abscesses, swellings, ulcers, and inflammation of the eyes are the principal troubles."He listed the medicines and supplies required to provide basic health services to the islanders, adding that surgical instruments, when needed, were available in the *Abarenda*'s sick bay.

Commandant Tilley approved Dr. Blackwell's report, noting for the record that Blackwell ". . .has given nearly all his time to the gratuitous treatment of sick natives." The Navy

Fita Fita at flag-raising ceremony in front of Administration Building. Circa 1910.

Sadie Thompson Hotel. Circa 1930.

The Amercan Sāmoa Commission, also known as the Bingham Commission, gathering at the Poyer School, Anua, last week of September, 1930.

Surgeon General also recommended acceptance of Blackwell's request, requesting the use of emergency funds in this circumstance. Despite the proven need to construct a dispensary, no funds became available until 1906. Also, it was not until that same year that the Naval Surgeon General formally authorized the regular expenditure of Navy Medical Department supplies for the Sāmoan population.

Dr. Blackwell found a vacated wooden building owned by an island trader in Fagatogo and there he established the island's first dispensary. Beside the dispensary he had a Sāmoan *fale* erected for Sāmoan patients. Blackwell noted that his Sāmoan patients ". . . thrive best in a building of their own type of construction." He added further that the ventilation provided by the traditional Sāmoan house was ideal for the humid

tropics. The building needed repairs, but once completed it provided space for surgery and a three-bed ward for naval patients. The little facility became known as "The Government Hospital" and served the community until 1906, when the first permanent naval dispensary and a larger Sāmoan *fale* were erected.

Prior to the construction and use of the first naval dispensary, Sāmoans had never seen or experienced the use and application of "modern" medicine. Throughout their history Sāmoans had relied on traditional Sāmoan healers, all known as *foma'i*, of which there were three particular kinds: the general *foma'i*, the old women of the family, and the spirit doctors.

The *foma'i* was normally a specialist and held a respected place within his village. He learned his skills from his elders and passed such skills to certain younger members of the *aiga*. The older women practiced their medical knowledge normally within their own families. These women were often experts in the use of leaves and plants to create liquid medicines for both internal and external use. The spirit doctors were usually employed in cases of *ma'i aitu*, or spirit illnesses. They used fetishes, charms and chants to exorcize the perceived illness.

Foma'i generally specialized in certain injuries or illnesses. Surgeons used scalpels of shark's teeth or sharpened objects to lance abscesses, used seawater to flush the wound, and used medicinal leaves as poultices and bandages. Specialists in fractures were quite knowledgeable in basic anatomy. They set breaks, splinted the broken bone, and used massage to aid the healing process. Compound fractures

were flushed with seawater and the bones re-set, usually with success.

Both women and men earned reputations as expert masseuses and numerous injuries were mended through the Sāmoan art of massage. Internal illnesses were sometimes thought to be spirit-induced, and therefore spirit doctors were sought to exorcize the evil spirit from the body through various incantations. But certain internal illnesses, such as diarrhea, were treated with liquids made from leaves or plants which contained tannic acid, often with good results.

Despite the reliance on these, and other, traditional forms of Sāmoan medical practices throughout millennia, Sāmoans in time came to trust the concept and practice of *palagi* medicine. By 1905 Naval records note that 169 patients were admitted for treatment, with an average of 10 outpatient visits per day. Diseases listed were "simple and complicated fevers," — most likely filarial fever – as well as bronchitis, typhoid, pneumonia and dysentery. The surgical ward of the dispensary was the most active, with 120 operative cases that year, including forty-five amputations due to elephantiasis. The term "elephantiasis" is used to describe the end stage of repeated exposure to mosquitos carrying the filariasis parasite. The large number of amputations indicates the prevalence of that disease during the decades of the early 1900s.

In 1908 vital statistics reported that the population of American Sāmoa had grown to 6,780, of whom 145 were non-Sāmoan. There were 6,361 Sāmoans, 172 part Sāmoans, 102 natives of other Pacific Island groups, and 12 Asiatics, eight of whom worked at the naval station. That same year there were 200 recorded births and 230 recorded deaths. This discrepancy indicates that the registration of births was not complete.

In 1909 the concept of a broad policy in the field of health – and disease prevention – began to become a reality. Filariasis – and the resulting elephantiasis – was a serious health problem. Hookworm infestation was endemic throughout the population. And the notion of general sanitation in the villages was unknown – nor was it understood.

The transmission of filariasis was misunderstood in 1909. It was known to be mosquito-borne, but Navy doctors thought it was passed on to humans through drinking water. Dr. David Jordan, a biologist, believed the answer to the problem was to insure a pure and safe supply of drinking water. Although the concept was wrong, and therefore the fight against filariasis was ineffective, the improvement of the drinking supply greatly reduced water-

Fale āfolau, Pago Pago. Circa 1930.

borne diseases and proved to be the first big step in preventative medicine in Tutuila. The villages of Pavaʻiaʻi and Leone were the first to complete properly protected water tanks.

In November 1909, Dr. P.S. Rossiter, who later became Surgeon General of the Navy, found that 82.5 percent of tested Sāmoans, including an equal percentage among members of the Fita Fita Guard, were infected with hookworm. Based on these numbers, Dr. Rossiter concluded that possibly half of the total population was infected.

The transmission of hookworm among the general population was well understood. The eggs of the parasite were deposited on the ground with the carrier's excreta. If the ground was moist the eggs hatched and the larvae penetrated the skin of anyone who came in contact with them. The chain could be broken by everyone wearing shoes, which in Sāmoa was an impossible solution. The only solution was the construction of public latrines and enforcing their use.

To deal with the problem Governor Parker issued "An Act to Preserve Public Health." He appointed a Board of Health and empowered the board to publish and enforce regulations. The act required each village to furnish itself with a latrine and made failure to use it punishable by fine or imprisonment. The board went to work against hookworm with purpose, naming a sanitary inspector to visit villages and enforce the law.

To educate the population and win public support, Governor Parker called a special session of the Fono. The facts regarding hookworm and how it is spread, as well as its effect on the human body, were explained to the district leaders. High chief Tufele, speaking for his fellow chiefs, thanked the Governor for his efforts. Now that they understood the disease, and the effect it had

U.S. Naval Station, Tutuila. Top left, Enlisted Men's Club, below, left to right, Fita Fita Barracks, Jail, Bakery. The large roof to the right of the Bakery is the Navy Enlisted Men's Barracks, known as the *Fale Seila* by Sāmoans. Circa 1940.

upon the population, Tufele promised full cooperation by Sāmoa's leaders to eradicate hookworm.

The population did support the fight against hookworm. In less than six months the beaches were lined with outhouses, soon to be known as *fale sami*. Though the crude structures were a terrible eyesore, they did contribute greatly to a significant reduction in hookworm cases. Large supplies of the curative drug, thymol, were ordered, and the population was dosed throughout the villages.

The campaign of 1909-1910 was not a complete success, however. Hospital statistics four decades later showed that roughly 21 percent of the population continued to carry the disease. The health campaign was still considered a

success by Navy officials for it provided an impetus in the prevention of diseases in general, and aroused the Sāmoans' interest in the concept of preventative medicine. The campaign proved that health facilities were inadequate, and along with the construction of the new dispensary came the demand for a proper hospital.

With the completion of the new hospital at Malaloa in 1912, a major step had been taken to improve the overall health of the general population. While the Navy Department approved the hospital project, it clarified that funds from the U.S. Treasury could not be used for construction. A Sāmoan hospital fund was created to finance the cost of construction, which, when completed, came to a total of $2,284.94. Monies collected for the fund were deposited with the Treasurer of the Island Government and managed by a medical officer. The fund was authorized to collect fees for services rendered, to operate a drug store for the

benefit of the hospital, and to accept charitable donations. Fees were instituted for medical treatment and the purchase of prescriptions. Outpatient visits cost 10 cents and surgical fees ranged from $1.00 to $25.00. Prescription medicines were sold at a cost of 10 cents per prescription. The charge for bed occupancy was 25 cents, plus 25 cents for each attendant brought along by the patient. There was no charge for food, as each patient was fed by his relatives. In the first year, the hospital collected $1,623 in revenues.

To raise the quality of health care in American Sāmoa to a more "modern" standard, Governor William Crose, and his successor Commander Clark Stearns, realized that it was necessary to establish a professional medical authority with department head rank within the government. This goal was accomplished in 1914 with the establishment of the Public Health Department of American Sāmoa, which replaced the Board of Health. The Senior Medical Officer of the Naval Station served as the department director.

During the first year of the hospital's operation it became very clear that using family members in the care of hospital in-patients was inefficient. The original hospital staff consisted of only two Navy corpsmen, one "female nurse," and one janitor. As a result of the small staff, family members were needed to provide "bedside" care. When the beds became filled with patients, the ward became crowded with family members. Prescribed medicines were not properly administered, if administered at all, and family members most likely did not follow the diet ordered by the doctor for the patient.

Governor Crose, together with his medical officer, conceived the idea of establishing a nursing school to train young Sāmoan women as nurses. Crose contacted the Navy's Surgeon General and secured his support for the project. On August 26, 1913, five months after Crose's term as governor was completed, the Surgeon General ordered that "A school is hereby directed to be established in American Sāmoa for the purpose of training native Sāmoan women in the principles of nursing with a view to their making use of this teaching in their own country, and among their own people. For this purpose, two members of the Nurse Corps, United States Navy, will be ordered to Sāmoa who, together with the medical officer of the Navy attached to the station, will give the necessary instruction."

On February 14, 1914, the Sāmoan Nurses' Training School began its long and respected career with Acting Chief Nurse Humphrey and Nurse Anderson in charge of three young nursing students. The three young ladies – Pepe, Se'iloiga and Initia – were graduates of Atauloma Girl's School. As the first nursing students in American Sāmoa, the three ladies went on to serve as nurses into the 1950s, earning for themselves a reputation for devoted and professional service to the people of American Sāmoa, as well as setting a standard of excellence for all Sāmoan nursing students to follow.

▼ ▼ ▼

On February 14, 1913, three American Sāmoan boys were sent to the Hilo Boarding School in Hawai'i aboard the SS *Ventura*. The three boys, sent to school at government expense, were the first to be given the opportunity to attend school outside of Sāmoa. They also represented Governor Crose's strong belief that education was the key component to American Sāmoa's future. The three boys were Fa'atoia from Manu'a, son of Tufele; Nelesone from Leone, son of Uaine; and Toalei of Leone, son of Leoso.

Three years earlier, within a year of his appointment as governor in 1910, Commander William Crose determined that education in American Sāmoa was entirely inadequate. American Sāmoa's islands, he said, "are so far away from the United States and so isolated that the public does not know or care . . . by our treaty . . . it is plainly the duty of the American people to lead the Sāmoans on toward civilization," but he was disheartened that the Navy's requests to Congress for educational funds ". . . have regularly been either ignored or acted upon adversely."

Commander Crose was not the first naval governor to be frustrated by a complete lack of federal support in his attempt to establish government education in the islands. Previous naval commanders, most notably Commander Tilley and Captain Sebree, had made a concerted effort to secure federal aid for education, but met with no success.

Commander Tilley's executive officer, Lt. Commander E.J. Dorn, made the first official request for federal aid. He suggested that the Navy ask the Commissioner of Education of the Department of the Interior to propose an educational program. The Commissioner recommended an expenditure of $347.50 for school equipment, and proposed the educational program be turned over to the Interior Department, with an annual allotment of $5,000 for operational expenses. The Secretary of the Navy, however, rejected the plan, stating he was unable to accept the proposal on the grounds Sāmoa was too small and too remote to

A 1920s model pick-up truck provided the earliest motor transportation in Tutuila. Circa 1940.

hold representatives of two departments of the federal government.

Commandant Sebree asked the Navy Department for $5,000 in 1902 to be used to establish a public school system with an American Director of Education. When Sebree realized the money would not be forthcoming, he made an arrangement with the Roman Catholic Mission to provide a government subsidy to establish a boys' school near Leone on a non-sectarian basis. Sebree, who was committed to a policy of public education, was not happy at having to rely on a religious organization to provide schooling for Tutuila's children. Such education, Sebree believed, should come at public expense.

The following year a number of European and part-Sāmoans in the Pago Pago bay area requested a school be established for their children, as well as for many Sāmoan children in the vicinity. In response, the Commandant established the first public school on Tutuila at Fagatogo, allocating $1,000 from the copra fund for the purpose. Since this was to be a public school, the Commandant requested that students be nominated from the Eastern, Western and Manu'a districts. The Commandant reserved for himself the right to choose students from the non-Sāmoan and part-Sāmoan population.

The school proved to be a success, as did the popularity among Sāmoans for the concept of public education. The Western District, unable to secure government funding for their own school, raised $5,000 to get their district school started. By 1909 the government had three schools in operation, though the funds to operate the schools came largely from the private sector. From 1909 to 1911 there were no further attempts to organize a public school system. It would be

Tennis players gather to complete during the Ernest Reid Memorial Cup competition. Front row, left to right: Sam Scanlan, unknown, Eddie Meredith. Standing, left to right: unknown, George H.C. Reid, Peter Reid, Sr. Circa 1935

The original Burns Philp store with adjacent copra dock and rail line. The store was located between Malaloa and Happy Valley. Circa 1900.

Governor Crose who pushed hard for recognition by Washington of the need for public education in American Sāmoa.

Crose first compiled a report of the educational system in the islands and sent it to the Secretary of the Navy. The report defined the many needs required to establish a public school system and noted the complete lack of funds available. The report concluded by asking for advice and financial aid. The report completed, Crose called a conference for all foreign teachers in Tutuila and Manu'a. The conference was attended by all invited teachers except the Catholic mission. The conference proved to be a great boost to the concept of public education by adopting a resolution calling for compulsory education. The resolution enabled Crose to frame his "Regulation to Enforce the Educational Rights of Children," published on February 23, 1912.

The Secretary of the Navy responded to Crose's report by asking the Interior Department's Commissioner of Education, Mr. P.P. Claxton, for his assistance. Claxton responded to the Navy Secretary's request on January 4, 1912. He based his recommendations upon the premise that it would be a mistake to try to force the pace of education among a primitive people. He stated he believed there were too many schools in American Sāmoa which were not large enough to be efficient. He proposed an annual budget of $20,000, half to be provided by island funds, half by the federal government. The funding would be used to establish a Department of Education to be supervised by an American director and staffed by assistants, at least ten of whom would be Americans. Claxton stated, that in his opinion, the curriculum should consist of English, arithmetic, practical geometry, field science, industry and morals. Schools should be in session four hours a day throughout most of the year.

Claxton further suggested the creation of a normal school to train Sāmoan teachers, and suggested that promising Sāmoan boys and girls, not over ten years of age, be selected for special training and sent to Washington, D.C., to live in American homes and attend the public schools in the District of Columbia.

Encouraged by Claxton's report, Governor Crose called a second conference of teachers, which this time was attended by representatives of the Catholic mission. The teachers agreed upon a general program, a curriculum and a number of text books. Crose announced he would provide $10,000 a year from local funds, and when the conference adjourned the delegates were confident that a new system of public education was about to be permanently established.

Much to the disappointment of Governor Crose and the missionary teachers, the federal money upon which public education depended was never allotted. Without federal funding, Crose was left with only a voluntary organization of private schools, over which he had no administrative authority.

Despite the disheartening setback, Crose was still able to bring a sense of island-wide cooperation among the missionary teachers. This voluntary teachers association resulted in stimulating the interest among the population for an improved system of education.

Though it was not practical to send Sāmoan children to the United States for schooling, everyone understood the benefit of off-island education. The Fono proposed that three promising youngsters be sent to school in Hawai'i. After consulting with Sāmoan leaders, Governor Crose chose the two boys from Leone and one from Manu'a. Once the boys arrived in Hilo their progress was closely followed by educators and Sāmoan leaders. Sadly, Toalei died soon after arriving in Hilo. Both Nelesone and Fa'atoia proved successful as both did well in their school work. The two young men would later emerge as leaders in their respective lives.

During the first fourteen years of Naval administration of American Sāmoa, Navy governors both recognized and defined the need to establish public education in the islands. Their efforts were frustrated by the repeated inability of federal agencies in Washington, as well as Congress, to recognize the federal government's responsibility to establish a system of public education in American Sāmoa and provide federal funding to that end.

Despite these continual setbacks, Naval governors pursued the concept of education. On July 28, 1914, Naval governor Commander Clark D. Stearns issued "The Education Regulation of 1914." The regulation established a Department of Education and outlined its duties. The act defined "three classes of public schools, the duties of the taxpayers of a village to provide suitable buildings for pupils and for the teachers." It provided for "tracts of land for playgrounds and other tracts for school plantations. Every public school was to be open for instruction for a least four hours a day, Fridays, Saturdays, Sundays and holidays were excepted. The age for commencing school was five years."

One month earlier, in June, Governor Stearns also issued a report which stated there were "in addition to village pastors' schools, eight recognized schools in Tutuila. Six were sectarian, two island government (schools), three for boys, three for girls and two for both boys and girls. These schools were being taught by a teacher from the United States, by Catholic Marist Brothers, by Catholic Marist sisters, by representatives of the London Missionary Society, and by Mormon elders."

Prior to his transfer to his next duty station, Governor Stearns completed a library building and equipped it with 3,000 volumes which he personally solicited from his friends in the United States. The library remained operational until 1950, when it was incorporated into the new library of the High School of American Sāmoa in Utulei.

Flag Day dancing in front of Fita Fita Barracks. Circa 1927.

Ua uō, uō foa

'First friends, then broken heads.'
War or disagreements happen. — Proverb

Chapter 10

War, The Mau, And The Bingham Hearings

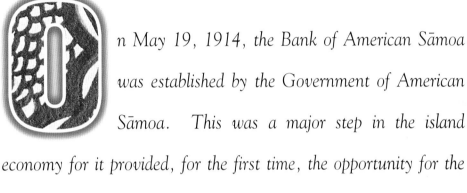n May 19, 1914, the Bank of American Sāmoa was established by the Government of American Sāmoa. This was a major step in the island economy for it provided, for the first time, the opportunity for the government and independent merchants and traders to conduct private business in a professional manner.

From the day the American flag had been raised on Tutuila in April, 1900, the lack of banking facilities had been a continuing obstacle to the transaction of private and government business in the islands. Both the island's merchants and government had to bank by mail. The time involved, plus the fact that shipping to and from Australia and San Francisco was oftentimes unreliable, made banking transactions a laborious and time-consuming problem.

Without a bank Sāmoans had no opportunity to learn the use of money as a medium of exchange. They understood the value of gold and silver coins, but were reluctant to trust postal money orders. When they wished to send money out of the islands to make purchases or contribute to church organizations, they shipped gold.

Governor Clark D. Stearns created the new bank by subscribing $5,000 in capital from the Government of American Sāmoa to get the bank started and by employing the first civilian bank manager. Although it took some time for Sāmoans to learn to use the bank and understand the value of money, it proved to be a boon to local merchants and the island's economy.

Six weeks following the opening of the new bank, Governor Stearns issued his "Annual Report to the Secretary of the Navy." Under the heading "Improvement of Grounds," Stearns informed the Secretary that "1800 feet of concrete walks, four feet in width, have been constructed where necessary to connect buildings. Cinders from the power plant and station ship have been used as available on the roads through the station, furnishing a light thoroughfare by being well tamped and covered with crude oil. Many trees and shrubs have been planted, such as mango, papaya, kapok, candle nut, avocado, breadfruit and other native shade trees. The total number of trees and shrubs planted is 1,541."

In August, 1914, all appeared quiet in Tutuila and Manu'a, but events in Europe would soon find their way to both German Sāmoa and American Sāmoa. On August 6th German Sāmoa's new governor, Dr. Erich Shultz-Ewerth, learned via the wireless that war had begun. Only the day before Shultz-Ewerth, knowing that war was inevitable, met with his administration and decided not to resist an invasion by British forces, as he knew that Sāmoan loyalty to German interests was doubtful. Upon learning that war had broken out, Shultz-Ewerth sent the German steamer *Elsass* to Pago Pago for internment, along with his gunboat, the *Solf*.

The same day Britain's Secretary of State, Sir Lewis Harcourt, sent a telegram urging New Zealand's Governor General, the Earl of Liverpool, to seize German Sāmoa and take control of the radio station. He reminded Liverpool that any territory thus occupied "must at the conclusion of the war be at the disposal of the Imperial Government for the purposes of an ultimate settlement." Liverpool replied immediately, agreeing to capture German Sāmoa.

One week following the declaration of war an expeditionary force of 1,473 New Zealanders sailed from Wellington for New Caledonia. At Noumea the expedition was reinforced by the British battle cruiser HMS *Australia*, the light cruiser HMS *Sydney*, and the French cruiser *Montcalm*. With this superior naval force, the New Zealanders sailed for German Sāmoa on August 23rd with a stop in Suva.

On the morning of August 29th anxious German citizens in Apia saw the large naval convoy gathering beyond Apia harbor. The convoy had been joined in Suva by New Zealand light cruisers HMS *Psyche*, HMS *Philomel* and HMS *Pyramus*. The New Zealand expeditionary forces, commanded by Lt. Colonel Robert Logan of the New Zealand Army, came ashore with 1,473 men. Governor Shultz-Ewerth, after destroying the radio station to "keep it out of British hands," left Apia for a meeting with Sāmoan chiefs, leaving the official surrender of German Sāmoa to his subordinate, S.N. Rimberg. Not a single shot was fired by either side. In a matter of hours German Sāmoa had ceased to exist. On August 31, 1914, Lt. Colonel Logan raised the New Zealand flag at Vailima, Robert Louis Stevenson's former home and the official residence of the German governor. The flag-raising was accompanied by a 21-gun salute from the cruiser HMS *Psyche*.

With the arrival of the New Zealand forces in Apia, Lt. Colonel Logan proposed that German civilians remain at their posts and continue their duties. The Germans did not accept Logan's suggestion and left him no alternative but to take them prisoners. On September 11th the Allied convoy sailed for New Zealand, taking the German prisoners into captivity.

Meanwhile German Admiral Graf von Spee, based in Tsingtao, China, commanded the German Pacific Squadron of two heavy cruisers and four light cruisers. He determined that he had two choices: go back to Europe to join the main German fleet or stay in the Pacific and raise havoc with Allied shipping. In early September von Spee learned that the New Zealand expeditionary force had landed in Apia and that the accompanying naval convoy was bottled up in Apia harbor. He thought that if he surprised the

Commander Clark D. Stearns, 9th Naval Governor, 1913-1914.

Allied fleet at anchor in Apia he could inflict heavy damage. He hastened to Apia with his two heavy cruisers arriving on September 14th, but he was too late. The Allied ships had left three days earlier.

Bringing his ships close to shore he could see the Union Jack flying from flagstaffs and khaki-clad soldiers along Beach Road. A few hours later as he passed through the strait between 'Upolu and Savai'i he was hailed by two Germans in a rowboat who explained that the New Zealand forces were poorly-trained and expressed the opinion that von Spee's forces could easily recapture 'Upolu. Von Spee, however, saw that recapturing the island would only serve a temporary purpose. He decided to steam eastward for Cape Horn and head into the Atlantic. On December 6th von Spee encountered a superior British fleet at the Falkland Islands and suffered complete defeat, ending seventy years of German power in the South Pacific.

Despite the scale of military acitivity in 'Upolu, American naval personnel in Pago Pago, together with the Sāmoan population, remained merely spectators just beyond the view of the war. The only real activity in American Sāmoa, beyond the internment of the German ships *Elsass* and *Solf*, was the enlargement of the capacity of the wireless station to enable direct communication with Honolulu.

While American Sāmoa was spared direct involvement in the war, the islands were not so lucky when it came to the whims of mother nature. On January 8, 1915, a powerful hurricane slammed directly into Manu'a, killing three people. While all the islands in the Sāmoa chain felt the hurricane's impact, Manu'a suffered by far the worst damage.

The full force of the hurricane hit during the night, as villagers fled from their collapsing *fales* to seek shelter by burying themselves in the ground or hanging on to trees. Metal roofing iron — very new to Manu'a – was swept into the sky and carried seven miles across the strait to Olosega. Large trees such as breadfruit were uprooted in great numbers and seventy-five percent of all coconut trees were uprooted. The village of Sili, located on a narrow shelf between the beach and mountain on Olosega, was washed away. A boy drowned at Fitiuta when towering waves rushed inland and swept through the village. A man at Ofu was decapitated by a flying sheet of metal, and at Olosega village a woman was crushed by a falling tree. When dawn finally broke, Manu'ans found complete devastation of their villages, plantations, and their livelihood.

The radio station was destroyed, leaving Manu'ans unable to send word of the disaster to Tutuila until late in the day.

Immediate help for Manu'a from Tutuila was impossible for weeks. The three vessels at Pago Pago, the USS *Princeton*, the western district schooner *Leone*, and the Manu'ans own boat, the *Manu'a*, were themselves damaged from the storm. The *Leone* was lost at sea for weeks due to the storm, the *Manu'a* was cast up on the reef, and the *Princeton* was under repair due to grounding.

Despite logistical problems and the 60-mile distance to Manu'a, Tutuilans gathered their resources to help their brothers in the eastern islands. Within the first weeks, however, the Manu'ans had to rely on ancient and time-proven methods to survive the disaster, as they knew it would take time before Tutuila could provide assistance. Fortunately Manu'a's water supply was not damaged, but nearly one hundred percent of all food crops and food-bearing trees were destroyed. Famine was the most immediate threat. Buried foodstuffs – *masi* — such as taro, yams and other similar plants, which fermented, provided the major source of nourishment for weeks. Finally, the *Princeton*, her repairs completed along with the USS *Fortune*, began shuttling rations of flour, rice and biscuits to Manu'a. Nearly two-thirds of Manu'a's population, estimated to be about 2,000, left their villages for Tutuila aboard the ships to stay with relatives to wait until food plants could be replanted and begin bearing again. A complete year would pass before Manu'a's residents finally returned to their villages.

The Manu'a hurricane of 1915 is notable for two reasons. It marked the first time in American Sāmoa's history that the United States Congress voted to send financial aid to the islands in the form of hurricane relief. The amount, $10,000, was the first direct Congressional assistance to the territory. Second, the American Red Cross donated $2,000 for disaster relief, the first such time this international organization involved itself with American Sāmoa.

▼ ▼ ▼

World War I provided American Sāmoans with an opportunity to demonstrate their loyalty to the United States, which they considered their adopted country. High chiefs from throughout the islands offered their services to the U.S. Navy, as well as those of their families, to whatever duties the Navy deemed necessary. Fortunately for all concerned the war remained far from Sāmoa and there was

Captain Edwin T. Pollock, 15th Naval Governor. 1922-1923

Matais gather for photo in front of *fale tele*. Circa 1930.

little need for the Navy to require Sāmoan assistance in the war effort.

The only anti-American problem encountered in Tutuila came from Willie Huch, of part German and Sāmoan ancestry, who expressed his loyalty to the German cause by stating that he intended to blow up the power plant in the event that either a German cruiser showed up in the vicinity or that Germany lost the war. Huch was arrested and tried for making seditious and treasonable statements against the government of American Sāmoa. He was found guilty and sentenced to hard labor for the duration of the war, the court later recommending clemency in view of his good reputation.

Soon after the war ended, the Sāmoas were hit with another disaster which, like World War I, had its origins at the opposite end of the globe. Spanish influenza was sweeping across Europe and North America taking millions of lives, eventually finding its way to New Zealand.

In November, 1918, the steamer *Talune* anchored in Apia harbor, having sailed from Auckland a few days earlier. Though it has not been proven beyond complete doubt, evidence suggests that a missionary, returning to 'Upolu after taking leave in New Zealand, was himself infected with the flu. With symptoms no worse than a slight cough, he possibly infected other passengers aboard the *Talune*.

The day the Talune dropped anchor, the citizens of Apia were holding a victory parade down Beach Road to celebrate the allied victory in World War I. It was a hot day, and dust filled the air throughout the town. The passengers from the *Talune*, many of them now carrying the disease, passed through an informal health inspection before coming ashore, then began mixing among the crowds who had crowded into Apia

from many outlying villages. Infection among the hundreds of people was swift and deadly. Within two days many took ill and began to die.

When the pestilence finally ended, some four to six weeks later, the people of British Sāmoa could finally mourn their dead and assess the damage. Nearly 9,000 people had died – about one-fifth of the population. Luck was with American Sāmoa, however, as swift and decisive action by Governor John Poyer prevented the epidemic from reaching Tutuila and Manu'a.

Governor Poyer, knowing that the *Talune* had sailed from Auckland, and also knowing that the flu epidemic was already in New Zealand, sent word to Apia that American Sāmoa was quarantined from all outside shipping and that the *Talune* could not land in Pago Pago. The Navy relentlessly enforced the quarantine around American Sāmoa, making the islands one of the few places on earth spared from this terrible pestilence.

Very soon after the flu's outbreak in Apia, Governor Poyer offered to send volunteer medical personnel to British Sāmoa to assist in the treatment of flu victims. Lt. Colonel Robert Logan, British Sāmoa's Administrator, pocketed Poyer's telegram and disconnected the telegraph, because he was "too stubborn" to accept aid, and "didn't like Americans." Nearly one-fifth of the population died during the epidemic. This terrible mortality rate placed British Sāmoa among the highest of any country on earth.

▼ ▼ ▼

On December 8, 1919, Peter Coleman was born in Pago Pago. Coleman would go on to become American Sāmoa's first Sāmoan Attorney General, the only Sāmoan appointed civil governor, the first elected Sāmoan governor, the longest-serving governor in the history of American Sāmoa, and the only person in the history of the United States and its territories who served as governor in five consecutive decades.

Sixteen days later, on December 24, 1919, Aifili Paulo Lauvao, later to become known as A.P. Lutali, was born on the island of Aunu'u. During his lifetime of public service, Lutali served as a sergeant in the First Sāmoan Battalion during World War II, was a founding member of Sāmoana High School, Speaker of the House of Representatives, President of the Senate, the second elected Delegate to Washington, D.C., and second elected Governor of American Sāmoa, later being elected to a second term as Governor.

Earlier that year, on June 10th, Governor John M. Poyer returned to the United States after serving as governor since March 1, 1915. Poyer

took office as American Sāmoa's 11th naval governor. He was the territory's longest-serving naval governor, serving four years, two months and ten days in office. He was one of only two naval governors, the other being Captain Henry F. Bryan, USN ret., who had retired from the Navy prior to their terms as governor.

Poyer had a number of accomplishments during his tenure in office. The one for which he is remembered is the establishment of the New Government High School in January, 1918. The new school, built at Anua, was later named the "Poyer School." The school, built for a total cost of $25,000, remained in operation for nearly three decades. It educated some of American Sāmoa's most outstanding young men who emerged as the territory's political and business leaders in the 1950s, 60s and 70s.

Another event that transpired during Poyer's term of office was the arrival, on December 15, 1916, of English writer Somerset Maugham. Maugham was allegedly accompanied by a missionary and Miss Sadie Thompson, both of whom became the major characters in Maugham's famous short story "Rain."

Governor Poyer's replacement was Commander Warren J. Terhune, who assumed the post of commandant and governor on June 10, 1919. Terhune quickly found himself embroiled in a number of issues which would ultimately bring unbearable pressure on Terhune himself.

The first issue involved one of his naval officers who, Terhune reported to the Navy Secretary, was ". . . conducting financial and mercantile operations in American Sāmoa, such action viewed with extreme disfavor" by both Terhune and his predecessor, Governor Poyer. Terhune requested that the officer "be forever kept out of the Sāmoan archipelago."

Terhune faced other difficulties involving both naval personnel and unattached *palagi* men living in the islands. The problem involved relationships between these men and Sāmoan women. Previous governors had apparently adopted a "hands off" policy in these matters, allowing each individual situation to work itself out through the natural course of events. For some reason, however, Terhune felt compelled to take a public stand on the

issue. In November, 1919, he issued a Naval Station Order forbidding the ". . . marriage of American naval personnel to Sāmoan women" without the consent of the Commandant.

Soon after the order was issued, a Navy petty officer requested permission to marry a Sāmoan woman with whom he was living. Since the petty officer already had a wife and family in the United States, Terhune refused to authorize the marriage. While Terhune was acting within his power as commanding officer, and his position was in keeping with public morality in the United States, his decision was very unpopular among the Sāmoans who perceived Terhune's actions reflected badly upon themselves.

Problems were also festering at the hospital. The LMS requested permission to install a missionary nurse at the hospital because they believed Navy nurses were rotated too frequently. They also believed it was not certain whether Navy nurses would be sympathetic to Sāmoan patients or that they would have Christian and moral values. Secretary of the Navy Josephus Daniels noted the implied affront to the Navy Nurse Corps in declining the request by the LMS. He also declined the request based on the reason that a missionary nurse working under the auspices of the U.S. Navy would find herself in the impossible position of trying to serve two bosses. Further, the Navy Secretary commented that it did not appear ". . . that the natives are not receiving proper medical attention and nursing care."

Governor Terhune faced further problems with another group of missionaries. This time it was the Latter Day Saints and their mission at Mapusaga. The Mormon mission of Tutuila occupied twenty-two acres of land at Mapusaga and rented 386 adjoining acres which it used as a farm to teach boys agriculture and provide an income for the mission by selling the produce.

The issue with which Terhune and the Mormon mission disagreed was taxation. The mission itself and the Mormon missionaries were exempted from taxation, as were the missionaries of other faiths. In 1919 taxes were assessed in each district by a board of assessors composed of the Secretary of Native Affairs, the District Governor

Captain Edward S. Kellogg, 16th Naval Governor. 1923-1925

Commander Warren J. Terhune, 12th Naval Governor, 1919-1920.

and the county chiefs of each respective district. The tax in the western district that year was set at 150 pounds of copra per taxpayer year or, alternatively, at $11.34 in cash. To this the western district added a special school tax of $1.80 per person, payable in copra or in cash.

The head of the Mormon Mission, John Q. Adams, took exception to the levying of the school tax upon the inhabitants of Mapusaga and objected to the taxes upon the young men from 'Upolu attending the school. He presented his views to the district matais but they did not agree with him and ordered the taxes be paid. Adams filed a complaint with Senator Reed Smoot of Utah citing the "unjust and unreasonable taxation," but the Navy Department was able to demonstrate that Adams' statements were inaccurate and let the taxes stand.

When Terhune assumed command of the Naval Station and Governor of American Sāmoa, he was considered to be "an upright officer" who began his term of office energetically and enthusiastically. Soon after he took office, however, his health began to fail. Those around him apparently did not realize how serious Terhune's health problems were. As his health deteriorated the problems he faced became more serious. He was in no condition to handle the events which would unfold during the year 1920.

Pepe Tufele Haleck, one of the first three Sāmoan ladies to enter Nurses Training School in 1914. Circa 1925.

Very early in 1920 a movement began in Tutuila in opposition to the Navy's administration of American Sāmoa. Since 1900 the Navy had generally been quite popular among the Sāmoan population. The Navy's decisions during the flu epidemic in 1918 to quarantine American Sāmoa, and the successful enforcement of that quarantine, were very well received by Sāmoan leadership. Everyone realized that the Navy's quick and decisive action had prevented a tragedy as the people in British Sāmoa had suffered.

By early 1920 the only points of concern between Sāmoans and the Naval Administration were: 1. the marriage regulation; and 2. the question as to the fitness of Secretary of Native Affairs A.M. Noble and his assistant, L.W. Cartwright. The question regarding both Noble and Cartwright were raised by one of Tutuila's most recognized leaders, Mauga Moi Moi of Pago Pago. For reasons unknown, Governor Terhune took no steps to address these two issues. As a result a movement began in Pago Pago which in time would grow into vocal opposition to the Naval Administration.

The movement would be called by various names in 1920 and 1921. It was known as the "Committee of Sāmoan Chiefs," the "Sāmoan Movement," and the "Sāmoan Cause." Later on it would acquire its Sāmoan name, the "Mau." For purposes of clarity we shall refer to it by that title.

The Mau began in earnest in February and March 1920 with a series of *fonos* in Pago Pago. High chiefs and talking chiefs of numerous ranks gathered together with other individuals to begin the game of Sāmoan style politics with lengthy oratory, discussion and intrigue. The meetings became so consuming that during the months of April, May and June no copra was cut and the source of the island's economy evaporated.

Since no records were kept during the Mau's early proceedings it is not known whether the grievances were entirely Sāmoan in nature, or whether they were inspired – or fueled – by individuals from outside Sāmoa. Whether Sāmoan or inspired from outside, the Mau can be grouped into two categories: 1. Sāmoan grievances; and 2. the legality of the authority of the United States in American Sāmoa.

The question of the legality of United States authority in American Sāmoa had its roots in a land dispute involving a proposed trading business to be established in Leone by the Ripley family. Mr. Samuel S. Ripley, the eldest of the second Sāmoan-borne generation who descended from Mr. E.V. Ripley and his Sāmoan wife who had settled in Leone in the mid-nineteenth century, proposed to start a planting and trading business in Sāmoa. Mr. Ripley had migrated to California in 1904, served in the U.S. Army in France in World War I, demobilizing as a sergeant at the end of the war. His wife, Madge Ripley, a Californian, was a graduate of the University of California. The Ripleys, through Ripley's niece, were connected to Mr. Arthur A. Greene, a lawyer by training, who was at the time the city editor of the Honolulu *Star-Bulletin*.

The project proposed by Ripley to develop family lands would have been entirely proper in the United States or Hawai'i. But the Native Lands Ordinance of 1900, which forbade the alienation of Sāmoan lands, prevented such a project in American Sāmoa. The perspective of the Naval Administration was clear: the original

Ripley had acquired the lands, estimated to be as much as 300 acres, through marriage to his Sāmoan wife. The land therefore remained Sāmoan property, usable and transferable only in accordance with Sāmoan custom. The obstacle to Ripley's plans was clear and unequivocal, the land could not be developed as he proposed.

The legal approach Ripley's lawyers – or advisors – took at the beginning, show that they recognized that unless the Naval Administration could be forced to change the law or could be removed and replaced by a more agreeable administration, they could not expect to achieve their goals.

The Ripley family began their pursuit to establish their business March, 1920, with the arrival of Mr. and Mrs. Arthur A. Greene from Honolulu. The following month Mr. C.S. Hannum, a lawyer in Richmond, California, whose secretary had been Ripley's wife, wrote a letter to the Secretary of the Interior. In his letter, Hannum said he understood ". . . that the United States has not acquired the islands . . . that the Sāmoan Government still functions . . . and succession of land titles and distribution of estates is still governed by its laws and customs."

At the same time in Sāmoa, Arthur A. Greene took the position that the treaties between the United States and the Sāmoans contemplated only the right of the U.S. Navy to use the facilities of Pago Pago Bay. The strategy of the two men was perfectly clear. The authority of the United States in American Sāmoa was to be challenged. And secondly, the activities of its administering agency, the Navy Department, were considered illegal.

When Greene arrived with his wife in Tutuila, the meetings of Sāmoan chiefs regarding their grievances with the Navy had been carrying on for nearly two months. Greene would later deny that he ever organized the Sāmoan chiefs into a protest movement, but from his point of view the Mau could not have begun at a better time. Greene was soon asked to act as counsel to the Mau. One of his first recommendations to Mau leaders was that they draft a bill of complaints, but he was told this had already been done and that it had been ignored.

In their list of grievances, the Mau asserted that Sāmoans were kept in ignorance of the laws because they were not published in the Sāmoan language, and that the newspaper, *O Le Fa'atonu*, which was supposed to keep them informed, was not published promptly. They said they received no accounting for the Island Government's revenues nor of the expenditures of their money. They called the roads outside the Naval Station

Village *aumaga* circles guest house while important ceremony takes place. Circa 1935.

inadequate and the school system backward, both as to size and quality of instruction. They noted the lack of an agricultural station for teaching and research. They alleged that justice was harshly administered, that the governor forbade meetings of the chiefs and "Government of Sāmoa." They considered the drug store of the Sāmoan hospital to be exploiting the people. Finally, they objected to the "violation" of Sāmoan girls and to the "marriage regulation" of the Naval Station.

This list of grievances by Mau leaders clearly indicated their concerns. Many considered these complaints to be in many ways entirely reasonable. At the same time, however, the record showed that past Navy administrations had tried to improve the conditions in Tutuila but had received no support from Congress.

On many occasions former naval governors had sought federal aid for schools and agriculture but their requests were ignored in Washington.

The condition of the roads throughout Tutuila – which were admittedly very poor — had been a concern of every governor since Tilley. Again, no funds were ever budgeted in Washington to improve the island's roads.

In regard to the Mau's other grievances, the quality of justice administered and the "violation" of Sāmoan girls were matters of opinion and therefore subject to debate. The "exploitation" by the drug store was without foundation, and not taken seriously. The marriage regulation was considered the exclusive business of the Navy administration.

The failure of the local administration and a lack of imagination among administration personnel can be seen as reasons for a number of problems about which Mau leaders were unhappy. It was American disinterest in Washington for Sāmoa, however, that lay behind each of the grievances which had a foundation in fact. Unfortunately, the Navy had not kept Sāmoan leaders informed through the years about their own frustrations as to Washington's unwillingness to provide even the smallest amount of financial aid for basic improvements.

In May, 1920, Lt. Commander C.S. Boucher, USN, reported as the new executive officer for the Naval Station. Within a very short period of time Boucher became closely associated with the Mau and its objectives. Though Boucher's total stay in Tutuila was last little more than three months, during which time he could not possibly become an expert in the Sāmoan affairs of the time, he displayed a willingness to act with little understanding of all the facts involved.

When Boucher arrived, Governor Terhune was said to have been in rapidly failing health. There are few official records which explain Boucher's impression of Terhune or his health condition, nor are there any records indicating why Boucher so quickly supported the Mau. As a naval officer, Boucher had two choices upon arrival: subordinate his personal views to those of Governor Terhune – who was his commanding officer; or, relieve Terhune of many of his duties and assist him in much of the decision-making in an effort to calm the situation.

Boucher, however, followed neither of these two courses. Instead he represented himself as a secret agent, went about carrying a side-arm, and met repeatedly with Mau leaders in an effort to promote further hostility. Terhune confined Boucher to his quarters as a warning, but this did not deter Boucher from continuing his course of action. Terhune then requested Boucher's recall, stating "To strike at the root of the disaffection

and uphold law and discipline, it is imperative that he sail next steamer."

In July, 1920, just as Mau displeasure was coming to a boiling point, Samuel S. Ripley and his wife, Madge, arrived in Tutuila. Ripley joined the Mau and named himself agent for "The Sāmoan Government." He also secured the services of Mr. C.S. Hannum as the Mau's counsel. Hannum took the approach that the Mau was the legitimate successor of the Sāmoan government of the previous century and as such represented an "independent nation," attempting to convince Mau leaders that this was their status.

While Ripley kept busy with Mau activities in Pago Pago his wife stayed at Leone. She immediately found Sāmoan living unpleasant and determined that it should be modernized. She complained about the Navy dispensary in Leone and the lack of proper health care throughout Tutuila. She criticized Naval administration of the island, inferring that American Sāmoans were among the most disadvantaged of Pacific-island peoples. Though many of her statements were without foundation, they did contribute to the tension and disaffection that was growing within the Mau movement.

Through the months of August and September, Terhune was unable to make necessary decisions to decisively deal with the growing crisis. The measures he took did not satisfy Mau leaders. He dismissed Mauga and Satele from their district governorships, replacing them with Le'iato and Fai'ivae. He evicted the Greenes from the private home in which they were staying and made them move into the Sadie Thompson Hotel. He secured Boucher's removal, hoping that his replacedment, Commander A.O. Kail, USN, would provide him with a reliable assistant. Much to Terhune's disappointment, Kail immediately aligned himself with the Mau after meeting with Greene, Ripley and other dissidents. Within a very short period of time Kail began taking action independent of Terhune, further aggravating an already delicate situation.

It is not clear whether the Navy Department was entirely informed of the rapidly accelerating problems in Tutuila during the months of August through October. Governor Terhune had sent a wireless dispatch requesting Boucher's removal. The wireless must have alerted Navy officials in Washington that trouble was brewing. Following his departure from Tutuila, Boucher arrived in San Francisco with a petition signed by Mau leaders to President Wilson. In August Navy Secretary Daniels appointed a court of inquiry to proceed to Sāmoa

to investigate the situation and recommend what steps should be taken.

On November 3, 1920, Governor Terhune entered a room on the second floor of Government House which overlooked the entrance to the bay of Pago Pago and shot himself with a pistol. His body was discovered by the Government House cook. Two days later, on November 5th, the Naval Court of Inquiry, presided over by Captain Waldo Evans, USN, arrived aboard the battleship USS *Kansas* to investigate the Mau and the Naval Administration's dealings with it. Immediately upon arrival they learned of Governor Terhune's suicide. Six days later, on November 11th, Captain Evans was appointed the 13th naval governor.

The Court of Inquiry concluded its business on November 24th. Governor Evans sent a wireless to the Navy Secretary which stated, "Have completed Court of Inquiry. No evidence legal, financial, or political irregularities. Recent unrest of natives influenced by Commander Kail, Lieutenant Commander Boucher, and an American citizen named Greene. It is recommended that Boucher be court martialed on the following charges: conduct unbecoming, conduct prejudicial to good order and discipline; drunk on duty; disrespect to President, SecNav, and superior officer. Greene will be deported as undesirable . . ."

In Washington Rear Admiral C.F. Hughes, USN, was not impressed with the Mau's petition. He exonerated the traders, whose implication in the dissension had been suggested. He expressed the opinion that Secretary of Native Affairs Noble had lost the confidence of the Sāmoans and recommended he be replaced. Admiral Hughes concluded his findings by stating the unrest would recede once the active participants in the crisis had left the island and sufficient time had passed to permit animosities to fade away.

On November 31st Governor Evans deported Greene. As the city-editor of the Honolulu *Star-Bulletin*, Greene continued to write about, and stay involved with, American Sāmoa for a number of years. Lt. Commander Boucher was sentenced by a general court martial to dismissal from the Navy. Navy Secretary Daniels recommended execution of the sentence, telling President Wilson that he considered presidential approval of the sentence of the highest importance, for he believed Boucher's reprehensible conduct might have led to an insurrection.

Following the return of the Court of Inquiry to Washington from Tutuila, Daniels met with Major R.B. Creecy, USMC, its judge advocate, and received a detailed briefing on the entire matter of the Mau and the behavior of the Navy officers. Daniels summarized the entire sad state of affairs in a letter to Governor Evans. "I know," he wrote, "something of the very difficult job you have in hand. You may be sure that I am in full sympathy and will cooperate in every way possible . . . Major Creecy has been good enough to give me a very illuminating story of the whole situation. It is most deplorable. It shows how careful we have to be in sending officers to remote places. I have always tried to send men of judgement and character and ability, but could not of course know about the younger men who, in this instance, have created so much trouble and, as a matter of fact, are probably in conscience guilty of the death of a kind and good man."

On March 4, 1925, Swains Island, which had also been known as Gente Hermosa, Quiros Island, Olosega, Olohenga and Jennings Island, was annexed by the United States Congress under the provisions of Public Resolution No. 75, 68th Congress, to become part of American Sāmoa.

Five months later, on August 11, 1925, Margaret Mead, age twenty-four, arrived in Pago Pago harbor aboard the SS *Sonomato*, to begin the fieldwork for her doctoral dissertation in anthropology at Columbia University. Miss Mead conducted the first segment of her fieldwork in Tutuila, then sailed to Taʻū, Manuʻa, where she remained for the rest of her study of Sāmoan life and culture. Mead's dissertation became famous in the publication, "Coming of Age in Sāmoa."

One year later, on August 12, 1926, the first case of a mild form of influenza was reported in the Pago Pago bay area. An epidemic of serious proportions followed, spreading rapidly throughout Tutuila, lasting approximately six weeks. When the epidemic subsided, there were 4,000 to 5,000 cases.

In December, 1926 a survey of church membership was taken in American Sāmoa. The membership of the four primary religions in Tutuila and Manuʻa was: London Missionary Society, 6,985 members; Wesleyan Methodist Mission, 295 members; Roman Catholic Mission, 1,047 members; and the Mormon Mission, 353 members.

Captain Waldo Evans,
13th Naval Governor,
1920-1922.

Raising the stars and stripes on Swains Island. Circa 1940.

Catholic church, Nu'uuli. Circa 1927.

On October 1, 1927, Naval Governor Captain Henry F. Bryan, USN, issued his report "American Sāmoa: A General Report by the Governor." The report listed the territory's population as of September 30, 1926, as follows: Eastern District of Tutuila, 4,221; Western District, Tutuila, 2,395; Manu'a District, 2,060; and Swains Island, 87, for a total of 8,763 people. Of this total, 2,260 were listed as taxpayers.

From 1925 through 1929 debate continued over the political and administrative status of American Sāmoa. Much of the debate occurred not in American Sāmoa itself, but in California, Hawai'i and the Navy Department in Washington, D.C.

Once the Naval Court of Inquiry had completed its mission and Captain Waldo Evans assumed management of American Sāmoa as governor, he moved quickly to restore order and encourage productive enterprise. He recalled a number of naval officers who he believed could no longer execute their duties properly and set a new, exacting standard of performance for the naval officers stationed in Tutuila.

Governor Evans then turned his attention to municipal matters. Evans himself believed that many of the complaints voiced by the Mau were a reflection of the feelings of previous naval governors. His first step was to improve public education, which had been long delayed due to a lack of federal aid. When Evans began his term as governor there were three public schools in the public school system. When he left two years later, nineteen schools were in operation. For their management he appointed a Board of Education which consisted of the Chaplain of the Naval Station, as chairman, the Public Health Officer, the Secretary of Native Affairs, and two local residents, Mr. George Reid and Mrs. B.F. Kneubuhl.

Evans' next priority were the roads. In 1920 the road between Pago Pago and Leone, a distance of about eight miles, was in such terrible condition that it took nearly an entire morning to make the journey. Evans budgeted $30,000 for road building, with one result being the "Leone Rapid Transit" business starting

operations, offering two round trips a day between Leone and the town area.

Evans' efforts in the area of commercial enterprise also produced results. Although copra cutting had declined dramatically by March, 1920, the production of this commodity began again in November. The tonnage produced by the end of the year, added to that of the first three months of 1921, was enough to make 1920 the second best year in the economic history of the islands since 1900.

In 1921 the Secretary of the Navy, Edwin Denby, issued a statement regarding American Sāmoa as it compared to other U.S. territories. "Although the Congress has provided liberally for Puerto Rico, Hawai'i, the Philippines, and even for Cuba," Denby wrote, "American Sāmoa has been overlooked and the development of a fine race has been delayed." Denby added that "island revenues were pitifully small" and that developmental funds would have to come from the outside.

In July, 1921, Governor Evans called a meeting of high chiefs and leading talking chiefs to ascertain, once and for all, their feelings regarding the Navy's administration of American Sāmoa. Evans asked the chiefs directly to state whether they were or were not satisfied with the Naval Administration, then left them to discuss the matter amongst themselves. He received his answer the next day. The answer was in the form of a letter to the President, signed by Satele, Tufele, Mauga, Tuitele, Pele, Leoso and others, in which they expressed their satisfaction with the Navy's administration, and requested that any papers filed previously which denounced the Naval Administration, be disregarded.

This position by the high chiefs was not entirely unopposed. A number of lower ranking matai assembled at Faleniu where they decided to object to the position of the high chiefs and draw up a protest petition. The meeting degenerated into a "bush-war" assembly where some of the members present threatened to kill High Chief Letuli. When Governor Evans heard what was developing, he sent Chief of Police Hunkin to investigate. Hunkin was told the bush was full of armed men and reported this information to the governor. Evans sent a contingent under Lt. W.A. McDonald, USN, to round up the men. He arrested seventeen *matais* and escorted them back to town to face charges of conspiracy and rebellion against the high chiefs. The group was tried in a court consisting of S.D. Hall, Leoso and Molino'o. Sixteen of the accused confessed their guilt, and were convicted and sentenced to terms varying from seven and a half to twelve years as well as the loss of their *matai* titles. This particular case would drag on until 1924 when the prisoners were offered a parole, provided they take an oath of allegiance and agree to renounce their *matai* titles. They were not prepared to renounce their titles, but the following year agreed to the terms and were released, soon thereafter to receive full pardons.

Naval officials and Sāmoan leaders gather in front of Administration building, the site of today's High Court building. Circa 1920.

Bingham Commission
member Rep. Carroll
Beedy of Maine with
taupou, October, 1930.

Bingham Commission
member Rep. Guinn
Williams of Texas.

On February 20, 1929, the United States Congress approved the cessions of Tutuila, which had occurred on April 17, 1900, and Manu'a, which was signed by Tui Manu'a Elisara on July 14, 1904 and recorded at the Courthouse on July 16, 1904.

The bill calling for the approval of the cession was introduced into the 70th Congress by Senator Hiram Bingham of Connecticut, the Hawai'ian-born son and grandson of missionaries. The bill further provided that, pending action by Congress, the President should continue to appoint the Governor of American Sāmoa; that the land laws of the United States should be inapplicable there; and that the President should appoint a commission consisting of two senators, two members of the House of Representatives, and two Sāmoan "chiefs" to visit the islands and to recommend to Congress "such legislation as they shall deem necessary or proper."

President Herbert Hoover named Senator Bingham and Senator Joseph Robinson, of Arkansas, together with Representatives Carroll Beedy of Maine and Guinn Williams of Texas as members of the Commission. The President then directed Governor Stephen Graham to nominate two appropriate Sāmoan "chiefs" as members. Governor Graham believed that both Tutuila and Manu'a should be represented on the Commission, and he submitted the names of High Chiefs Mauga Palepoi and Tufele Fa'ato'ia as the best representatives from their islands. Governor

Graham also believed that the Mau should be represented on the Commission, and accordingly recommended Sāmoan membership on the Commission be increased to three and include Magalei Siasulu, the Mau leader. The governor's suggestion was approved by Congress which modified the act, by Public Resolution Number 3, 71st Congress, which permitted the naming of three Sāmoan members.

The Commission's visit to American Sāmoa and the hearings were finally scheduled for 1930. Before their departure from Washington, the American commissioners invited all interested persons to appear and be heard. They received and heard proposals for an organic act from three former naval governors of American Sāmoa, the current governor and the Secretary of Native Affairs and the Officer in Charge of the Navy Department's Office of Island Governments.

In American Sāmoa the Mau Committee, including Commissioner Magalei Siasulu, outlined its ideas in a letter addressed to Mr. Thurston and Mr. Bruce Cartwright of the Bishop Museum staff and A.A. Greene of Honolulu. The committee's proposal included its desire for territorial status, removal of the Naval Administration, and an appropriation of $1 million to establish the future Sāmoan government.

The Congressional commissioners boarded the USS *Omaha* at San Pedro, California on September 11, 1930. They were accompanied by Captain W.R. Furlong, USN, officer in charge of the Navy's Office of Island Governments, who acted as aide and paymaster for the expedition. On board the *Omaha* they found a good collection of official documents and pertinent books and publications concerning American Sāmoa, which they studied during their time at sea.

The commissioners arrived in Honolulu on September 18th and were joined by Albert F. Judd, who had been designated counsel for the commission. The commissioners visited the Bishop Museum where Dr. Peter Buck addressed them on "The Sāmoan System of Chieftainship" and expounded on the social and political organization of Sāmoa. Formal hearings began on September 19th, with Senator Bingham opening the session by expressing his regret that the Sāmoan commissioners could not be present due to the problem of time and distance from Sāmoa.

Four members from the Bishop Museum, including Dr. Buck, appeared by invitation as expert witnesses. They confined their comments to social and economic matters and avoided discussion of political matters. One individual urged caution in order to prevent Sāmoan culture being swallowed up by American culture and another member expressed his concern that Sāmoans be protected from exploitation by traders and degradation by tourists. All four members saw no objection to ownership of Sāmoan land by half-castes on the same basis as full-blooded Sāmoans.

Mr. V.S.K. Houston, a delegate of the Territory of Hawaiʻi in Congress with part Polynesian ancestry, delivered the most important testimony in Honolulu, and possibly the most important of all the hearings. Houston had previously recorded his approval of the Navy's health program in American Sāmoa and of its rigid protection of Sāmoan lands. Stated Houston, "With the restricted amount of land this policy or its continuation is absolutely necessary, for the natives have nowhere else to go."

In his testimony Houston went beyond the issues before the commission to address future areas of concern. He stated the basic assumption that statehood for the remote islands was not practical and proposed a "dominion" type of government for American Sāmoa, similar to what later evolved in Puerto Rico. He favored American citizenship for Sāmoans, incorporation of the Bill of Rights in their basic law, and full protection of Sāmoan land and traditional political organizations.

One non-Sāmoan who testified in Honolulu was Lorrin A. Thurston. He favored a civil government aided by American leadership, personal ownership of private property, even at the cost of private ownership of the land, and equal rights for half-castes with Sāmoans. In one of his more interesting statements, Thurston said that because the cession had given the United States the finest harbor in the South Pacific, American taxpayers should be willing to pay for it.

Other non-Sāmoans testified in Honolulu, along with four Sāmoans living in Hawaiʻi. The third Sāmoan witness was Napoleone Tuiteleleapaga, then a twenty-one-year-old student at the University of Hawaiʻi. He said that Sāmoans had been "enraged" when *malagas* were prohibited and when the Public Health Office forbade swimming in polluted Pago Pago Bay. He believed that the governor had too much power, but hoped that white people would not be allowed to buy land, citing the example of his own *matai*, who had been willing to sell family land for a very small sum to send him to school in Hawaiʻi.

The testimony in Honolulu convinced the members of the commission that they faced a difficult and complex task. As they voyaged toward Sāmoa aboard ship they realized that their

commission would have to move carefully, for the introduction of certain American legalities, such as all of the provisions of the Constitution of the United States, would create chaos in the islands. They recognized that common sense demanded they listen carefully to the views of their Sāmoan colleagues before offering any of their own. "We are not going to Sāmoa," said Senator Bingham, "with a platform in our pockets with orders to sign."

The Bingham Commission members left Honolulu on September 20th for Pago Pago aboard the USS *Omaha*. They were joined by Albert F. Judd, legal advisor; William S. Chillingworth, reporter, Reuel S. Moore, representing the United Press, and Joseph R. Farrington, managing editor of the Honolulu *Star-Bulletin*. Merl LaVoy, Pathe News photographer, had boarded the *Omaha* at San Pedro.

When the USS *Omaha* steamed into Pago Pago Bay on September 26, 1930, rainclouds were gathering overhead. As the large Navy ship entered the bay dozens of canoes and numerous small watercraft put into the water to get a closer look. The Fita Fita Band paraded to the dock, where they played "The Star Spangled Banner." Sāmoan commissioners Mauga Palepoi, Tufele Faʻatoʻia and

Naval Governor Stephen Graham with aviators of the airplane "Southern Cross." Left to right, Captain Lancaster, Lt. Commander Harry Lyon, radio operator James Warner, Mrs. Graham, Governor Graham and Mrs. Miller. Photo taken at Government House, June, 1928.

Captain Stephen Graham (center) at ceremonies on the Fagatogo *malae*. Circa 1928.

Bingham Commission delegates and village chiefs, 1930.

Magalei Siasulu stood at the dock to welcome their fellow commissioners. The three chiefs knew full well the importance of this commission and of their historical place as members.

On the afternoon of their arrival the first executive session of the Bingham Commission was held at the Poyer School in Anua. Senator Bingham recognized the solemnity of the occasion by distributing medals struck for the occasion by the United States Mint and announced that the commissioners would wear them when in official session. Bingham formally indicated the precedence of the commissioners as prescribed by President Hoover by announcing the names of each commission member. After this first executive session concluded, the commission called formally

upon Governor Gatewood S. Lincoln, who was given a 17-gun salute from the *Omaha*.

Governor Lincoln announced that he and his staff would not attend the hearings unless they were summoned, as he did not want to influence the testimony of the witnesses. Preparations for the hearings were made by Judge H.P. Wood, who selected Pago Pago, Leone, Nuʻuuli and Taʻū in Manuʻa as official sites for the sessions. The Poyer School would serve as the central site for the hearings because its concrete buildings were considered one of the best facilities on Tutuila.

At the opening of the hearings Commissioner Magalei Siasulu requested that the names of Joseph Steffany and Alex T. Willis be added to the list of witnesses. Commission members approved his request. A total of fifty-nine witnesses would testify before the commission in Sāmoa, of whom four were non-Sāmoans from outside the islands. Two were naval officers, Governor Lincoln and a member of his staff, who were called upon to answer specific questions. Forty-nine of the Sāmoans to testify were *matai*. Among this number were nine high chiefs and seven orators of high rank. There were two young untitled witnesses who also testified, and a young man of mixed Sāmoan blood by the name of Chris Young, who at the time was a claimant to the title of Tui Manuʻa.

There were three official interpreters, George Peters, George Reid and Alex T. Willis. Two interpreters were required at each session,

Flag day dancing on Fagatogo *Malae*. Circa 1927.

who debated the translations until all were satisfied that their translations were accurate. The testimony was recorded by the clerk of the high court of American Sāmoa, a qualified court reporter, and his staff.

On Sunday, September 28th, commission members arose early to attend the services at the LMS church at Pago Pago, with "approximately 300" Sāmoan worshipers in attendance. The following day the commissioners traveled to Leone to hear testimony. Senator Bingham presented Tuitele with a cane made of Hawai'ian koa wood. The cane bore a silver plate, with Tuitele's name inscribed on it. Four days later, on October 2nd, the commission traveled to Ta'ū aboard the *Omaha*. Official documents state that "members of the commission and their party were landed in two whaleboats and a Sāmoan long boat, rowed by sturdy natives through the surf via a channel which had been blasted in the reef." The commission returned to Tutuila on October 4th, conducting the final three days of hearings at the Poyer School.

Witnesses appearing before the commission were not required to confine themselves to set topics. They were invited to speak freely, and at times the commissioners would rely on direct questioning in an attempt to get specific answers or opinions. The one major topic which all witnesses except three testified upon was the desirability of the continuance of the Naval Administration or its replacement by a civilian agency. Of the Sāmoan *matais* who testified, forty expressed support of the Naval Administration, while nine wished to have it replaced. Of the two untitled Sāmoans testifying, one favored maintaining the Navy, the other wished to see the Navy removed.

There were three other topics of serious concern to the witnesses. There was a strong desire by the witnesses for United States citizenship. There was only a small objection to the ownership of Sāmoan lands by half-castes upon the same basis as full-blooded Sāmoans. On this subject High Chief Tuitele said it was the business of each *matai* to decide who belonged to his family. The third topic was the alienation of Sāmoan land which was overwhelmingly opposed.

The Mau designated three speakers to represent their thinking. Two of the Mau leaders were Fanene and Galea'i. Fanene claimed the loyalty of 6,000 Sāmoans, which the commissioners concluded to be a large exaggeration. Responding to this number High Chief Le'iato responded, "When the Mau committee comes

they are all in the Mau. And when the other side comes, they are all on the other side. So you can't tell how many are in the Mau."

At the hearings in Nu'uuli, a noted Mau center, the principal witness was Galea'i, who introduced into the record a letter alleged to have been signed by 711 people, the legitimacy of whose signatures he could not verify. He admitted that the letter had been prepared by Samuel Ripley, who had received more than $2,500 in payments in the past four years, and who had been continuing his dispute with the Navy during this time. Commissioner Guinn Williams of Texas, after listening to Galea'i's testimony regarding the payments to Ripley, proceeded to lecture the Mau leaders about the uselessness of sending money to private individuals in the United States. Williams stated such expenditures

Senator Hiram Bingham, center, flanked by village *manaia* and other participants in Bingham Commission hearings, 1930.

Bingham Commission delegates gather outside meeting *fale* after commission hearings.

Chiefs gather for Fono, Ta'ū, Manu'a. Circa 1930.

Bingham Commission delegates depart American Sāmoa, October 7, 1930.

accomplished nothing, and for the record encouraged Sāmoan leaders in the future to make their wishes known by writing directly to the President or a member of Congress.

Two American witnesses were Benny Kneubuhl and Joseph Steffany. Both men, who operated their own businesses, testified that for years they had been facing unfair competition from the government. Steffany was clearly resentful over the situation, admitting his inability to find a remedy to the injustices which he had suffered. Kneubuhl supported Steffany's testimony, but felt he had a solution. He stated that he objected to the fact that the government was supported largely by customs revenues and a poll tax, believing the customs revenues unfair to the residents of the territory and the poll tax to be unrealistic. Kneubuhl pointed out that as a merchant he had to pay a license fee and customs duties on his importations, while his landlord paid only a few dollars a year as a poll tax. He thought that if the customs duties were removed and business allowed to operate freely that the economy would expand and the islands might eventually become self-supporting.

Once all the witnesses had testified, Chairman Bingham invited comments from the Sāmoan commissioners. Mauga Moi Moi reviewed at some length the history of events since the cession of 1900. He said that most of the troubles in recent years were due mainly to the activities of irresponsible *palagis*, both naval and civilian, and added that as early as 1921 he had informed Governor Terhune that ". . .the laws that are now governing Sāmoa are not laws that have been forced upon the people of Sāmoa because the way the government makes their laws and handles the government is exactly the way the Sāmoans handle their own customs."

High Chief Tufele simply voiced his gratification over the visit of the Bingham Commission and expressed the hope that such a body would revisit the islands from time to time. Chief Magalei of the Mau concluded his statements by saying, "I certify to all what Mauga has said to be

true." Magalei added that he gladly left the decision as to whether the Navy Department should remain in charge of the local government, or should be superceded by a civilian government, to the judgement of the commission.

On October 7th over 300 people, "mostly *matais* and higher chiefs," gathered at the Poyer School to hear the announcement of the decisions of the Bingham Commission. Governor Lincoln and his staff were present by special invitation. The Commission Chairman, Senator Hiram Bingham, read aloud from a list of the Commission's recommendations.

American Sāmoa, said the commissioners, should be governed in accordance with an organic act, which they proposed to draft, and United States citizenship should be conferred on its inhabitants. The inhabitants should enjoy both Sāmoan and American citizenship, qualifications for American Sāmoa citizenship to be determined by the *Fono*. There should be no differentiation between part- and full-blooded Sāmoans in regard to citizenship. An appeal from the decision of the High Court to the U.S. District Court of Hawai'i was to be authorized, and a bill of rights incorporated into the organic act. The governor could be either a military officer or a civilian, according to the choice of the President, but his powers should be curtailed to the extent that his veto could be over-ridden by a two-thirds vote of the *Fono*, in which case the point at issue would be referred to the President for final settlement. Finally, Swains Island was to be left administratively apart from American Sāmoa and was to continue as an appendage of the Naval Station.

The commissioners agreed unanimously to file a report to the President based upon the preliminary statement they had presented to the assembly. On the afternoon of October 7th, the commissioners boarded the *Omaha* for the return voyage to Honolulu and the west coast.

Three months later, on February 14, 1931, Captain William R. Furlong, USN, who had been the naval adviser to the Bingham Commission, prepared a report on the territory after returning to Washington. He noted that the ". . . naval station had no naval yard facilities, and that it existed only to administer governmental affairs." The naval station, he reported, ". . . and the buildings in it, built and maintained by the Navy, constitute the capital of the island." He noted that naval officers were paid by the U.S. Government and not by the Island Government.

Captain Furlong's report also stated that besides Navy personnel and Sāmoans, twenty-five white civilians and 818 "halfcastes" lived in American Sāmoa. Furlong concluded his report by stating he believed American Sāmoa was the only place in the South Pacific where the natives had thrived in population and physical well-being. The situation came about, Furlong said, ". . . because of the policy of non-alienation of land ('Sāmoa for the Sāmoans') and the attention the Navy had given to health."

Ben Kneubuhl, Sr., at 53. Photo taken in 1938 on "Boat Day" near Centipede Row.

O le malie ma le tuʻu malie

'Every shark has its price.'

Every act receives its reward. — Proverb

Chapter 11

World War II

n July 17, 1931 Captain Gatewood Sanders Lincoln relieved Lieutenant Commander Arthur Tenney Emerson and became American Sāmoa's 18th naval governor. The appointment was Captain Lincoln's second tour as naval governor. He was one of two naval governors to serve two non-consecutive terms. Lieutenant Nathan W. Post was the other naval governor to serve two non-consecutive terms, the first term from 1929 to 1931, the second in 1931 and 1932.

One month following his return to Tutuila, Captain Lincoln prepared a report for the Chief of Naval Operations, Admiral William V. Pratt, in which he stated that the naval station was "capable of furnishing an anchorage, dock, radio communication, a limited amount of coal and water to ships, and doing a limited amount of repair. Personnel assigned to the station were there for the purpose of conducting the civil government of Sāmoa."

Naval station tennis courts with Fita Fita Barracks, left. Top right, Naval Station Barracks.

Lincoln noted that 72 sailors and one Marine First Sergeant were assigned to the station. They carried out the following duties: twelve enlisted men assigned to the operation and maintenance of the main radio station; twenty-three enlisted men assigned to the Medical Department, Public Health and village dispensaries; six men worked in the Ice and Power Plants, the Machine Shop and Public Works, and upkeep of Navy buildings and grounds, vehicles and naval station roads; two men assigned to the Fita Fita Guard and Band; three enlisted men in the Commandant's Office; one sailor to navigational aids; and the remaining men performed duties concerning discipline, mess service, commissary service, naval clerical work and the care of naval equipment.

Though there had been considerable controversy in the territory prior to the Bingham Commission, life in American Sāmoa was generally quite tranquil through the latter half of the

1920s and early 1930s. An article appeared in the Honolulu *Star-Bulletin* in 1927 which said that many Western Sāmoans envied their relatives under American control, ". . . due to the attitude (of the government) in American Sāmoa of keeping hands off native affairs, maintaining a rigid sanitary inspection, and devoting its attention to keeping the natives free from all white man's exploitation . . ."

That same year, however, naval Governor Captain Stephen Graham made the comment that the only mission for the Naval Administration he could derive from all the orders issued to his predecessors and to himself was ". . . to govern the people of American Sāmoa in such a manner as to facilitate the maintenance of the naval station."

Governor Graham believed that there was no basic plan aimed either at preserving the Sāmoan way of life or at transforming them into citizens of the twentieth century. For his own administration, Governor Graham adopted the previously noted policy of "Sāmoa for the Sāmoans," which later was expanded by Governor Landenberger which said, "Sāmoa for the Sāmoans, no alienation of lands, and no exploitation of the natives." The Sāmoan people were, in practice, left largely to themselves to devise their own means of adjusting to the modern world which was now encroaching upon their ancient way of life. A few social scientists later noted that the Navy's "hands-off" policies during these decades was most likely a fortunate benefit for the Sāmoans, since natural adaptation to changing times is often superior to the schemes of well-intentioned planners.

The Bingham Commission's hearings in American Sāmoa resulted in two major political reforms: A Bill of Rights; and the separation of the positions of Judge and Secretary of Native Affairs, which had originally been held by one person. The Bill of Rights was drafted by former Governors Bryan and Kellogg and Judge H.P. Wood, and incorporated into the Code of American Sāmoa. The Chief Judge, on nomination by the President, was appointed by the Secretary of the Navy, and would be entirely independent of the local administration. The Chief Judge was to devote his attention exclusively to the administration of justice.

To deal with the non-judicial functions relating to "native affairs," the post of Attorney General was created, to be filled by a naval officer with legal training. The many responsibilities heretofore held by the Chief Judge, including the position of government counsel, secretary of

Sāmoan affairs, collector of taxes and revenues, government secretary, passport officer, prison supervisor and manager of the copra fund, were now under the Office of the Attorney General.

The sleepy routine of the Naval Station was interrupted every three weeks when steamers of the Matson Line called in from their voyages between San Francisco and Sydney. The local agent for the Matson Line was Benny Kneubuhl, a successful merchant and community leader.

Kneubuhl was one of approximately a half-dozen or more expatriates, or *palagis*, as they were more commonly called, who had arrived in Tutuila in the early decades of the century, liked what they saw, and made it their home. Kneubuhl was born in Burlington, Iowa, in 1885 and joined the U.S. Navy as a young man. While serving in the Navy he was stationed at the U.S. Naval Station Tutuila. During the course of his duties, young Ben met Atalina Pritchard, daughter of Alfred James Pritchard, the grandson of George Pritchard, the LMS missionary to Tahiti in 1827, and the first British Consul for Sāmoa in Apia. Alfred Pritchard had married Lemusu Fuiavailiili of Savai'i and the couple moved to Leone in 1890, where they settled down and opened a store.

In time Kneubuhl proposed marriage to young Miss Pritchard, who accepted. Navy regulations, however, forbade marriages between naval personnel and Sāmoan citizens. Kneubuhl was determined to marry Atalina and make Tutuila his permanent home. Upon being transferred to Honolulu, he took early retirement from the Navy and returned to American Sāmoa and married Atalina. The couple settled in Aitupini and began raising a family. When the opportunity presented itself, Kneubuhl, bought a building in Fagatogo from the Ho Ching family. He opened a general store in the building which carried "every kind of merchandise imaginable," and which proved to be successful from the outset. Within a few years the Kneubuhl business branched out to include a travel agency, shipping and the Matson agency. In later years he would have the Pan Am agency and his shipping business would greatly expand.

Benny and Atalina would raise seven children, Jim, Ben, Jr., John, Margie, D.C., Mike and Frances. Ben Jr., Margie and Mike would become involved in the family businesses during the ensuing decades, while John went on to become a well-known Hollywood screenwriter and later, upon returning home to American Sāmoa, a highly-respected researcher and writer on Sāmoa's people, culture and history.

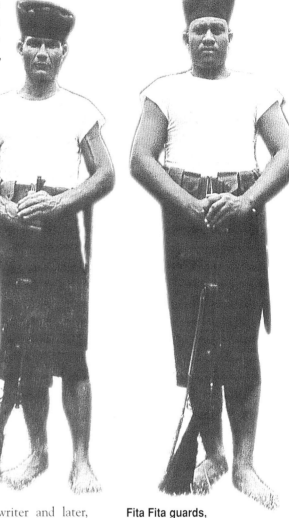

Fita Fita guards, Circa 1939.

Administration Building, later to become the High Court Building. Circa 1935

Businessman Benny Kneubuhl with children, left to right, Ben, Jr., Jim, John, and Fale holding Margie, in 1922.

Atalina Pritchard Kneubuhl's parents, Alfred and Lemusu, raised five children, Atalina, Nellie, Jack, Frank W., and Ronald. Their uncle, William T. Pritchard, the author of "Polynesian Reminiscences," had succeeded his father George as British Consul for Sāmoa and later was appointed the first British Consul for Fiji. Between Alfred and Lemusu's five children, there would be more than twenty-five grandchildren, a number of whom would become well known in American Sāmoa.

Frank W. Pritchard, the second youngest, started an export business in the 1930s. The business started exporting Sāmoan artifacts such as floor mats, tapa cloth, table mats, hand fans, carved wood artifacts and hula skirts to Honolulu.

Matson liner docking at the naval station dock. Circa 1938

The exportation of Sāmoan curios and handicrafts was an important source of income for Sāmoans during the 1930s and 40s. The goods were sold to exporters, or to passengers from the Matson liners who called at Pago Pago on a regular basis during these years.

The youngest child, Ronald E., married Mary Jewitt, later to become famous as Mary Pritchard. Later in her life Mary would revitalize the ancient – and dying – art of Sāmoan tapa making, and reintroduce the art of tapa cloth and tapa art to the people of American Sāmoa. Mary's two daughters, Marilyn and Adeline, were to become renowned tapa artists in their own right, and carry on the art after Mary's death. Ronald and Mary's youngest son, Ron, was to become a successful businessman who served as the Pan American agent for many years. Ron started Sāmoan Airlines and was a pioneer in airline expansion in American Sāmoa for more than two decades.

There were many other palagi traders, adventurers and sailors who settled in American Sāmoa during the first half of the 19th century, married local women, and began families who would become influential in the territory's history. Among them was a German named Max Haleck.

Max Haleck was born in Dessau, Germany in 1892. As a young man he had always been interested in the South Pacific. In 1910, at the age of 18, young Max left home with the intention of exploring the Pacific. He arrived in Sāmoa in 1914 and took a job with the German trading firm, South Seas Trading Company. He was posted to the village of Alofau that same year as a trader, where he traded fishhooks for copra and sold the copra to the government for export. He was later transferred to Ta'ū, where he met a young lady named Louisa, whom he married in 1915. Max and Louisa had two children, Lottie and Otto. Young Otto was born in 1920 and attended Marist Brothers School in Atu'u. After Louisa unexpectedly passed away, Max remarried. In the ensuing years Annie, Max, Jr., Ernest and Gerhard were born. In time

it was Otto who became directly involved with the Haleck family enterprises.

In 1932 Max Haleck started his own business by leasing a Ho Ching building in Fagatogo, and there he began his general merchandising business. He later purchased the Sadie

Thompson building on a sealed bid. The Haleck business would expand over the decades by establishing "bush" stores in villages throughout Tutuila. The war years would not be easy for Haleck, who was a German citizen. Once the war was over, however, Max Haleck would pursue his dream to become an American citizen. Although Max, Sr. suffered a stroke in 1961, he became a U.S. citizen in 1963.

The same year that Max, Sr. suffered a stroke, Otto took over the family business. He expanded into groceries and hardware, and later into real estate and development. The Haleck enterprises remain a viable and progressive business.

▼ ▼ ▼

Vital statistics from 1920 through 1940 showed a rapid resurgence in the population of American Sāmoa. At the turn of the century the population stood at approximately 5,000. Because of high infant mortality, a number of social scientists voiced fears that the Sāmoan race could follow the Hawaiians into obscurity.

By 1920, however, the population had grown to a little over 8,000. By 1940 the population had reached nearly 13,000. Since the birth rate remained constant at about 40 per thousand of population per year, the increment reflected largely the prolongation of life by the Public Health Department, but even so, the health of the general population was not ideal.

Passengers disembark Oceanic steamship at naval station dock. Circa 1927

Handicraft and curio vendors gather on the Fagatogo *malae* (top) to wait for steamship passengers. Left, canoe-maker shields himself from the sun as he waits for customers. Circa 1927

Businessman Max Haleck in 1935.

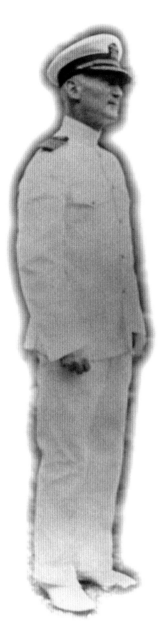

Endemic diseases known to Sāmoans for centuries still plagued the islands' citizens. Eye and vision problems due to conjunctivitis, cataracts and glaucoma affected nearly ten percent of the population. Even a higher percentage suffered from filariasis, among which twenty-five percent suffered from the end result of the disease, elephantiasis. Both tuberculosis and yaws remained a serious concern, though the health department had been successful in greatly reducing the number of reported cases.

As the population grew so did the demand for increased production of food. In 1932 Governor Landenberger, recognizing the need to expand and improve the production of agricultural products in the territory, created the department of agriculture. Since 1917 Tutuila had been plagued by the rhinocerous beetle, which had first been discovered in Poloa, having most likely drifted over from 'Upolu on a log. The beetle threatened the quality and quantity of copra production, one of the few cash crops farmers could rely upon. Under the new agriculture department an experimental farm was established at Taputimu. Sadly, the farm received little support or interest from the island's farmers, and little was accomplished.

In the pre-war years education remained a source of open concern among the population. Navy administrations had always supported an improvement in schools, teacher training and expanded educational opportunities for school-age children. As had been the case since 1900, Congress and the federal government provided no support to the territory in this regard and education languished.

About 1930 a young American from Hawai'i, Frederic DuClos Barstow, arrived in Pago Pago aboard a Matson liner. While wandering through the open market he met an 11-year-old Sāmoan boy who invited him to his village, located on the islet of Aunu'u. Barstow did visit the island, and stayed with the boy's family for a week or more. The young boy's name was Aifili Paulo Lauvao. In later years this young boy would become American Sāmoa's second elected Sāmoan governor and be known as A.P. Lutali.

As a result of his visit to American Sāmoa Frederic Barstow became deeply interested in the Sāmoan islands and people. He was very interested in the state of education in the islands and expressed an interest in trying to help improve the situation. Barstow, who came to be known to Sāmoans as "Feleti," died unexpectedly not long after leaving Sāmoa. To perpetuate his memory, his parents established the Frederic DuClos Barstow Foundation, and provided about $200,000 in capital to get the foundation started. The purpose of the foundation was to "educate young Sāmoan men in the American and Sāmoan way of life, so as to prepare them for leadership of their people." The ex-officio trustees of the foundation were the presidents of the Kamehameha School of Honolulu, the Board of Trustees of O'ahu College, and the Bishop Trust Company of Honolulu. The sole stipulation imposed as to the management of the fund was that one-half of the income must be spent to

educate young Sāmoans abroad and the other half for educational activities in Sāmoa.

▼ ▼ ▼

On January 20, 1936, Captain MacGillivray Milne relieved Lieutenant Commander Thomas B. Fitzpatrick and became the 25th naval governor. Milne remained governor for two years. He was then relieved by Captain Edward W. Hanson, who served as governor from 1938 to 1940.

During Captain Milne's tenure as governor a major step was taken in opening the Pacific to air travel. On March 17, 1937 a trans-ocean flying boat, bearing the name Pan American Clipper, lifted off the waters of San Francisco Bay and headed westward. Ahead lay the assignment of opening up a 7,000-mile aerial trade route across the South Pacific to link the United States and Australia. The aircraft, a Sikorsky S-42B, was subsequently named the Sāmoan Clipper. The aircraft pioneered the San Francisco to Kingman Reef to Pago Pago to Auckland route. The clipper landed in Pago Pago Bay on March 24th on the first leg of her maiden flight from Honolulu to Auckland.

The Sāmoan Clipper would continue her voyages across the Pacific for the next nine months until January 11, 1938, when she exploded after departing Pago Pago. Shortly after take-off Captain Edwin Musick notified the naval station by radio the clipper had developed an oil leak. In order to lighten the airplane and make a safe landing, Captain Musick decided to jettison his excess fuel. His last message, at 8:27 a.m., said, "We are going to dump gas and we can't use the radio during the dumping. Stand by." The fuel apparently streamed over the lowered flaps and struck a hot exhaust manifold, thus igniting and causing the airplane's fuel tanks to explode. Sāmoan *fautasi* and the seaplane tender USS *Avocet* were sent to look for survivors, but found none. Only an oil slick and some uniform coats and pieces of aluminum were found floating on the surface. Beside Captain Musick, the Sāmoan Clipper was carrying a crew of five.

Four months following the crash, in May, 1938, Frank McKenzie of Pan American Airways, was given the task of surveying Canton Island for Pan Am to determine the suitability of the island to use as a base for Pan Am's flying boats. McKenzie departed Pago Pago harbor on May 22nd aboard the USS *Ontario*, a coal-burning tug stationed in American Sāmoa. The *Ontario* arrived at Canton on May 26th, and McKenzie surveyed the island for two days, returning back to Pago Pago on June 2nd. Canton Island would

Naval station buildings and private businesses surround the Fagatogo *malae*. Circa 1938

later become an important island for trans-Pacific flights and for use by the United States.

▼ ▼ ▼

On March 22, 1940, the Chief of Naval Operations, Admiral Harold R. Stark, informed the Commandant of the U.S. Naval Station Tutuila, Captain Edward W. Hanson, that

Sāmoan *fale* next to Jean P. Haydon Museum, Fagatogo.

Fita Fita unit marching in Fagatogo. Circa 1940

Fita Fita assembling in front of barracks, Fagatogo. Circa 1930

Captain Alfred R. Pefley, USMC, would be coming to American Sāmoa to draw up defense plans for Tutuila and outlying islands.

By July 16th, following a review of Captain Pefley's defense plan, Governor Hanson moved to inform the Chief of Naval Operations, Admiral Harold R. Stark, that defenses recommended by Captain Pefley must be augmented by additional facilities totalling $1,325,000. Four months later, on November 7th, the expansion of the U.S. Naval Station Tutuila was authorized by the Director of the War Plans Division in Washington, D.C. Twenty-eight days later Admiral Stark directed that Captain Pefley's plan for the defense of Tutuila be implemented immediately.

On December 11, 1940, an advance detachment of the 7th Defense Battalion sailed from Marine Corps Base in San Diego. The battalion was commanded by Captain H. McFarland, under whom were First Lieutenant R.H. Ruud and twenty enlisted men. Five days later the 7th Defense Battalion was organized at Marine Corps Base San Diego with a total strength of 424 men.

By the end of the year 1940, the U.S. Navy and Marine Corps were moving with all possible speed to provide for the defense of Tutuila. As Japan continued to take military action in various countries on the Asian continent, defense planners realized that American positions in the Pacific were vulnerable not only to Japanese attack, but in most cases to being overrun should the Japanese military decide to invade them.

On December 20, 1940, Admiral Stark directed the Governor of American Sāmoa, Captain Laurence Wild, to make suggestions for the establishment of "a Native Insular Force, not to exceed 500 men, to be officered and trained by the U.S. Marine Corps, and to be employed ashore in Sāmoa, mainly at outposts and as guards at beaches." Governor Wild replied by recommending the establishment of a Native Insular Force separate and distinct from the Fita Fita Guard, which was to function under and to be paid by the Government of American Sāmoa.

The defense of the islands of Tutuila, Aunu'u and Manu'a were not the only concerns of the United States Navy. The islands of Western Sāmoa, which had been under the administration of New Zealand since August 29, 1914, when an expeditionary force landed in Apia and accepted Germany's surrender, were considered crucial in the defense of Sāmoa. The Navy understood clearly that the islands of 'Upolu and Savai'i must be defended. It was not known to the Navy, however, if New Zealand troops would have enough manpower to carry out such an assignment.

In early January, 1941, a board of four U.S. Naval officers, chaired by Lt. Commander N.W. Sears, prepared a joint plan for the defense of Sāmoa (Tutuila), based on the recommendations of Marine Corps Captain Alfred Pefley. The defenses included four 6-inch guns, six 3-inch guns and fourteen 50-caliber anti-aircraft guns. Provisions were also made for patrol vessels, coastal lookouts and mine warfare. One month later plans were made to construct "a double anti-torpedo net extending from Blunts Point to Whale Rock, and then about 300 yards further to the east, leaving a channel of about 300 yards on the eastern side of the entrance" to Pago Pago Harbor.

The U.S. Marine Corps 7th Defense Battalion arrrived in Pago Pago Harbor aboard the USS *William P. Biddle* with a total strength of 443 officers and men on March 15, 1941. Two days prior to the arrival of the *William P. Biddle*, plans began to build an airstrip on Tutuila, and to lay a mine field to protect Pago Pago Harbor. Three days after arrival in the harbor, the 7th Defense Battalion boarded trucks which transported them to Camp Samuel Nicholas, located at the village of Faga'alu.

In early July, 1941, the organization of the First Sāmoan Battalion, U.S. Marine Corps Reserve, began. All recruits were enlisted as privates, paid seventy cents a day, and given a uniform allowance of $5.00. One month later Sianava Robert Seva'aetasi became the first Sāmoan to enlist in the First Sāmoan Battalion. His enlistment followed the physical examinations of possibly a thousand young men, of which approximately 700 were considered to be physically fit to become marines. On September 24th the commanding officer of the First Sāmoan Battalion recommended that his unit be called to active duty for a six-week training course in Mapusaga Valley.

As the First Sāmoan Battalion was being formed, construction of the four six-inch guns at Blunts and Breakers Points continued apace. The four guns were placed high on steep ridges and surrounded by thick concrete bunkers. The placement of the heavy guns with their long barrels and extraordinary weight provided Navy and Marine Corps engineers with a special challenge, as the four guns had to be lifted from the shorelines below each ridge to each ridgetop. A track was constructed with winches and other

engineering devices to lift the guns into place–a remarkable feat considering the limited amount of materials available to the military engineers at the time.

On August 28, 1941, the two new guns at Blunts Point fired eight rounds each at a target floating in Pago Pago harbor. The sound of the guns' discharge echoed off the mountainsides of Pago Pago Bay startling many bay area residents. The day following the firing of the guns' first live rounds of ammunition, Pita Fiti Sunia was born. Pita Sunia would later take the matai title Tauese and become American Sāmoa's third elected Sāmoan governor. Eight days after the guns at Blunts Point had been tested, ten rounds were fired from each of the two newly-situated guns at Breakers Point. The guns' discharge could be heard for miles.

Sāmoan marines marching in Nu'uuli. Circa 1942

The last week of October, 1941, the Commanding Officer of the 7th Defense Battalion, Lt. Col. L.A. Dessez, USMC, informed the Commandant of the U.S. Naval Station Sāmoa (the name "Sāmoa" had replaced "Tutuila" once the military buildup had begun) that only 160 Sāmoans had been enlisted in the Sāmoan Battalion and that only 50 prospects remained to be enlisted. Lt. Col. Dessez recommended that the Sāmoans working for the navy contractors and the public works officer be made available for recruitment as these men were highly skilled, spoke some English, and were very motivated. Governor Wild agreed with Lt. Col. Dessez and authorized him to "confer directly" with the Officer-in-Charge of the Pacific Naval Air Base and to make arrangements for "recruiting men employed by the contractor."

Rainmaker Mountain as seen from Tafuna.

happened that morning. "As we sat on the mountaintop overlooking the bay area we could see hurried activity on the roads in Utulei and Fagatogo far below. We heard the siren blow. For a Sunday morning all the traffic and movement of the military seemed out of place. The four of us sat there and wondered what was going on. We decided to get down the mountain as quickly as possible to find out what had happened."

When the group arrived at the road in front of Aua village they were picked up in a military jeep. The driver told them that the Japanese had attacked Pearl Harbor. With the base-wide alert already sounded, men were ordered to battle stations where they remained for nearly two months, until January 23, 1942, when the 2nd Marine Brigade arrived.

As soon as word spread throughout the villages that Pearl Harbor had been attacked and that American Sāmoa was threatened with a Japanese attack, young men from around the island arrived at the Naval Station in large numbers, armed with bush knives, volunteering to do anything necessary to help defend Tutuila. Two days later, December 9th, Captain Laurence Wild placed the First Sāmoan Battalion on active duty "for an indefinite date."

The afternoon of December 7th Captain Wild, as Governor, ordered all women and children evacuated from the U.S. Naval Station and moved to Atauloma Girls' School for reasons of safety and security. A Japanese attack on the naval and docking facilities was considered to be a very real threat. In the ensuing weeks the six-inch guns at both Blunts and Breakers Points began firing their guns at towed targets near the harbor entrance.

As the last weeks of November drew to a close, preparations for the defense of Tutuila continued at a fast pace. On November 26th Tutuila was unexpectedly struck by a hurricane which caused serious damage to plantations, Sāmoan *fales* and military tents. U.S. Navy defense planners could not concern themselves with hurricane damage, however, for as December approached, they could see just how vulnerable American Sāmoa remained to a serious military assault.

▼ ▼ ▼

On Sunday morning, December 7, 1941, the people of American Sāmoa prepared for church services in the traditional manner. The military installations at Utulei and Faga'alu were quiet. There was almost no military traffic in the bay area as people prepared to walk to church wearing the customary white church clothes.

That morning twenty-two year-old Aifili Paulo Lauvao, later to be known as A.P. Lutali, met with two Marine Corps officers and a Navy nurse. The officers had asked Aifili to guide them Sunday morning on a hike to the top of Mt. Pioa, which had come to be known as Rainmaker Mountain. The group assembled in Utulei very early and caught a ride on a jeep to the village of Aua. Aifili led them on the Rainmaker trail arriving at the top of the mountain some time around 11 a.m. Later in his life, A.P. Lutali explained what

Admiral Chester W. Nimitz, USN, Commander-in-Chief, Pacific Fleet, World War II.

On the last day of 1941 a boatload of Sāmoans from "outlying islands" docked at the Naval Station. The people of Tutuila, in traditional fashion, found families for the displaced refugees, many of whom remained in Tutuila through the first years of the war.

▼ ▼ ▼

Following the attack on Pearl Harbor the Japanese military were in actual—or potential–control of the entire Pacific Ocean west of a line drawn from Hawai'i to Sāmoa, and north of a line from Sāmoa, through Fiji, to New Guinea. Had the Japanese been given time to consol-

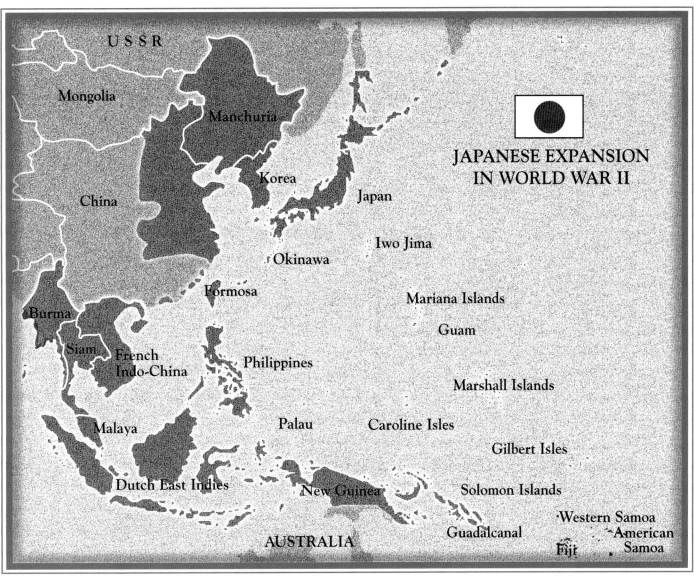

USSR

Mongolia

Manchuria

Korea

China

Japan

**JAPANESE EXPANSION
IN WORLD WAR II**

Iwo Jima

Okinawa

Formosa

Mariana Islands

Guam

Burma

Siam

French
Indo-China

Philippines

Marshall Islands

Malaya

Palau

Caroline Isles

Gilbert Isles

Dutch East Indies

New Guinea

Solomon Islands

Western Samoa

American
Samoa

AUSTRALIA

Guadalcanal

Fiji

idate their positions throughout this vast region of the Pacific, it would have been only a matter of time before they moved further south and east to interrupt communications between the United States and Australia and New Zealand.

Strategically the United States could not rely on either Australia or New Zealand to provide the military defense for the southwest Pacific, for the majority of their military forces, as members of the British Commonwealth, were already engaged in North Africa and the Middle East. In the early months of 1942 both Australia and New Zealand were in serious danger of being overrun by the Japanese, and should Japan have launched an invasion on either one of these two countries, they might well have fallen, leaving the United States pinned back against its own west coast. The disastrous consequences of such an event were unmistakable, and Fleet Admiral Ernest J. King, USN, ordered that the Hawai'i-Sāmoa-Fiji-New Guinea line be held at all costs. In 1942, as the Pacific war against Japan unfolded,

American Sāmoa stood in the center of the last line of defense.

The potential invasion of Sāmoa or Fiji by Japanese forces was illustrated by their naval establishments and airfields in the Marshall Islands to the northwest of Sāmoa, which they held under a League of Nations mandate. Their hold on the Marshalls soon spilled over to the British-mandated Gilbert Islands, placing the Japanese Navy within easy striking distance of Sāmoa and Fiji.

This ominous fact was proven on the morning of January 11, 1942, when, at 2:26 a.m., a Japanese submarine surfaced about 10,000 yards off the north coast of Tutuila in the vicinity of Fagasa Bay and fired about fifteen shells from its 5.5-inch deck gun at the U.S. Naval Station. The attack lasted approximately ten minutes. Ironically, the first shell struck the rear of Frank Shimasaki's store, one of Tutuila's few Japanese residents. One shell inflicted light damage on the naval dispensary, another shell landed behind the

American Sāmoa's key strategic position in the Pacific is illustrated in this map of Japan's maximum expansion during World War II.

171

Looking toward naval station docks along Officer's Row, often called "Centipede Row." Circa 1927

Matson liner approaches naval dock prior to outbreak of World War II. Matson liners ferried Navy and Marine Corps personnel to American Sāmoa from the west coast in the early months of the war.

naval quarters known as "Centipede Row," while a fourth shell hit the seawall outside the customs house. The other shells fell harmlessly into the harbor.

Return fire against the Japanese sub did not happen, though, according to various reports, "the Sāmoan Marines were eager to test their skill against the enemy." This would be the only time the Japanese launched an attack against Tutuila during the war, but Japanese submarines, which had been patrolling Sāmoan waters prior to the attack on Pearl Harbor, would continue to send sea and air patrols into the area throughout much of the war.

Six days following the attack on the Naval Station, the Commander-in-Chief, Pacific Fleet (CINCPAC), Admiral Chester W. Nimitz, USN,

appointed Brigadier General Henry L. Larsen, USMC, as Military Governor and Island Commander of Tutuila. This created an unusual situation, since the Governor of American Sāmoa, Captain Laurence Wild, USN, was senior to Larsen in position, but junior to him in rank. Nimitz's telegram attempted to clarify the situation as follows:

"... You are appointed military governor of American Sāmoa X Subject orders of CINC-PAC you are authorized and empowered to exercise exclusive authority and jurisdiction over American Sāmoa including the entire control of the Government thereof X Governor of American Sāmoa heretofore appointed or his successor shall continue to execute and fulfill duties of the Office of Governor of American Sāmoa according to law but will in all respects and particulars be subject your orders and directions ... designation of objective and exercise of such coordinating control as you deem necessary is vested in you X but you are not repeat not authorized to control administration and discipline of naval forces nor to issue any instructions to such forces beyond those necessary for effective coordination X Your present orders modified accordingly X Written orders being mailed." Two days following Nimitz's telegram, January 19th, a flight of planes launched from the carrier USS *Wasp* roared over Tutuila, and a float plane from a naval cruiser landed in Pago Pago Harbor. The planes and ships were part of the task force launched in San Diego on January 6th. On that date the 2nd Marine Brigade, 4,798 strong,

departed aboard the Matson liners *Lurline*, *Matsonia* and *Monterey*, accompanied by a fleet oiler and ammunition ship. The fleet was escorted part way by the USS *Yorktown's* carrier group, and later joined, on January 19th, by the USS *Enterprise's* task force, commanded by Vice Admiral William F. Halsey.

The 2nd Marine Brigade, with Brigadier General Henry L. Larsen in command, arrived in Pago Pago Harbor. Three days later Vice Admiral William Halsey's carrier task force arrived, along with the Matson Line ships carrying the 8th Marines, 10th Marines and 2nd Defense Battalion. Halsey's carrier task force remained for only two days before departing for Howland Island, 1,000 miles northeast, for refueling. From there Halsey's task force steamed to the Gilbert and Marshall Islands to launch air strikes against the Japanese bases there. The attack destroyed enough of the enemy's naval and air potential to temporarily reduce the danger of Japanese attack against Sāmoa.

In February Lt. Col. William Bales, USMC, after two weeks surveying 'Upolu and Savai'i in Western Sāmoa in concert with New Zealand authorities, presented his report on the larger islands to Brigadier Henry Larsen. His report stated that ". . . 'Upolu, with its harbor facilities, road net and several potential airfield sites made it readily susceptible to base development . . . Savai'i, on the other hand, had no major safe anchorages and its lava-encrusted surfaces did not offer airfield sites that could be developed quickly by Japanese or anyone else." Bales concluded his

report by saying that "In its present unprotected state, Western Sāmoa is a hazard of first magnitude for the defense of American Sāmoa. The conclusion is inescapable that if we don't occupy it the Japanese will and there may not be a great deal of time left."

Approximately five weeks after Lt. Col. Bales filed his report Western Sāmoa's Administrator, Alfred C. Turnbull, informed American Sāmoa's Military Governor Henry Larsen that New Zealand's Prime Minister had informed him that "Americans can have full and free use of all land and other facilities for all war purposes and every possible assistance . . ." Two weeks following Turnbull's message to Henry Larsen, March 27th, the USMC 7th Defense Battalion arrived in Apia Harbor aboard the USS *President Garfield*. Lightweight anti-aircraft guns were quickly installed along the harbor's seawall. Vehicles, bulldozers and tractors were landed from naval barges at Vaiala. Temporary camps were established at Ifiifi and Moata'a.

The first airplanes of Marine Air Group 13 landed at partially completed Tafuna Air Base on April 2nd "just as the airstrip was brought to a usable state." The Marine Air Group was supported in its defense efforts by a tank company, a heavy weapons platoon, a three-inch gun battery, and one section of the island's barrage balloon squadron. The conditions surrounding the Tafuna airstrip were primitive and difficult. The area was surrounded by dense jungle. Rain made the construction of an adequate camp difficult, and the heat in the area could become intense. Four days following the air group's arrival the first runway at Tafuna was

Naval officers and men in front of navy Commissary Building, Fagatogo. Circa 1939

Aerial view of navy Officer's Quarters, Naval Hospital, Government House, Quarantine Station and Goat Island. Circa 1928

The Poyer School, Anua, Tutuila. The building was converted into a machine shop for ship repair during World War II.

completed by the Utah Construction Company, with Marine Corps assistance. The airstrip was 2,500 feet long and 250 feet wide.

At the same time mine laying operations along the approaches to Pago Pago Harbor were being completed. A total of 400 mines in six fields were laid by the USS *Ontario*, USS *Kingfisher*, USS *Swan* and the USS *Turkey*. The mine fields were located south of Cape Fagauso; near Taema Bank; west of Leone Point; south of Cape Taputapu, west of Southworth Point; and near Afono Bay.

On April 25th the USMC 1st Raider Battalion, the 2nd Barrage Balloon Squadron, the 7th and 8th Defense Battalions, the 3rd Battalion, 11th Brigade and the Navy 2nd Construction Battalion (Seabees) arrived in American Sāmoa, swelling the number of military personnel on Tutuila dramatically. Soon afterward the Sāmoan Defense Group was established, to be commanded by Major General Charles F.B. Price, USMC.

From May 5th through May 12th Marine Corps manpower and supplies arrived in Apia in ever-increasing numbers. Five large ships docked in Apia Harbor unloading construction materials, military supplies and equipment. During this time the USMC 7th Defense Battalion in Western Sāmoa came under the control of the 3rd Marine Brigade, commanded by Maj. General Charles D. Barrett. Companies A and B of the 2nd Naval Construction Seabees Battalion arrived in 'Upolu to build an airfield at Faleolo, 22 miles west of Apia. By May 18th the 3rd Marine Brigade was firmly

established on 'Upolu and Savai'i, with a strength of 4,853 officers and men.

Unbeknown to the CINCPAC command, the Japanese Imperial General Headquarters ordered, on May 2nd, the raising of a new army for military offensives against New Caledonia, Fiji and Sāmoa. American military planners and strategists for the Pacific theater, though unaware of Japan's plans for the new offensive, suspected such an operation was forthcoming nonetheless. Suspecting that time was very short, huge amounts of war materiel and manpower continued to pour into Sāmoa to prepare for a Japanese invasion.

On May 30th a board of officers from the Department of the Navy arrived to conduct an inspection of Tutuila's defense capabilities. The senior member of the group was the famed Antarctic explorer, Rear Admiral Richard E. Byrd. The group only took one day to finish its inspection and filed its report, which stated that there were ". . . 7,995 Navy and Marine Corps personnel on Tutuila, plus 100 men in the Fita Fita Guard." The report went on to say that Tutuila's defense force was strong enough to repel minor raids and landings, but not strong enough to deter a major assault. Only five days following Byrd's report the Japanese 7th Army was formed. Its mission: to capture New Caledonia, Fiji and Sāmoa in July. Two battalions of the 41st Infantry Regiment, then fighting in the Philippines, were assigned to capture Tutuila.

Sāmoa's position as a front line of defense was to last throughout much of 1942. But while the threat of an all-out Japanese invasion lasted only a few months, the results of the war had tremendous impact upon the Sāmoan people and their way of life.

The entire island of Tutuila had become an armed camp. During 1942 it was estimated that Marine Corps and Naval personnel outnumbered the Sāmoan population. Added to this was the fact that the Sāmoan Islands formed a strategic base to Allied operations in the Pacific, in which Western Sāmoa was as important as American Sāmoa. When the Marines moved to 'Upolu and Savai'i to provide for those islands' defense, it resulted in a temporary reunification of the islands and their people.

The sheer numbers of military men and materiel dramatically upset the ancient rhythms of Tutuila. Thousands of men were filing through the island on their way to battles farther to the west. Marines trained in Tutuila fought in Guadalcanal and later the Gilbert Islands — most notably the invasion of Tarawa. The concrete buildings of the Poyer School were commandeered and converted into machine shops for a ship repair unit. The Feleti School was discontinued, its buildings and grounds used for military purposes. In many villages the Marines occupied the school houses and used them as headquarters. Concrete pillboxes were placed on every beach that offered the slightest possibility of a landing

from the sea. The pillboxes were manned night and day by Marines quartered in nearby villages.

The single-lane roads which had long been adequate in connecting Alofao in the east to Amanave in the west were now grossly inadequate for military requirements. They were quickly replaced by a two-lane, coral-rock-surface road, along which jeeps and military vehicles moved along raising huge clouds of coral dust. A new road from Alofao to Amouli to Tula needed to be built, as well as the difficult task of cutting a

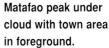

Matafao peak under cloud with town area in foreground.

Aerial view of shoreline and underwater reef between Fagatogo and Pago Pago. Circa 1927

road across the ridge between Pago Pago and Fagasa. A communication and radar station was required on the top of Tutuila's central ridge line above the village of Aoloau, necessitating the clearing of a square mile of land on top of the plateau and the building of a long and winding mountain road up to the top from Mapusaga.

Two airfields would be constructed. Besides the airstrip at Tafuna another one was built at Leone. A new oil dock was constructed in Fagatogo along with a tank farm in Utulei, with the two facilities being connected by an oil pipe. The original power plant, which had lighted the Naval Station was now insufficient. Two larger power plants, located in Pago Pago and Utulei, were constructed and provided power for ship repair and other vital wartime installations.

SS *Sonoma* beside the naval station dock. Circa 1927

One particular event which would transform American Sāmoa dramatically in the years ahead was the enlistment of young Sāmoan men in the Navy. These young men would be stationed throughout the Pacific and elsewhere, such as Chief Machinist Edward Hunkin, USN, who was stationed in Iceland. Others went to Pearl Harbor to work in the shipyard and many were employed locally in stevedoring and construction. The widespread Marine Corps and Naval installations had other positive impacts on the general population. The presence of the U.S. Naval Mobile Hospital No. 3, located at Mapusaga, resulted in the improvement of the general health of nearby villagers.

From the very beginning of the military buildup in American Sāmoa in 1941 the local population had welcomed the presence of the Navy and Marine Corps with open arms. As Marine Corps units were stationed in remote villages, those villages treated the marines as special guests in traditional Sāmoan fashion. Individual families would house and feed small groups of marines, wash their clothes and tend to their housekeeping, whether in military-issue tents or in Sāmoan *fales*, which the marines found much more comfortable. Deep and sincere friendships developed between the marines and Sāmoan villagers. Sāmoans taught young men from Iowa or Vermont how to fish with nets or spears, how to climb coconut trees and husk the nuts. Marines gave military gear and clothing to their Sāmoan families and friends – military belts, canteens, k-rations, hats, fatigues, shoes, as well as those special items loved by everyone: candy and chocolate. The Sāmoans treasured these gifts and the marines treasured their friendships with the villagers.

When the time came for special marine units to ship out to join other battle units in the western Pacific, there was heartfelt sadness by both Sāmoan and marine. There were many young sailors and marines who had become romantically involved with the island women. American military personnel were naturally attracted to the beauty and charm of Sāmoan "teine." Intimate relations between American marine and naval personnel and the young ladies of Sāmoa became a fairly common occurrence. The military command understood the situation, and though certain military regulations prohibited such "fraternizing," navy and marine corps officers tended to look the other way. The end result, after nearly five years of a large military presence, were the births of a number of children whose navy and marine corps fathers were fighting in faraway battles, many of them never to return.

▼ ▼ ▼

On July 29, 1942, the Matson luxury liner SS *Lurline*, carrying units of the 22nd Marine Regiment bound for Sāmoa, was attacked by a Japanese submarine 24 miles northeast of Tutuila. Marine Private Edwin C. Bearss, who later became the Chief Historian of the National Park Service and a noted authority on the American Civil War, recorded the incident, writing that "Fortunately, the submarine commander had set his 'long lances,' (torpedoes) to run too deep, and one passed under the *Lurline's* bow, and the other hard astern."

The *Lurline* arrived in Pago Pago without further incident. After unloading "hundreds of bags of mail" and personnel from specialized military units, the *Lurline* weighed anchor at 11:30 a.m. bound for Apia, arriving there at 4:30 p.m. Two days later work parties from the 22nd

Marines began unloading war materiel in Apia harbor. Private Bearss wrote: "This was a time-consuming operation, because the gear and supplies had to be first off-loaded into landing craft and barges. These craft then made the run into shore, tying up at either the jetty or the Burns & Philip dock. The equipment was then handled again, as other fatigue parties shifted it up out of the craft and onto trucks that hauled it to various depots. The sun beat down, and we lamented, 'It will take us a long time to get used to the heat.'"

By the month of August the U.S. Navy's Mobile Hospital No. 3, (MOB 3) had forty buildings in Mapusaga – where the American Sāmoa Community College is presently located. The facilities included an X-ray facility and a second operating room. At the beginning of the month there were 51 patients in the hospital, but many more beds were soon needed to accommodate the wounded from the Guadalcanal campaign, which began on August 7th.

On August 13th, General Henry Larsen, USMC, Commanding General of the Sāmoan Defense Group, provided for the needed expansion of MOB 3. Forty-five Marine Corps carpenters arrived at Mapusaga and began construction

on new medical facilities. In less than a week, a morgue, laboratory and dental clinic were completed. The carpenters then constructed a urology clinic, two urology wards, a receiving ward, and an eye, nose and throat ward. When these buildings were completed, two more surgical wards were built. When completed, MOB 3 at Mapusaga had a facility that included sixty-five buildings, including wards for 140 beds. So large was the complex that two streets were needed to clarify the various areas. One was named Upper Pearl Street, the other Sands Street.

On August 27th and 29th wounded sailors and marines from the battle at Guadalcanal began arriving in Tutuila and were transported from the harbor to MOB 3 at Mapusaga. The battle at Guadalcanal had been a fiercely contested confrontation, and the wounded, who had come from Tulagi, Solomon Islands, overwhelmed the facilities at MOB 3. Seabees from the 11th Battalion quickly began constructing more buildings to accommodate the wounded.

On the last day of the month 130 Navy Seabees from Construction Battalion 111 began construction of 45 additional quonset huts. Working ten hours a day, seven days a week through October 1st, the Seabees barely kept pace

Isolated beach between the villages of Amanave and Poloa, western Tutuila.

177

First Lady Eleanor Roosevelt, wife of President Franklin D. Roosevelt. Mrs. Roosevelt visited the U.S. Naval Station, Tutuila, in 1943, the first wife of an American President to visit the Territory.

with the arrival of the large number of casualties from the Guadalcanal campaign.

At the same time the defense buildup of Sāmoa continued. By October 9th the United States military population of the Sāmoan Defense Group stood as follows: Tutuila – 9,320; 'Upolu – 5,051; Wallis Island – 3, 191; and Funafuti – 1,195. Soon thereafter the Vice Chief of Naval Operations ordered a mine disposal unit to duty at the Naval Station Tutuila. This followed, by approximately two months, the installation of a new "heavy indicator net" to replace the old net in the area near the entrance to Pago Pago harbor.

One of the more famous patients at MOB 3 during this time was Captain Edward "Eddie" Rickenbacker, America's leading "ace" in World War I. Rickenbacker and his companions had spent 22 days in a raft after their B-17 went down on a flight to Australia. They were rescued by an airplane and PT boat near Funafuti, Ellice Islands, and taken to Sāmoa for medical care. While at Tutuila Rickenbacker wrote, ". . . Tutuila was alive with all kinds of military activities; and from being one of those so-called island paradises of the South Seas it was fast becoming an ocean fortress. The scenery is wonderful, and in many other respects the South Seas is the most attractive place in the world to fight a war. But the region has its drawbacks. The rainy season has just begun, and you have my word for it, it doesn't just rain out there – the ocean tilts up and swamps you."

In December the USMC 1st Replacement Battalion arrived in Tutuila from North Carolina for jungle training. After observing the jungle combat in Guadalcanal, Lt. General Thomas Holcomb, USMC, suggested a Jungle Warfare Training Center be established in Tutuila. The 1st Replacement Battalion was the first Marine Corps unit to receive jungle training in Sāmoa at Malaeimi, known as "Mormon Valley." This unit was followed by the 3rd, 5th, 7th, 13th, 15th and 19th Replacement Battalions. The training program "stressed conditioning marches and exercises, individual combat, cover and concealment, field fortifications, infiltration tactics and countermeasures, infantry weapons, jungle warfare, small unit tactics, and amphibious training."

A Marine veteran of three Pacific campaigns – Bougainville, Guam and Iwo Jima – later wrote that ". . . the worst experience (he ever) went through was the training program in Sāmoa. Everything from that ordeal on was rela-

tively easy, and this from a scout-sniper, a Marine who operated behind enemy lines. . ."

The day after Christmas fifteen pilots from Marine Air Group 13 (MAG-13) were transferred from Tutuila to Guadalcanal. This left a contingent of only twenty-six pilots. A short time later a number of the remaining MAG-13 pilots were sent to Guadalcanal, leaving behind an even smaller number of pilots. Then, one month later, in January 1943, six Douglas SBD-3 Dauntless dive bombers from Marine Corps Scout Bombing Squadron 151 and nine Grumman F4F-4 Wildcat fighters left Tutuila to reinforce the Wallis Islands, which were part of the Sāmoan Defense Group.

Four days following the departure of the fighter planes to Wallis the total manpower of the First Sāmoan Battalion, USMC Reserve, was listed at 515 men. The unit's official history states that ". . . these late increases can be attributed to the coming-of-age of the younger boys who waited until 18 to enlist."

At the end of February, 1943, the designation of the "First Sāmoan Battalion, USMC Reserve, Tutuila, Sāmoa" was changed to "First Sāmoan Battalion, USMC Reserve, 2nd Defense Battalion, Reinforced, 2nd Marine Brigade." A month later it changed again to "First Sāmoan Battalion, USMC Reserve, 2nd Defense Battalion, Reinforced, Fleet Marine Force, in the Field."

▼ ▼ ▼

On August 24, 1943, a very special guest arrived in American Sāmoa. First Lady Eleanor Roosevelt was in the Pacific visiting American troops. On this date the First Lady inspected the Fita Fita Guard and Band, and the First Sāmoan Battalion at the U.S. Naval Station Tutuila. Mrs. Roosevelt was the first wife of an American President to visit American Sāmoa. The only other First Lady to visit the territory would be Lady Bird Johnson, in 1966.

The following month the membership of the First Sāmoan Battalion was listed as "11 Marine officers, 1 Navy officer, 530 enlisted men, including six Navy hospital corpsmen. Sāmoan Marines totaled 494 men."

On the last day of September the Marine Corps fighter air strip at Leone was completed. Only two planes ever took off and landed at the air strip. Following those trial landings, the strip was never used again due to turbulent air currents and was eventually abandoned two years later. On the same date the United States military population of the Sāmoan Defense Group was listed as follows: Tutuila – 7,950; 'Upolu – 1,541; Wallis Island – 2,726; Funafuti – 1,838; Nanumea – 1,221; and Nukufetau – 947.

On the first of October members of the First Sāmoan Battalion were reassigned to new duty posts and assignments. Units were dispersed from Cape Matatula in eastern Tutuila to Amanave on the western end. Company A had two officers, four U.S. Marines, one enlisted Navy, and 67 Sāmoan Marines at Alega. Two U.S. Marines and 30 Sāmoan Marines were stationed at Auto. One U.S. Marine and 29 Sāmoan Marines at Matatula. Company B had one officer, three U.S. Marines, and 57 Sāmoan Marines at Aua; one officer, two U.S. Marines and 46 Sāmoan Marines at Afono Bay; and one officer, three U.S. Marines, five Navy enlisted boat crewmen, and 46 Sāmoan Marines at Fagasa Bay. Twenty of the Fagasa Sāmoan Marines were attached to Battery C, Harbor Defense Group, Fleet Marine Force. Company C had one officer, three U.S. Marines, 99 Sāmoan Marines and two Navy enlisted personnel at Pavaiai; and one officer, two U.S. Marines and 50 Sāmoan Marines at Amanave.

The last week of October Lt. Commander C.T. Gilliam, USN, completed his Facilities Survey Report for the U.S. Naval Station Tutuila. He recommended that Tutuila be used for these purposes in the future war effort: (1) As a central headquarters for the Sāmoan Defense Group; (2) As a rear logistic supply depot; (3) As a supporting defense link in the front ring of island bases; (4) As a fueling depot; (5) As an anchorage, watering station and repair station; (6) As a search and weather station for observation planes; (7) As a hunter-killer station for antisubmarine warfare, and (8) As a jungle training area. In time, the USNS Tutuila would perform all eight of Lt. Commander Gilliam's recommendations.

Three months following the completion of his Facilities Survey Report, Lt. Commander Gilliam completed a second report, the Establishment of Facilities and Allowance for Tutuila. On January 10, 1944, Lt. Commander Gilliam presented his report to the Commander, Service Squadron, South Pacific Force. The report included all Army, Navy and Marine Corps personnel on Tutuila.

In his report Gilliam proposed that "the personnel allowance for Tutuila be cut down to 77 officers and 1,717 enlisted men by June 1944." In the redeployment program this would not be accomplished until January, 1945. Lt. Commander Gilliam also proposed that "all salvageable materials be shipped to forward areas as soon as they were available." One week later Gilliam proposed that the U.S. Marine contingent on 'Upolu be reduced to three officers and 26 enlisted men, adding that salvage operations, similar to those on Tutuila, be undertaken. At the time that Lt. Commander Gilliam released his report, the aggregate strength of the defense force on 'Upolu was listed as U.S. Army, 2,539; U.S. Navy, 529; U.S. Marine Corps, 26; and the New Zealand Defense Force, 119.

Only two weeks later, as the war in the Pacific moved farther to the west, 110 officers and 2,080 enlisted men of the U.S. Army's 147th Infantry Regiment departed 'Upolu for Noumea, New Caledonia.

Three days following the departure of the 147th, the Commandant of the U.S. Naval Station Tutuila, Captain John G. Moyer, assumed control of the Marine Barracks. Moyer's assignment to the Marine Barracks signaled that the military importance of Tutuila, as well as the Sāmoan

Navy SNJ trainer at Tafuna air base. Circa 1942

Young girl ironing clothes with a charcoal iron as a friend looks on. Circa 1940

Defense Force, was rapidly decreasing as the war moved not only westward, but northward, in the final push for the Japanese Islands. Two days following Captain Moyer's new assignment, Captain Allen Hobbs relieved Moyer and became American Sāmoa's 30th naval governor, on February 8, 1944.

▼ ▼ ▼

The month of February, 1944, marked the beginning of the end of the great war effort of the United States military in the Sāmoan Islands. Even with the rapid redeployment of the majority of military units, Tutuila would remain important to the U.S. Navy throughout the remainder of the war.

On February 17th the U.S. Naval Station Tutuila's destroyer repair base, located near Anua and Atu'u, was completed, and was officially designated as "U.S. Naval Ship Repair Unit, Navy 129." The total cost for construction of buildings at this new unit was estimated at $884,860. Machinery costs were listed at $344,232, and vehicles at $48,489.

Forty-eight hours after the opening of the destroyer repair base, "Operation Roll-Up" began. This ocean-wide operation would eventually close all unneeded South Pacific bases and "move them to other locations." Within a month many barracks in Tutuila, as well as mess halls and administrative buildings, had been removed. At the same time the Navy 1st and 2nd Construction Seabee Battalions left Tutuila for the United States. By the end of February the military pres-

ence on Tutuila had been reduced to 2,016 men, from nearly 8,000 men only four months earlier.

On March 1st the command of the Sāmoan Defense Group reverted to the Navy, as Captain Allen Hobbs, USN, relieved Major General Charles Price, USMC, and assumed the title "Commandant of the Sāmoan Defense Group." With the north and westward progress of the Allied Pacific offensive, American Sāmoa had become, within a period of less than six months, a military strategic backwater. The USMC 7th Defense Battalion departed Tutuila for the Ellice Islands on March 9th. Within two weeks of their departure plans were begun to remove the anti-torpedo net materials from the entrance to Pago Pago harbor. At the same time the Navy's Mobile Hospital at Mapusaga, MOB 3, began to disassemble and departed Tutuila on April 1st.

As the Pacific battlefronts moved towards Guam and the Japanese Islands, orders came from the Commander, South Pacific Area and Force instructing the Commandant of the U.S. Naval Station Tutuila to "institute a program of redeployment of personnel and materials for use in forward areas." The program was completed in December, 1944.

By January 1, 1945, all excess military equipment had been sent from Tutuila to forward military areas. The U.S. Naval Station began preparations to close down to "peacetime operations." Soon after Captain Ralph W. Hungerford relieved Captain Allen Hobbs to become the 31st naval governor, the Naval Ship Repair Unit in

Pago Pago was inspected by the Commander of the South Pacific Area and Force, Vice Admiral W.L. Calhoun, who recommended "drastic cuts" be made in unit personnel. Soon thereafter the Navy's Construction Battalion Maintenance Unit left Tutuila, and the Public Works Department reverted to a peacetime footing. Finally, on August 15, 1945, the U.S. Marine Corps Barracks, Tutuila, was closed. For American Sāmoa, the war was over.

▼ ▼ ▼

World War II had a tremendous — and nearly incalculable — social and economic impact on American Sāmoa. Like most of the other South Pacific island groups which served as military bases for the United States military, American Sāmoa inherited material assets and wants far beyond the territory's ability to support and maintain. The marines had brought first class roads, electric power and telephones. The military provided wage-paying jobs, highly preferable to young Sāmoans who otherwise would be working in taro or banana plantations or tending to family needs. When the majority of jobs left with the navy and marines, young Sāmoan men were reluctant to return to the drab work of farming or fishing.

The military also introduced the younger Sāmoan generation to the tastes of America: ice cream, movies, ready-made clothing, accessible transportation, even shoes. The military had departed, but the people of American Sāmoa had experienced new American ways and they were eager to maintain them. Life in Tutuila would never be the same. The war had brought enormous change. That change would accelerate in the decade to follow.

Reef fishing near Lauli'i.

Cruise ship passengers are greeted at the main dock, Pago Pago.

O le aso e loaloa

'The day is long.'

A wise man waits until the truth is known. — Proverb

Chapter 12

The Interior Department

n April 17, 1950, American Sāmoa celebrated the fiftieth anniversary of the cession of Tutuila and the raising of the United States flag.

Months of preparation preceded the occasion, and for weeks in advance of the celebrations nothing seemed to be on the minds of the people except the approaching anniversary. Numerous villages and schools practiced their singing and dancing, and selected chiefs prepared their speeches. In the eastern district High Chief Le'iato's aumaga, 300 men strong, rehearsed their knife dance to perfection. At dawn the calm waters of Pago Pago Bay found boat crews in their fautasi rowing through the morning mist, as village oarsmen from Tutuila, Manu'a and 'Upolu trained in preparation for the three-mile race.

Flag Day is celebrated every April with traditional dancing and singing.

As the sun rose on the morning of the 17th, hundreds gathered on the *malae* in Fagatogo in preparation for the day's events. While happy Sāmoan nurses manned a first-aid station, distinguished guests gathered on the podium. The special guests included Admiral Arthur W. Radford, USN, then Commander-in-Chief, U.S. Pacific Fleet, the Honorable G.R. Powles, High Commissioner of Western Sāmoa, and the respected holders of the *tama aiga* titles of Western Sāmoa, Malietoa, Tamasese and Mataʻafa.

The program included a two-hour address by High Talking Chief Pele Tuiolemotu in both English and Sāmoan, dances and songs from many villages, numerous athletic events and finally, a parade by 3,000 people – young and old – led by the Fita Fita Guard and Sāmoan Nurses.

At mid-century, the people of American Sāmoa were proud, vigorous and enthusiastic about their future. It appeared everyone looked forward to the next fifty years under the United States flag.

▼ ▼ ▼

Nineteen years earlier, in 1931, when the U.S. House of Representatives defeated the Bingham Bill, then again defeated the bill a second time one year later, Congressional apathy toward these American islands returned and lasted until the attack on Pearl Harbor. World War

II, however, left the United States in possession of a vast area of the Pacific which had formerly been under Japanese control. The United Nations recognized these island groups as a trust territory and turned them over to the United States to administer. Under this arrangement, continued Naval Administration of American Sāmoa became an anachronism. Plans for a civilian government needed to be formulated.

The Department of the Interior had long been interested in American Sāmoa. Over the course of the first two decades of naval administration, the Navy had sought Interior's advice on education in the islands as well as on other matters. After World War II the Interior Department became actively interested in supplanting the Navy in Sāmoa and other Pacific island groups. Since Interior had been responsible for Indian Affairs and the administration of other U.S. territories for decades, the department seemed to be the logical agency to replace the Navy. Toward that end, Interior Secretary Harold L. Ickes mounted a campaign following the war directed at assuming administrative authority over Tutuila and Manuʻa.

Apparently, little thought was given at Interior as to what kind of administration the Sāmoans themselves wanted. Not since the Bingham hearings in 1930 had the Sāmoans spoken out in regard to their desires – whether to

retain the Naval Administration or replace it with a civilian government. The relationship between American Sāmoa and the United States had been firmly cemented through fifty years of friendship culminating with the Sāmoans' exuberant patriotism during World War II. With the second half of the 20th century upon them and the world's political winds rapidly shifting away from military administrations, the final outcome of the territory's administrative future could not be in doubt.

Historically there is little documented fact as to what kind of administration the Sāmoans wanted in 1950. A plebiscite had not been held or even called for. Even in hindsight it is hard to guess how such a plebiscite might have turned out. It is a fact that the western district leaders of Tutuila favored a civilian administration. High Chief Tuitele and High Talking Chief Leoso were quite outspoken in this regard. There is also no doubt that certain Manu'an leaders supported a Naval administration, as Talking Chief Tauanu'u publicly announced in 1950. But even with the outspoken declarations of these traditional leaders, it is difficult to come to a firm conclusion as to the true feelings of the general population.

Nevertheless, on June 18, 1947, the Secretaries of Interior, State, War and Navy Departments jointly recommended to President Harry S. Truman that responsibility for American

Sāmoa, together with Guam and the Trust Territories, be vested in the Department of the Interior. On May 14, 1949, President Truman directed the Secretaries of Interior and the Navy to draw up plans for the transfer. The two secretaries, by joint memorandum, agreed upon the date of July 1, 1951, as the official date for the transfer of administrations in American Sāmoa.

The Interior Department sent Mr. Emil J. Sady of the Division of Island Territories to Pago Pago to begin the transition. In May, 1950, a planning committee arrived in the territory, headed by the U.S. Commissioner of Indian Affairs John R. Nichols. The committee included Dr. Gordon MacGregor, a noted anthropologist well-known in Sāmoa, Lloyd Furstenau, a personnel administrator, and Marshall Spaulding, a management engineer, who was to study and define the islands' future administrative needs.

The biggest uncertainty facing the committee was the future of the islands' economy. The group faced the fact that removal of the Navy would eliminate all of the indirect subsidies it provided – which were substantial. A solution would have to be found to replace the financial vacuum created by the Navy's departure. The committee eventually proposed a direct federal grant in aid of $790,000 a year.

On February 22, 1951, Captain Thomas F. Darden, USN (Ret.), the last of the twenty-seven naval governors, stood waiting on the dock with members of his staff to meet the *Manu'a Tele* bringing in his designated relief, Mr. Phelps Phelps. Accompanying Phelps was Dr. Gordon MacGregor, the new attorney general. The following day, Governor Phelps, representing the Navy Department until the actual transfer date of July 1, 1951, formally relieved Governor Darden at ceremonies on the malae at Fagatogo.

Fa'aluma–dance leader–performs with his dance and singing group in Flag Day celebrations on Fagatogo *malae*.

Biscuit tins make good drums as dancers perform during Flag Day.

185

Rainmaker Mountain overlooks busy port of Pago Pago.

Phelps Phelps, first appointed civilian Governor under the administration of the Department of the Interior, 1951-1952.

Max Haleck with Mr. MacMullin and Ed Johnson in Fagatogo. Circa 1948

As the territory's traditional Sāmoan leaders, Navy personnel and new civilian administrators gathered on the *malae*, members of the Fono passed out a program printed specifically for the occasion. A statement in the program said: "By means of the ceremonies set forth in the pages of this program, The Fono, in behalf of the people of American Sāmoa, wishes to place in the record of history the significance of the termination of 51 years of naval administration. Mutual respect, understanding and cooperation has been the keynote of our long relationship. Our appreciation for the guidance and leadership of the Navy in helping American Sāmoa to move forward is deep-seated and everlasting. Turning its head to the past, Sāmoa is sorrowful to bid farewell to a good and loyal friend, the Navy. At the same time, turning its head toward the future, Sāmoa bids welcome to the new administration under the Department of the Interior, and offers its loyalty, cooperation, and obedience with bright hopes for the future. May God grant strength, wisdom, and success to the new administration in its endeavors."

▼ ▼ ▼

The most serious problem facing Governor Phelps was the rapidly fading economy. The war had created what some referred to as a "false economy." Once the war ended and the navy departed, the economy had little foundation upon which to expand. Phelps hoped to bring in outside capital by using the oil storage facilities to sell oil to shipping and to lure airlines from the

growing South Pacific commercial airline market to the airport at Tafuna. He also made every effort to encourage Sāmoans to produce more copra for export and to make Sāmoan handicrafts for export to Honolulu to sell to tourists on the oceanic liners.

Despite his efforts, Governor Phelps was greatly disappointed. Due to the large oil capacity of transoceanic shipping, the sale of oil was not substantial. The facilities at the Tafuna airport did not meet the needs of the transpacific airline carriers, who continued to use Canton Island to refuel. While many Sāmoans did produce handicrafts and curios in sufficient quantity, the money received from the sales did not significantly impact the island economy.

Meanwhile in Washington, D.C. Interior Secretary Oscar Chapman and Emil Sady, Chief of the Pacific Division of the Office of Island Territories, hoped to provide American Sāmoa with a more clearly defined status under the United States by means of an organic act. While the idea seemed sensible on the surface, and had the support of a number of past naval governors, the idea behind such legislation was met with grave concern by Sāmoan leadership. These traditional leaders recognized that an organic act would bring all of the provisions of the Constitution of the United States into American Sāmoa, jeopardizing such ancient and sacred Sāmoan customs as the *matai* and land-tenure systems. In 1950 the Fono appointed a committee to design a way to safeguard the *matai* system against the pending organic act (HE 4500). Soon thereafter a special session issued a resolution stating, ". . . the Fono fully believes that neither Washington nor Miles' Subcommittee should evolve, instigate, create, or sponsor anything that would hasten destruction of the Sāmoan matai system."

In June, 1951, just before the transfer of administrative control to Interior, the Fono demanded that its status be changed from advisory to legislative. One of the primary reasons behind this demand was the Fono's wish to be able to speak with authority against the proposed organic act. The message from Fono leaders was clear: the Fono was determined to decide for themselves what the future political status should be – not what outsiders thought they should accept.

The most outspoken and eloquent Fono leader of the time was a high ranking orator from Vaifanua – Tuiasosopo Mariota. Tuiasosopo burst upon the stage of local politics in 1932 at the Annual Meeting of Chiefs instituted in 1905 as a means of bringing chiefs together from different

required that no law involving lands and titles be made or changed "unless first decided by the Fono." Though Governor Landenberger did not agree with the resolution, he stated in his report to Washington: "The instance . . . shows the importance that Sāmoans attach to their Fono . . ."

In 1935 the Eastern District again brought a resolution which requested the "establishment of a legislative body to be known as the Fono." The delegates elected Tuiasosopo to argue their case. The governor responded at the time that only the U.S. Congress had the authority to create a legislature, though that position would be reversed by another Navy governor thirteen years later. Tuiasosopo was not discouraged. He continued to

High Talking Chief Tuiasosopo Mariota, dynamic leader in the establishment of the modern day Legislature in American Sāmoa.

districts to discuss topics of common interest and recommend to the governor any laws they wished to be passed.

Soon after his appearance at the meeting in 1932, Tuiasosopo voiced the opinion that the Annual Meeting was called by the governor only to keep the chiefs happy. He soon resolved to begin the process to create a real legislature. In 1933, the Eastern District, under Tuiasosopo's leadership, introduced a resolution which

press for the creation of a Fono continuously for nearly ten consecutive years.

The Annual Meeting of Chiefs was terminated during the war, but when the Annual Meetings resumed in 1945, Tuiasosopo had emerged as the territory's most prominent leader. In 1946 he orchestrated the chiefs of Tutuila and Manu'a into agreeing to a General Assembly outside of the Annual Meetings called by the governor for the purpose of drafting initial legis-

Late at night a family gathers in a Sāmoan *fale* in Saʻilele to discuss an impending celebration. Fine mats are gathered, kegs of salt beef stacked and contributions made in the traditional manner.

Ceremonial head-dress–*tuiga*–is placed on the head of a young lady prior to a village celebration in Leone.

Richard B. Lowe, 5th appointed civilian Governor, 1953-1956.

lation for a territorial government. The assembly decided to appoint a committee to prepare draft legislation for submission to the governor. Tuiasosopo was elected leader of the committee which consisted of Manuʻa's two leading chiefs, Sotoa and Tufele, and two of Tutuila's highest ranking chiefs, Tuitele and Leʻiato. The two most serious obstacles facing Tuiasosopo were the inability of the chiefs to agree on the language of the draft and the fact that Governor Houser believed the expense of setting up a legislature was too heavy a financial burden for the government. But the skillful Tuiasosopo cleared

those obstacles and the draft legislation was presented to the governor.

In 1947 the new Navy governor, Captain Vernon Huber, reversed all previous denials and declared the governor did have the power to promulgate a law establishing a legislature. Unbeknown to nearly everyone, Governor Huber's reversal of previous decisions by prior governors was the result of months of quiet lobbying and confidential negotiations between Tuiasosopo and Governor Huber.

Tuiasosopo Mariota became Speaker of the House in the First Legislature called into session on October 26, 1948. Outsiders who observed the original Fono sessions remarked as to the serious decorum exercised by Fono members and the

correct protocol in their deliberations. To witnesses watching the proceedings one aspect was clear: Tuiasosopo was in complete command.

Once the Legislature of American Sāmoa became a reality many members thought their struggles were over. Tuiasosopo, however, knew that many battles lay ahead. In February, 1949, he issued the following statement to the newspaper *Fa'atonu*: "This government of American Sāmoa, has not by any means remained stationary in any year since 1900. It has made steady, forward progress step by step. The government passed the nursery or cradle stage. The Legislative Power vested in a Fono composed of two houses, House of Ali'i and the House of Representatives, is an established fact for Sāmoa and its government. Sāmoa is now faced with a really heavy responsibility which shall be proved a blessing through the matured and harmonious cooperation of all and a complete confidence and trust in Divine Providence. There remains another stage to be attained. That is building of the Sāmoan Government slowly step by step that in due time when we are ready we shall have a Government of Sāmoa by Sāmoans, for the happy and full enjoyment of life by all."

Tuiasosopo was clearly not satisfied with simply having a Legislature. He wanted a Legislature that had full authority to legislate. In 1951, only two years after the Fono was founded, Tuiasosopo introduced a resolution (HR No. 6) which called for the repeal of "all laws or provi-

sions in the Code of American Sāmoa which limit the power of the Fono or Legislature. . ."

This step was too fast for Interior's new governor, Phelps Phelps. He had just told the Fono in his inaugural speech that Interior's policy was a "step by step" government, with more measures of authority when Sāmoans have proven their ability to handle more responsibilities of government.

Undeterred, Tuiasosopo quickly embraced the idea of developing home rule, or self-government, on the basis of a constitution developed and voted on by the people themselves. Such a constitution, Tuiasosopo believed, would spell out and then protect the framework of a local government – one where Sāmoans would rule themselves, and equally important, where their customs and traditions would be protected.

In time Governor Lowe offered this idea in a speech before a joint session of the Legislature. Tuiasosopo was then the President of the Senate. The idea would develop a constitution that would create a Sāmoan Government, as opposed to an organic act which local leaders clearly did not want.

On January 26, 1956, the first official U.S. air mail was delivered to American Sāmoa. Later that year in October, Richard B. Lowe ended his term as the territory's fifth appointed civil governor. President Dwight D. Eisenhower replaced Lowe with Peter T. Coleman, age thirty-seven, who had previously been serving as the territory's public defender and attorney general.

Tuiasosopo not only faced unending political obstacles in his effort to bring a Sāmoan government to maturity, he also was forced to deal with his political foes. As the respected orator's political power grew, so did the voices of those who disagreed with him. Surprisingly, in 1956, his foes combined to remove Tuiasosopo from his position as President of the Senate. His removal from office had a double effect, for it also removed him from the Constitutional Committee on which he served in his capacity as Senate President. He was therefore unable to inject his views and proposals into the Constitutional process. Tuiasosopo later remarked to Salanoa Aumoeualogo that being left out of the Constitutional process was one of his greatest sorrows. Later that year Tuiasosopo Mariota died unexpectedly at the age of fifty-one.

▼ ▼ ▼

One of Governor Coleman's earliest accomplishments was improving both air and sea transportation between American Sāmoa and the U.S. mainland. The Matson Liners began calling regularly at Pago Pago, as did other freighters, bringing

A young girl learns to weave a floor mat. The Arts Council and Jean P. Haydon Museum sponsor programs in which senior citizens teach youngsters the arts and crafts of traditional Sāmoa.

Salanoa S.P. Aumoeualogo, President of the Senate, 1969-1971, 1973-78, gives a Flag Day address in front of the Fono Building.

Peter T. Coleman, 6th appointed civilian Governor, 1956-1961.

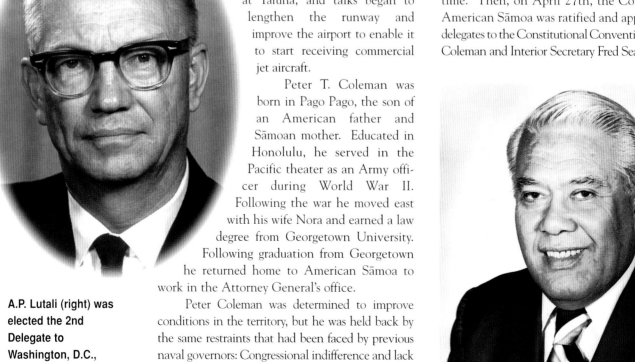

Fautasi racing is the highlight of every Flag Day. The Televise crew, from Utulei, were the champions of Tutuila and 'Upolu from the late 60s through the early 70s.

H. Rex Lee was appointed the 7th civilian Governor by President John F. Kennedy in 1961, serving through 1967. Lee returned to American Sāmoa as the last appointed Governor, serving for seven months in 1977-1978.

A.P. Lutali (right) was elected the 2nd Delegate to Washington, D.C., serving from 1975-1978.

in much needed supplies, mail, food, and building materials. Lawrence Coleman organized Sāmoan airways which commenced regular air service between Tafuna airport and 'Upolu. By 1959, transpacific airliners began landing occasionally at Tafuna, and talks began to lengthen the runway and improve the airport to enable it to start receiving commercial jet aircraft.

Peter T. Coleman was born in Pago Pago, the son of an American father and Sāmoan mother. Educated in Honolulu, he served in the Pacific theater as an Army officer during World War II. Following the war he moved east with his wife Nora and earned a law degree from Georgetown University. Following graduation from Georgetown he returned home to American Sāmoa to work in the Attorney General's office.

Peter Coleman was determined to improve conditions in the territory, but he was held back by the same restraints that had been faced by previous naval governors: Congressional indifference and lack of federal aid. Between 1956 and 1960 government wages averaged about $6.00 a week. American Sāmoa was held in such disregard by Congress and Interior that it was excluded from Congressional aid

bills. Governor Coleman was forced to operate his government with very little funding.

In April, 1960, two events of significance took place. On Flag Day, the territory's 60th anniversary under the United States flag, American Sāmoa's new flag was raised for the first time. Then, on April 27th, the Constitution of American Sāmoa was ratified and approved by 68 delegates to the Constitutional Convention, Governor Coleman and Interior Secretary Fred Seaton.

In the election of 1960, John F. Kennedy was elected President of the United States. Within four months of taking office Kennedy appointed H. Rex Lee as the territory's seventh appointed civil governor. Prior to Lee's arrival, the territory was visited by Clarence Hall, a writer from the United States. Hall toured Tutuila and interviewed a number of community leaders. In July, 1961, his article appeared in *Reader's Digest*. The article was titled, "Sāmoa: America's Shame in the South Pacific." In 1961 *Reader's Digest* was one of the most widely-read magazines in the United States. Hall's article would have a tremendous impact on both President Kennedy himself and the members of Congress.

In one of the article's more memorable quotes, Hall said, "While we (the U.S.) have been doling out billions to underdeveloped nations, we have let our only South Pacific possession sink to the level of a slum."

The article contained numerous quotes from Sāmoan leaders. One quote was from A.P. Laovao, later to be known as A.P. Lutali. "All we ask," said Lutali in the article, "is to be treated as brothers, not sons or stepsons. We ask nothing but enough technical aid to help us start doing for ourselves, to prove to the world that Sāmoans can stand on their own feet – like real Americans."

The article jarred President Kennedy and Congress into action. Governor Lee was given both the funding and Presidential support he needed to begin the modernization of American Sāmoa. Between 1961 and 1967, under Governor Rex Lee's direction, the island of Tutuila changed dramatically.

A new conference center, shaped like a turtle, was built in Utulei, to house the delegates for the 1962 South Pacific Conference. The building would come to be known as the *Fale Laumei*. The main road was paved from Fagatogo to the airport at Tafuna, and a new airport terminal constructed. Elementary schools were built throughout Tutuila, and high schools planned for Leone and Fagaʻitua. Lee shocked the territory's citizens when he announced he was going to install a television education system to broadcast lessons into elementary schools in remote villages. The educational TV system would become famous throughout the entire Pacific region.

On July 18, 1962, the first jet aircraft, a Pan Am Boeing 707, landed at Tafuna International Airport, carrying Interior Secretary Stewart

At a village celebration in Faleniu, Tutuila, a young boy provides his own interpretation of Sāmoan dancing (top, left). Above, a championship cricket match has just concluded at Vailoatai, Tutuila, as the teams gather to shake hands.

The village of Vailoatai has long been considered one of the most beautiful in American Sāmoa. Nestled against a dramatic coastline and built around a large grass *malae*, villagers line the roadside daily with flowers and keep their family compounds meticulously clean.

Udall. Negotiations were begun with Pan American World Airways to build a luxury hotel on a site in Pago Pago harbor known as "Goat Island." Pan Am would eventually place American Sāmoa in the center of its South Pacific flight network, linking the territory with Tahiti, New Zealand, Australia, Fiji and Hawai'i. By 1967 tourists began coming into the territory in large numbers and the island's economy began to greatly expand.

In 1966, a devastating hurricane smashed into Sāmoa the last two days of January. Tutuila reported gusts of 110 mph. By the time the hurricane moved away, five people were dead and nearly a thousand people were left homeless. The

hurricane would have a lasting impact on Tutuila. Hundreds of traditional Sāmoan *fales* were destroyed, never to be rebuilt. They were replaced by square, wall-less buildings which came to be known as "hurricane houses." Many of the islands' more beautiful and picturesque villages were irreparably damaged, their pristine visual charm, which had stood for centuries, vanished forever.

Later that year, on October 18th, President Lyndon Johnson became the first American chief executive to visit American Sāmoa. He was accompanied by his wife, Lady Bird Johnson, who dedicated the Manulele Tausala elementary school in Nu'uuli, which was named after her.

On August 1, 1967, Owen Aspinall was appointed governor, replacing Rex Lee. Aspinall, who had served as Attorney General under Governor Lee, would serve only two years as governor. Compared to the energetic pace of Rex Lee, Governor Aspinall's term was noted as a quiet, uneventful period. During Aspinall's tenure Apollo 10, after circling the moon, splashed down east of Rose Atoll, with astronauts Thomas Stafford, Eugene Cernan and John Young aboard.

John M. Haydon, a prominent publisher from Seattle, was appointed governor by Interior Secretary Walter Hickel on August 1, 1969. Haydon would serve as governor for more than five years, and, like Rex Lee, was a man of action. Though tremendous progress had been made in the building of island infrastructure through the terms of both governors Lee and Aspinall, John Haydon found such basic services as water and power to be woefully inadequate.

Like Rex Lee, John Haydon had friends in Washington, D.C., and he called on them continually to push for more federal funding to expand and modernize the territory's government services. His efforts were successful. During his term of office great strides were made in both expanding and modernizing the territory's water, sewer, electrical power and highway systems. Tutuila's new hospital, named the LBJ Tropical Medical Center, was, in the early 1970s, considered to be the best hospital in the South Pacific outside of Hawai'i and New Zealand.

The territory continued to be, during Haydon's term, an important part of the Apollo space program. On April 18, 1970, Apollo 13 splashed down in Sāmoan waters, carrying astronauts James A. Lovell, John L. Swigert and Fred W. Haise.

John Haydon was also a man of history. He held the title as the territory's first Historic

symbolic. During Haydon's tenure the political momentum on two vital issues moved forward at a rapid pace. The first was the election of a Sāmoan governor, to replace the appointed governors. The second was the creation of a seat in the U.S. House of Representatives for a Congressman from American Sāmoa.

The first step in creating an American Sāmoa seat in Congress was the election of a "Delegate-at-Large" to Washington, D.C. In 1970 A.U. Fuimaono was elected the territory's first Washington delegate in American Sāmoa's first territory-wide election in which ninety-five percent of the registered voters cast their ballots. Fuimaono began his term in January, 1971, and remained in Washington until the end of 1974, when he lost his bid for re-election for delegate to A.P. Lutali.

The election of Sāmoa's own governor was not as simple an issue as having a representative in Congress. There was strong opposition, both within the Fono and among the general public, to having a Sāmoan governor. Both Interior and Congress, however, were strong advocates of Sāmoans electing their own governor. Finally, in a referendum in 1974, Sāmoan voters approved the election of their own governor.

John Haydon completed his term as governor in October, 1974, and was replaced in an acting capacity by Lt. Governor Frank Mockler. Acting Governor Mockler was

Preservation Officer. During his term a number of former Navy buildings were placed on the National Register of Historic Places. Haydon's wife, Jean, established the territory's first museum, which later was named in her honor. The museum was dedicated by the famous anthropologist Margaret Mead, who had returned to the territory to visit Ta'ū island, the site of her renowned work, *Coming of Age in Sāmoa.*

On Flag Day 1973 the official seal of American Sāmoa, with the motto, *Sāmoa Muamua Le Atua,* (Sāmoa, Let God Be First) was dedicated. The dedication of American Sāmoa's own government seal was significant as well as

"It is unique for two very distinctive reasons. First, in a time when other island nations in the Pacific have sought their political independence, American Sāmoa has reaffirmed its desire to remain a part of the United States. We are Americans. We want to be Americans. We do not ever want to change that fact.

"Secondly, though we are a United States territory, we have our own constitution. This allows us to retain those aspects of our culture and way of life most dear to us. This makes our partnership with the United States government 'one-of-a-kind.'"

Governor Sunia continued. "Throughout this century American Sāmoans have proven their undying loyalty to the United States. Since the 1940s our men and women have served in the United States armed forces. American Sāmoans served their country in World War II. They have shed their blood in the snows of Korea, the jungles of Viet Nam, the skirmishes of Panama and Granada and most recently the Gulf War. Young men from our islands serve with the peace-keeping forces in Bosnia. We are proud of our service to the American military. We are proud to defend our nation."

In regard to American Sāmoa's Centennial, Governor Sunia concluded, "The one-hundredth anniversary of the signing of the Deed of Cession is very special to American Sāmoans everywhere. We recognize we have been blessed to have been part of the United States these past hundred years. And in return for this blessing, I do not think you will find a people more loyal, more proud to be American, than the people of American Sāmoa."

Clockwise from above: young boy builds his own toy; spear fishermen return home following an afternoon fishing on the reef; thatch is placed on *fale* roof; cricket on a village *malae*; little girls in church on White Sunday; children at play; woman hanging fine mats in the sun.

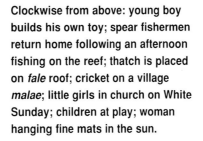

Nobody knows paradise better than your friends at Hawaiian Airlines.

CONTRIBUTORS

Eileen George

Eileen George is an artist and photographer who lived in American Sāmoa for three years. During her time there, she photographed hundreds of sights and events, a number of which appear in this book. She held three special art shows at the Jean P. Haydon Museum; her artwork commissions and paintings are now in collections throughout the world. As a special contribution to this book, Eileen George also served as editor and proofreader for the Centennial book text.

Bob Thomason

Bob Thomason is a member of the United States Coast Guard. He began his career in photography in 1982 in Key West, Florida. His photographs have been published in Florida Keys magazine, Pacific Islands magazine, local newspapers in Florida, and can be found on permanent display in Key West, Pago Pago and Honolulu. Mr. Thomason, stationed in Pago Pago from 1996-1998, took the portrait of Governor Sunia which appears with the Governor's message, as well as other photos included in this book.

Regina Meredith Malala

"Reggie" Malala grew up in Leone, American Sāmoa. She graduated from Washington and Jefferson College in Pennsylvania in 1982 with a degree in Visual Arts and Art Education. She received an M.F.A. in Painting and Drawing from San Diego State University in 1988. Since 1989 Reggie has taught art at the American Sāmoa Community College as well as serve as department chairperson of Fine Arts after teaching art at Sāmoana High School from 1982-1984. Reggie's artwork appears throughout this book, including her watercolor of a Sāmoan village scene in chapter three. She also is a major contributor to the art "background" of the book's theme, including Sāmoan cultural "texture" pieces through her photography and collection of Sāmoan cultural artifacts found on various pages throughout the book.

Sven Ortquist

Sven Ortquist is Master Carver for the American Sāmoa Council on Arts, Culture and the Humanities. He is Resident Artist at the Jean P. Haydon Museum where he teaches traditional Sāmoan woodcarving. In addition to being a master in the production of traditional Sāmoan wood-carving, Sven has developed his own interpretions of Sāmoan myths and legends through carved reliefs and sculptures. He was founder and first president of the Sāmoan Voyaging Society, Aiga Tautai o Sāmoa. He considers his greatest achievement to be the art work he designed and fashioned for the Roman Catholic Holy Family Cathedral in Tafuna, Tutuila. Sven's painting Tagaloa and Pava appears in chapter one along with many other pieces.

Louie DeNolfo

"Louie the Fish" is known throughout the South Pacific for his authentic bone carvings of fish and native Polynesian fishhooks. In 1970 he earned a B.F.A. in Painting and Ceramics from the University of Hawai'i. In the early 1970s he began carving Hawai'ian bone fishhook pendants and other pieces of miniature hand-sculpted bone art. Louie arrived in American Sāmoa in 1973. Over the following twenty-five years Louie spread the idea of bone-carving throughout Sāmoa, Fiji and Tonga. After living in New Zealand, Louie returned to American Sāmoa in 1996, where he continues to carve his bone sea life figures and authentic Sāmoan and Polynesian fishhooks.

Stan Sorensen

Stan Sorensen has lived in the Sāmoan Islands for twenty-five years. He presently serves on the staff of Governor Tauese Sunia as Historian for the Centennial 2000 project. Stan attended the University of Utah from 1964 to 1972, earning a B.S. in Geography and an M.A. in History. He served as a Peace Corps volunteer in (Western) Sāmoa for two years. He relocated to American Sāmoa in 1980, eventually serving as the American Sāmoa Government's Historic Preservation Officer. Stan has written a 200-page Sāmoan Historical Calendar and a Sāmoan Historical Chronology, which cover the period 1606-1998. In 1990 Stan received the Land and Water Conservation Fund's Distinguished Service Award from the National Park Service. Much of the historical data presented in this book is the result of years of research by Mr. Sorensen. Without the Sāmoan Historical Chronology as a reference, the historical detail in the text of this book would have been nearly impossible to attain.

Frederic K. Sutter

"Rick" Sutter is a professional anthropologist and photographer, who did his undergraduate work at Harvard and holds the degree of MS in education from Wagner College, New York, as well as a Ph.D. in anthropology from the University of Hawaiʻi. He has been involved in photographic anthropology since 1962, when he first taught in (Western) Sāmoa. By 1966, his photographic work had attracted recognition from National Geographic. His first photographic essay, "Sāmoa; A Photographic Essay," now in its fourth printing, grew out of subsequent work with Geographic. In addition, he has published two other photographic essays on Sāmoa titled "Amerika Sāmoa" and "The Sāmoans – A Global Family." The majority of color photographs appearing in this book were taken by Dr. Sutter.

H.M. "Hank" Taufaʻasau

Hank Taufaʻasau was born in Kalihi, Oʻahu, and raised in Mānoa. His home in Mānoa Valley serves as his art gallery where over the years he has painted depictions of Polynesians and Polynesian life, with a special interest in Sāmoa and its people. His art works are found in private collections throughout the world, including American Sāmoa's Jean P. Haydon Museum, the South Pacific Commission in New Caledonia, and in many homes in Hawaiʻi. "My focus is on our people . . . and the colors that makes our lives in Polynesia so special," he says. Hank's painting of the ancient voyaging canoe appears at the beginning of chapter two.

Adeline Pritchard Jones

Adeline Jones began her career in the art of Sāmoan tapa making in 1967. She served for several years under her mother, renowned tapa artist Mary J. Pritchard, author of the book "SIAPO, Bark Cloth Art of Sāmoa." Adeline has conducted and participated in numerous tapa demonstrations in several schools and universities in Hawaiʻi, the U.S. mainland, Alaska, Tahiti, New Guinea and Japan. She served as a tapa instructor at the Jean P. Haydon Museum for several years, and as a representative of American Sāmoa to the South Pacific Festival of the Arts. Since 1992 Adeline has operated as a freelance tapa artist out of her home in Pago Pago. She does tapa in both the "freehand" and "rubbing" method. Her work appears throughout this book.

Stan Jorstad

Commercial photography has been a very successful career for Stan Jorstad, but his real passion is nature photography. Stan opened PhotoMark in 1979, which has become a leader in the art of panoramic photography. In 1991-92 a collection of Stan's panoramic National Park photographs were exhibited at The Smithsonian's Museum of Natural History in celebration of The National Park Service's 75th anniversary. His photographs of America's National Parks brought Stan to American Sāmoa in 1996 to photograph the National Park in Tutuila and Manuʻa. Stan published his book "These Rare Lands" in 1997, which feature photographs of each of America's National Parks. Stan's photos of American Sāmoa appear throughout this book, including the cover photo.

Sina Liai Shaffer

The publication of a large book of this kind requires endless hours of systematic organization. For two years Sina Shaffer donated her time to make this special Centennial book project proceed as smoothly and efficiently as possible. During this two-year period Sina catalogued and filed hundreds of individual contents to be included in the book, kept computer files, searched for specific data to be included in the book, and organized photographs, artwork and other material into accessible classifications.

Marilyn Pritchard Walker

As a young girl growing up in Vaitogi, Marilyn Pritchard was surrounded by tapa makers who came to her home to make tapa with her mother, the renowned tapa artist, Mary Pritchard. In 1968, she began operating the Airport Restaurant, which was to successfully continue for twenty-eight years. Mary Pritchard often came to the restaurant where she would design her tapa. It was there that Marilyn began learning the art from her mother and soon had commissions to make tapa for gifts for the Vatican and the Israeli Embassy in Japan. She has given tapa-making workshops at the East-West Center in Honolulu, high schools in Hawaiʻi, as well as tapa design demonstrations at Honolulu City Hall and Jean P. Haydon Museum. Her work appears throughout this book.

Janet Stewart

People – their strengths, beauty and vulnerabilities – are the essence of Janet Stewart's paintings. Her work reflects the human element and natural beauty she finds around her. Her early watercolors of Polynesian people were of winning quality. Janet Stewart's work has been popular in the Hawaiian Islands since 1985 and the mainland U.S. since 1976. In April, 1998 she visited American Sāmoa for the first time. There she found "much inspiration in the friendly, beautiful people and lush tropical setting" for painting. Two of her watercolors appear in chapter three.

Leslie Wood

Leslie Wood began her professional tapa making career in 1974 when she was asked to assist in a University of Hawai'i, Mānoa workshop being taught by premier South Pacific tapa artist Mary Pritchard. As Mary's niece, she is a descendant of a long line of tapa makers. In 1978 Leslie began teaching siapo at the Bishop Museum. Upon her return to Sāmoa in 1984 Leslie had a private show sponsored by the Sāmoa Art Association. This show was a catalyst for her commercial career and she began selling her work in South Pacific galleries and handicraft shops. Leslie has three times received special recognition by various American Sāmoa governors – the Governor's Award for the Arts. She lives in her home in the Taputimu area of Tutuila.

Fa'ailoilo Lauvao

As the Executive Director of the American Sāmoa Arts Council and Jean P. Haydon Museum, Fa'ailoilo Lauvao is responsible for American Sāmoa's archival photos, documents and other historical data. Mrs. Lauvao graciously opened the Museum's archives and historical files making these priceless materials available for use in the book. Without Mrs. Lauvao's support, it would not have been possible to present these historical documents and photos in this publication.

Art Class — American Sāmoa Community College

Members of Art 170 class at ASCC have contributed their art to this book. The artists are Toalei Toalei of Pago Pago; Lin Martin Alenepi of Tafuna; Jay Leonard Maeva of Tafuna, and Tusiata Toafa, also of Tafuna. These art students study under the direction of Reggie Meredith Malala. Their artwork includes renderings of Sāmoan petroglyphs and other historical and natural elements.

SĀMOAN PRONUNCIATION AND GLOSSARY

Sāmoan vowels are pure, as in French, while the consonants are roughly equivalent to English in pronunciation. The accent is normally placed on the penultimate syllable, but vowels that are to be emphasized are indicated with a macron as in Sāmoa.

One of the more difficult sounds for foreigners is the "g" sound as in *palagi* (white person), pronounced "pah-LAH-ngee," as in the "ng" sound of "ping pong." Therefore, the village of Pago Pago is correctly pronounced "PAHNG-oh PAHNG-oh."

An okina before a vowel indicates a "glottal stop." The glottal stop is similar to a break between words, such as "oh-oh." Thus, the word ali'i (chief) is pronounced "AH-lee-ee."

The Sāmoan words which appear in the text are the following:

Geographic Sites or Locations

SĀMOAN SITE	LOCATION
A'asu	Site of massacre of French sailors, north coast, Tutuila
Aoa	Village located on the north-east coast of Tutuila
Apia	Capital city of (Western) Sāmoa, 'Upolu
Aunu'u	Small islet off south-east coast of Tutuila
Fagatogo	Village in Pago Pago Bay, Tutuila
Falefā	Site of early human settlement at time of Christ, 'Upolu
Faga'itua	Village and bay, south-east coast of Tutuila
Leone	Site of first missionary landing, west coast of Tutuila
Malua	Site of first missionary (LMS) school, 'Upolu
Manono	Small island between 'Upolu and Savai'i
Manu'a	Collective name designating islands of Ofu, Olosega, Ta'ū
Manu'atele	Sāmoan designation meaning "greater" Manu'a
Mulifanua	Site where Lapita-style ceramics found, western tip of 'Upolu
Mulinu'u	Peninsula west of Apia; burial site of Sāmoan royalty
Ofu	Island in Manu'a Group
Olosega	Island in Manu'a Group
Pago Pago	Village located at inland end of Pago Pago Bay
Sa'ilele	Village site of ancient temple, north-east coast of Tutuila
Savai'i	Largest island in Sāmoan island chain
Swains Island	Atoll 200 miles north of Tutuila annexed by the U.S. in 1925
To'aga	Prehistoric site with Lapita-style ceramics, south-east Ofu
Ta'ū	Largest island in Manu'a group
Tutuila	Largest island in American Sāmoa
'Upolu	Second largest island in Sāmoa group
Vailima	Site of Robert Louis Stevenson home near Apia, 'Upolu

SĀMOAN WORD	ENGLISH EQUIVALENT
'Āiga	Family, extended family, all relations however remote
Ali'i	Titled person; chief
Aualuma	Unmarried women's association
'Aumāga	Untitled men's association
'Ava	Kava, ceremonial drink
Auosoga	Ceremonial mourning for certain high chiefs
Fa'alupega	Ceremonial address of important titles and kinship groups
Fa'a Sāmoa	The Sāmoan way (of life); the Sāmoan manner of (doing things)

Fa'atonu	To instruct, order, demand
Faipule	Individual with power or authority; legislator
Fale	House; building
Fale sami	Outside latrine built over the water; lit. "sea house"
Fita Fita	Soldier; special military unit
Foma'i	Doctor; medical practitioner
Fono	Meeting; council; conference; legislature
Fusi	Bind or lash; belt; strap
Ipu	(Coconut-shell) cup; cup for the serving of kava
Kovana	Governor
Lavalava	Clothes; term for wrap-around cloth
Lotu Toga	Lit. "Tongan Church"; term for Methodist Church
Ma'i aitu	Lit. "Spirit sickness"
Malo	Loin cloth
Malo	Government; power in authority
Malae	Center of village; village green
Malaga	Journey; ceremonial visit according to Sāmoan custom
Manaia	Leader of 'aumāga; chief's son
Masi	Food made from breadfruit fermented in a pit
Masoā	Arrowroot plant; starch or paste for making tapa cloth
Matai	Holder of Sāmoan title; chief or orator
Mau	Keep; retain; hold fast; testimony; evidence
Niu	General name for coconut palm
Nu'u	Village
O'a	Tree from which brown dye is extracted from the bark
Oso	Digging stick (for planting)
Palusami	Dish made of taro leaves, coconut cream and sea-water
Papalagi; palagi	European; white person
Pilikaki	Pilchard; canned fish
Pisupo	Canned corned beef
Pola	Plaited coconut leaf wall screen
Popo	Ripe (mature) coconut
Pulenu'u	Mayor (of village); village authority
Siapo	Bark cloth made from the mulberry tree
Tagaloa	Sāmoan god
Taule'ale'a	Untitled young man
Taupou	Title of village maiden according to Sāmoan custom
Tautai	Master fisherman; boat captain
Tautua	Service rendered to one's chief; village or family
Teine	Girl
Tia	Platform
To'oto'o	Orator's staff; respect word for orator or member of legislature
Tui Manu'a	Lit. "King of Manu'a"
Tufuga	Craftsman; expert; specialist
Tulafale	Orator; talking chief
U'a	Paper mulberry tree used to make tapa cloth
Umu	Stone oven
Upeti	Wood tablet with raised pattern for rubbing designs for tapa
Va'aalo	Bonito outrigger canoe

Historical Documents

Tilly's letter to Washinton, DC., April, 1900

Tilly's letter to High Chief Mauga, 1899

U.S. Naval Station, Tutuila
April 18. 1900

No. 147.

Sir:

1. I have the honor to report that the American flag was hoisted at the Naval Station Pago Pago, on the 17th inst. at 10 o'clock A.M. with appropriate ceremonies.

2. The exercises were as follows:

1. Reading of President's proclamation and Navy Department General Order No. 540 by the Commandant.

2. Presentation of address by the Samoan people of Tutuila enclosed marked A. with translation marked B.

3. Religious exercises conducted by Rev. E. V. Cooper of the London Missionary

---

Society and by Father Meinauder of the Roman Catholic Mission in Tutuila.

4. Declaration of the Sovereignty and protection of the United States over the islands of the Samoan group East of 171° of longitude West of Greenwich - enclosed marked "C".

5. Hoisting of American flag by Comdr. B. F. Tilley U.S. Navy, Commandant.

6. Singing of America by the pupils and teachers of the London Missionary Society.

7. National salutes fired by the U.S.S. "Abarenda" and the German Cruiser "Cormoran".

8. Address by United States Consul General Osborn of Apia, enclosed marked "D"

3. Afterwards I received addresses from the

Missionary Societies. In the afternoon the natives gave several "taalolos" to me. The taalolo is a ceremony which indicates that those participating acknowledge the authority and promise allegiance to the person to whom it is given. It consists of a procession passing before the ruler and each native dressed in his aboriginal costume presents to the ruler some present of food such as a chicken, pig, fruit etc.

4. The other exercises were as indicated in the enclosed programmes marked E, F, and G and lasted until the evening of the 18th inst. Nearly the whole pop-

---

ulation of Tutuila was present and participated in the exercises and sports. They showed great enthusiasm and I think it is most gratifying to these people that the United States has taken charge of the island. I was treated with the greatest respect by the natives

5. The German Cruiser Cormoran came down from Apia to be present at the ceremonies. Governor Solf, the German Governor of Samoa and all the officials of the "Cormoran" attended the exercises on shore.

Very respectfully
B. F. Tilley

---

1 (Copy.)
United States Coal Depot
U.S.S. Abarenda
Pago Pago, Samoan Islands
December 6, 1899.

To the High Chief Mauga,
Pago Pago, Tutuila,
Samoa.

1. I arrived here yesterday from Apia.

2. While in Apia I received information that the three Great Powers; Germany, England and the United States of America had agreed to divide the Government of the Samoan Islands between Germany and the United States.

3. Germany will assume the government and protection of Upolu and Savaii and the United States will assume the government and protection of Tutuila, Manua and the other islands East of Upolu. England will withdraw altogether from the islands.

4. As the Senior Naval Officer of the United

States in Samoa, I have to express the wish that the chiefs will inform all the natives of the change of Government in Tutuila and that the chiefs will keep order as they are now doing. It is desirable that all the natives should resume their avocations, plant their gardens and settle down to habits of peace and industry. This course will soon bring great prosperity to the island of Tutuila.

5. All danger of war is now averted but the United States will punish all riots quarrels and crimes. The chiefs are urged to call upon me to assist them in punishing all persons who commit crimes or create disorder.

---

6. The authority of the chiefs, when properly exercised, will be upheld.

7. I shall sail for Auckland, New Zealand in the "Abarenda" tomorrow, December 7, but shall return to Pago Pago in a few weeks to complete the work on the wharf and buildings now being erected here.

Very respectfully.
B. F. Tilley,
Commander, United States Navy
Commanding U.S.S. Abarenda &
U.S. Naval Coal Depot,
Senior Naval Officer of the
United States of America in Samoa

TUTUILA
PAGOPAGO
2nd APRIL 1900

To His Susuga
    Commander B TILLEY

Acting-Governor for the United States of America
            at Tutuila.

Your Susuga :-

        SALUTATIONS !!

        We desire to make known with the greatest res-
-pect to your Susuga and His Afioga the President of the
United States of America, we are now exceedingly grate-
ful to the Great Powers for the care and protection in
this country in past days, we will continue thus to be
thankful. We rejoice with our whole hearts on account

[112]

Great Powers concerning Samoa are ended, their Declara-
-tions are thus :- " Only the Government of the United
States of America shall rule in Tutuila and Manua, other
foreign Governments shall not again have authority there."
We give great thanks to the Great Powers for that result
that Declaration is accepted by us with glad hearts.
NOW THEREFORE , LET YOUR SUSUGA KNOW, AND LET ALSO HIS
AFIOGA THE PRESIDENT OF THE UNITED STATES OF AMERICA
KNOW, AND LET ALL THE NATIONS OF THE EARTH KNOW AND ALL
PEOPLE DWELLING THEREIN , that in order to set aside all
possible doubts in the future concerning our true desire
at this time on account of the Rule of the United States
of America in Tutuila and Manua, We now, rightly appoin-
-ted according to the customs of Samoa to be the repre-
-sentatives of all the different districts in Tutuila
we do confirm all the things done by the Great Powers
for Tutuila, we do also cede and transfer to the Govern-
-ment of the United States of America the Island of
Tutuila and all things there to rule and to protect it.
We will obey all laws and statutes made by that Govern-
-ment or by those appointed by the Government to legis-
-late and to govern.
Our whole desire is to obey the laws that honor and dwe-
-lling in peace may come to pass in this country.
We depend on the Government and we hope that we indeed

[114]

---

and the Government will be prosperous, that the Govern-
-ment will correctly guide and advise us in order that
we may be able to care for and guard well and uprightly
our different villages and also our districts.
Let good and useful laws be made, let the foundations
of the Government stand firm for ever.
May your Susuga, the Acting-Governor live!
May His Afioga the President of the Government of Amer-
-ca live, and all the Government also !
We are, your humble servants
    I am Mauga of Pagopago
        Leiato of Fagaitua
        Faumuina of Aunuu
        Pere of Laulii
        Masani of Vatia
        Tupuola of Fagasa
        Soliai of Nuuuli
        Mauga (2) of Pagopago
    THE SUA AND THE VAIFANUA
(note. The Sua ma le Vaifanua is the term applied to
    and embracing the whole of the eastern district of
    Tutuila.)
FOFO and AITULAGI (Term applied to and embracing the
                       whole of the western district)
Tuitele of Leone
Faiivae of Leone
Letuli of Ililii
Fuimaono of Vailoa
Satele of Vailoa
Leoso of Leone
Olo of Leone
Namoa of Malaeola
Malota of Malaeloa
Tunaitaui of Pavaiai
Lutomana of Asu
Amituanai Ituau

[116]

TUTUILA
PAGOPAGO
2 APRIL 1900

Iland Susuga
    a Commander B Tilley
        O le SUI.KOVANA o le Unaite Setete o Amelika
            mo Tutuila.

Lau Susuga e :-

        SI OU MATOU ALOFA !!
Ua matou te fia faasilasila atu ma le ava tele i lau
susuga ma lana Afioga, le Alii Taitai o le Malo o le
Unaite Setete o Amelika, o lenei matou te matua faafetai
atu i Malo Tetele ona o latou tausisi ma faamamalu i
lenei atunuu i aso ua mavae, ua taupeapea matou ma le
faafetai tele. Ua olioli nei matou mo lo matou loto
atoatoa ona o tala ua ma ua ai matou ua faaiu nei fili-
-filiga o Malo Tetele ona o Samoa, ua faapea le latou
tautinoga " Tau ane le Malo o Amelika o le a pule i
Tutuila ma Manua, ua le toe aia si isi Malo Papalagi iai
Matou te faafetai atu i Malo Tetele ona o lena iuga, ua
talia foi lena tautinoga e i matou ma loto fiafia. O
lenei, IA SILAFIA LAU SUSUGA, UA SILAFIA FOI LANA AFI-

[113]

AFIOGA, LE ALII PULE O LE MALO O LE UNAITE SETETE O AMEL
-IKA, IA SILAFIA FOI MALO UMA I LE LALOLAGI, MA TAGATA M
UMA O LOO I AI, ina ia tea ese lava masalosalo uma lava
i aso amuli ona o lo matou loto faamaoni i ona po nei
ona o le pule o le Malo o le UNaite Setete o Amelika i
Tutuila ma Manua, o i matou nei, ua matou tofia tonu e
tusa ma le tu e masani ai Samoa, matou te faamaoni mea
uma sa faia e Malo Tetele ona o Tutuila, o i matou foi
matou te to atu ma foai atu i le Malo o Unaite Setete o
Amelika le Motu o Tutuila ma mea uma o i ai e pule i ai
ma faamamalu i ai. Matou te usiusitai tulafono ma faaton
-uga uma o le a faia e lena Malo poo e i latou ua tofia
e le Malo a fai tulafono ma pule.
O loo matou loto atoatoa seji usiusitai tulafono uma ina
taunuu i lenei Atunuu le manalu ma le nofolelei. Matou
te faalagolago atu i le Malo ma faamoemoe atu foi o lea
manuia lava tatou uma ma le Malo, o le a Taitai tonu mai
ma faatonu mai lelei le Malo a i a matou ina ia matou te
mafai ona tausi ma leoleo mo le lelei mo le tonu lo ma-
-tou nuu eseese ma lo matou itumalo foi-
Seji fai tulafono lelei ma aoga, seji mautu faavae o
le Malo ma le faavavau.

    Ia soifua, lau Susuga le Sui-Kovana
    Ia soifua lana Afioga le Alii Pule i le Malo o
Amelika ma le Malo uma.

    O i matou, o ausuna faamaulalo a outou

[115]

---

[117]

To the Chiefs and the People of the Islands
of Tutuila, Aunuu, and other Neigh
boring Islands.

Greeting:
    "Whereas the Chiefs and People of
the Islands of Tutuila, Aunuu and neighboring
small Islands have, of their own free will and
pleasure, for the promotion of the peace and welfare of the people of said islands, for the establishment of a good and sound government, and
for the preservation of the rights and property of
the inhabitants of said islands, solicited of the
United States of America its supervision and
protection; and
        "Whereas this desire has been express-
ed by the hereditary representatives of the people
of said islands in a Declaration dated the seven
teenth day of April, A.D. 1900, executed accord
ing to Samoan custom and pledging allegiance
to the Government of the United States of America;
        "Therefore, I, Theodore Roosevelt, President
of the United States of America, do hereby express to
the Chiefs and People of said islands the gratifi

---

cation of the Government and people of the
United States in receiving from the Chiefs and
People of the said islands this token of their
friendship and their confidence in the just and
friendly intentions of the United States. The local
rights and privileges mentioned in said Declara
tion will be respected and it is our earnest hope
that peace, happiness, and prosperity may make
their permanent abode with the good people of
these islands.

    White House, Washington,
        July the twenty-first, in the year of our
Lord one thousand nine hundred and two.

By the President: Theodore Roosevelt
    David J. Hill,
    Acting Secretary of State

Deed of Cession

Executive Statement by president Teddy Roosevelt (left)

213

170° 42'w

14°19's

Pago Pago

Tutuila

Aunu'

Samoan
Village